INDIAN HIGHER EDUCATION AT A CROSSROADS

"The Important and difficult Job is never to find the right answer, It is to find the right question"

-Peter Drucker

Indian Higher Education at a Crossroads

Khwaja M. Shahid

and

Bhanu Pratap Pritam

KALPAZ

ISBN: 9789351281535

Price: ₹ 490/-

Published by

Kalpaz Publications
C-30, Satyawati Nagar,
Delhi – 110052
E-mail: kalpaz@hotmail.com
Ph.: 9212142040

Laser Typesetting: Lucky Graphic, Delhi
Printed at: G. Print Process, Delhi

Contents

Foreword

"Indian Higher Education at a Crossroads" is a timely and important book in which Dr Khwaja M Shahid and Mr Bhanu Pratap Pritam have made a concerted effort to inform readers about developments within the domain of Indian higher education. The various chapters of this book that have been written by leading educationists in the country contain a detailed analysis of different aspects of contemporary issues in Indian higher education.

Areas covered in the present book include a historical background of how tertiary education was introduced in the country as well as current issues related to liberalisation, privatisation and globalisation in higher education. Apart from public private partnership, foreign direct investment in higher education sector, quality concerns in higher education, labour market issues in higher education, professional education sectors; engineering and teacher education, contemporary reforms needed in the higher education sector and the opinions of educational leaders of Indian higher education are discussed in detail. The international dimensions of Indian higher education; global university rankings, internationalization of Indian higher education through inbound-outbound mobility of students-teachers, etc. are topics covered in some of the important papers included in this book.

At the present time, there is a crisis in Indian higher education and the entire system is at a crossroads. The challenges that lie ahead of us, in my opinion, go well beyond mere numbers. As is widely discussed these days the demographic dividend that India has at this point in time—namely, the very large proportion of our citizens presently between the age of 10-20 years—has the implication that a very large number will enter the tertiary education system in the coming decade. Estimates of this number range anywhere from upwards of 100 million, and the challenges of providing suitable education to such large number is as much a management issue as its one of pedagogy and its methodology.

This apart, there is a significant improvement in outcomes when instruction is given in the mother tongue: in this sense there is a need to Indianise our education system. For most students in India there is this disconnect- we think in one language and are taught in another. Sometimes it is very clear that we think and speak in different languages as well. Therefore, the simplest form of Indianisation that is required in higher education is to make instruction available in a variety of languages. The scarcity of textbooks in all subjects in this regard is acute and this need is not being seriously addressed, not even for the major regional languages.

As educationists, we all have to concern ourselves with the all-important task of educating the India of the present as well as the India of the future. The bulk of the students that we will see in the classroom of the future will be first generation learners, and the majority will require education to enable skilled employment as quickly as possible.The requirement that these realities should be addressed forms the core of the several challenges that the management of higher education will face in the coming decades.

The editors of this volume deserve our gratitude as well as our admiration. Dr Khwaja M Shahid brings the rich experience of more than two decades in the higher education sector, as well as his own research work on the management of Indian higher education to this collection of essays. His work and developmental ideology is a great asset, and his work as an academic administrator at institutions such as the Jamia Millia Islamia, the Maulana Azad National Urdu University and several others have given him a keen insight into the important issues in the management of education. The understanding of the higher education sector displayed by Mr Bhanu Pratap Pritam is remarkable at his age, but well in keeping with his trajectory through the Banaras Hindu University, The English and Foreign Languages University as well as the National University of Education Planning and Administration. The research experience acquired by him at these important institutions has been brought to bear on this collection. I wish them both the very best.

I believe that this book is a significant contribution that will serve to highlight the contemporary concerns and challenges that confront higher education in India, and I warmly congratulate the Maulana Azad National Urdu University for highlighting these important issues, seeding the discussion and debate, and crystallising efforts to bring some solutions to the problems that all public Universities face now, and will face in the years to come.

Prof Ramakrishna Ramaswamy
Former Vice-Chancellor,
University of Hyderabad, Hyderabad

Acknowledgements

This book *"Indian Higher Education at a Crossroads"* has come out as a result of several efforts of academicians engaged in and experienced of higher education sector for decades. It took almost one year to finalise the chapters, gathering articles from different authors specifically on issues related to higher education. There are many who supplemented in order to come out with such book on higher education but due to paucity of space, we are including only few significant figures in this acknowledgement.

Firstly, some of the departments of the Maulana Azad National Urdu University (MANUU), Hyderabad have extended their support in materialising this book. Department of Management and Commerce of MANUU with its national seminar on management of higher education conducted in 2014 contributed some of the papers for this book which primarily needs acknowledgement. Apart from this, school of education and training of MANUU also supported in gathering articles and other supplements.

Most gracefully, we thank some of the great educationists who have spared their time to contribute papers out of their busy schedule namely; Prof Faizan Mustafa, Vice Chancellor of National Academy of Legal Studies and Research (NALSAR) Hyderabad, Prof Sunaina Singh, Vice Chancellor of The English and Foreign Languages University (EFLU),

Hyderabad, Prof. R. Ramaswamy, Former Vice-Chancellor of University of Hyderabad, Prof. D. N. Reddy, Member UGC and former Vice-Chancellor, Jawaharlal Nehru Technological University (JNTU), Hyderabad and Prof K Sudha Rao, former Vice-Chancellor of Karnataka State Open University, (KSOU) Maysore.

Most importantly, the authors contributed articles for this book need foremost gratitude without whom it would never been a successful publication of the book. Following is the list of contributors.

List of Contributors

1. Prof **(Dr) Khwaja M Shahid** (Pro. Vice-Chancellor, MANUU Hyderabad)
2. Prof Faizan Mustafa, (Vice Chancellor, NALSAR Hyderabad).
3. Prof Sunaina Singh (Vice Chancellor, The EFLU Hyderabad).
4. Prof. R Ramaswamy (Former Vice Chancellor, University of Hyderabad.)
5. Prof. K Sudha Rao, (Former Vice Chancellor, KSOU, Mysore)
6. Prof. D.N.Reddy Former Vice Chancellor, JNTU Hyderabad and Member UGC
7. Prof. F Rahman, Dean School of Sciences, MANUU
8. Dr. Saneem Fatima, Head, Dept. of Management and Commerce, MANUU.
9. Bhanu Pratap Pritam, Asst. Professor of Education, MANUU.
10. Dr. Pradeep Kumar Choudhary, ISID, New Delhi.
11. Dr. Tanu Shukla, Assistant Professor, BITS Pilani.
12. Dr. Fayaz Ahmad Bhat, Lecturer in Economics, Govt. College, Srinagar, J & K.
13. Dr. Shazli Hasan Khan, Asst. Professor of Education, MANUU.
14. Abdul Rasheed Shaik, Asst. Registrar, MANUU.
15. Dr. Gajendra Singh Chauhan, Assistant Professor, BITS Pilani
16. Dr. H. Akther Banu, Asst. Professor of Economics, GDC Karnool.
17. S.Mansoor Rahman Asst. Professor of Economics, Osmania College Karnool.
18. Syed Ahmed Shaad, Asst. Professor, AMU.
19. Syed Samiuddin Muzamil, Asst. Professor of Economics, Osmania College Karnool.

We also express our sincere thanks and gratitude to Maulana Azad National Urdu University (MANUU) Hyderabad and especially to Honorable Vice Chancellor of MANUU, Prof. Mohd. Miyan for providing such occasion and opportunity of an excellent academic atmosphere which made publication of this book possible within stipulated timeframe.

Introduction

The papers included in this edited book have been arranged thematically according to the concerned area of studies in higher education. This will further ease the readers in order to get the sectorwise understanding of entire higher education system in India. Below are placed the thematic brief abstracts of the several papers contributed in the book.

Development of Indian Higher Education — Dr Khwaja M Shahid (Pro. Vice Chancellor, MANUU, Hyderabad)

Firstly, Dr Khwaja M Shahid, the main author of the book has tried to summarize entire historical development of Indian higher education in the first chapter itself. This chapter/paper begins with brief note on ancient and medieval education system but largely it focuses on the British colonial system and its development in order to make a strong background for the book. Apart from this, the extensive discussion on several committees and commissions in pre-independence as well as post-independence period has also been placed in order to create the broad developmental understanding of development of Indian higher education. Subsequently, the author has placed issues and concerns in management of higher education system especially in post independent period. It further focuses on the nature and types of Indian Universities, organisational structure with administrative setup and finally the major issues of Indian higher education system.

Policy Issues in Higher Education

Secondly, Prof Faizan Mustafa in his paper "Management of Higher Education in India: Problems and Prospects" discusses about different facets of higher education in contemporary India. It deals with the economic approaches of developing and developed countries in terms of GDP contribution towards higher education. Further some of the issues like corporate social responsibilities and some of the legal aspects have also been placed along with its relationship with growth and development of higher education in India. Next to it, Prof K Sudha Rao in her monograph "Reforms in Higher Education: Facts and Impacts" involves the discussion on competitive relationship with countries like China, policy issues of last one decade in which growth in higher education is also placed. 11th and 12th Five Year Plans and its financial contribution have also been highlighted in this paper along with global university issues and many politico-legal legislations pending to reform higher education sector. Whereas Prof D N Reddy reveals in his paper "Challenges to higher education in India" briefly touched upon the impact of liberalisation, privatisation and globalisation of higher education in India and development of higher education in relation with other developing countries. Further it also analyses the role of Information and Communication Technologies and importance of English language.

Finally Prof Sunaina Singh in her paper "Taking Higher Education in India to the Future" brings readers to the present state of affairs and further leading towards the future of higher education. She refers to the dire need of assessment of time invested by the stakeholders and its questionable outcomes in Indian Universities/Institutions of higher learning. Industry institute linkages and the questions of employability have been a leading questions needs urgent attention apart from the larger goal of knowledge production rather merely knowledge transfer in such institutions. The competitive investment in education sector is as meager as one percent of GDP contribution on higher education whereas in other developing countries having more than three percent. India is growing fast in educational development with its noble policies but the actual implementations and impacts are always doubtful. The decreasing values and discipline among entire stakeholders of higher education are also needs immediate checks in order to maintain quality and purposefulness of Higher Education in India.

Contemporary Higher and Professional Education

Bhanu Pratap Pritam and Prof P.F. Rahman in their paper "Rashtriya Uchchatar Shiksha Abhiyaan" has placed the policy manifestation of Indian government. The recent past of Indian politico-economic scenario and its multi sectoral impact have manifested numerous changes in the country. In education, higher and professional sectors have largely participated and experienced such long lasting changes in terms of increasing GER upto 30percent by the year 2020, budgetary allocations and direct linkage of higher education with economic development of the country. This paper largely deals with the post-independent era policies of education in India leading to Rashtriya Ucchchatar Shiksha Abhiyan (RUSA) 2013. Demographic dividend, empowering slow and steady progress of state higher education sector and universalisation of school education are also some of the immediate reasons to launch such nationwide programme. Finally it also reflects on some of the key issues in planning and implementation of RUSA and status of low performing states which will largely face numerous challenges in order to accomplish the objectives of RUSA within the given timeframe.

Whereas Dr Pradeep Kumar Choudhury in his paper "Growth and Development of Engineering Education in India" situated the trends of increasing enrolments and institutions in last six decade after independence. The early phases of engineering education and the beginning of core sectors of engineering education leading to further extension of such core discipline to applied discipline based on marked demand have also been place in the beginning of the paper. Further he also discussed the regional and disciplinary imbalances along with the difference in several social categories in engineering education in the country. Finally, Bhanu Pratap Pritam in his paper "Teacher Education at Crossroad" as a part of professional education sector reveals the state of affairs of teacher education in India. The present scenario of extreme commercialisation leading to degradation of teacher education in India along with the recent report of Justice Verma Commission Report have also been critically place in the paper. Finally it ends with some of the suggestive areas for implementation of the report in a fruitful ways.

Economic Perspectives in Higher Education

In this sub-theme, Dr Saneem Fatima and Syed Ahmed Saad in their paper "FDI and Public Private Partnership in Higher Education" stated that India is a fast developing economy of the world and has become a favoured destination for FDI. The economic reforms of early 1990s paved the way for liberalised and more open economy for the private sector as well foreign investors. The service sector is booming and new investment alternatives are emerging like banking, telecom and education etc. Realizing the importance of education in a knowledge economy on one hand and potential market on the other due to the large number of students enrolling for higher education, government has given a liberal hand to private sector which attracted a lot of investment in recent past. In such times the scope of foreign direct investment and public private partnership has gain a lot of momentum. This paper discusses some issues related to foreign direct investment and public private partnership in the field of higher education in India. Whereas, Dr H.Akther Banu, Syed Muzamil & S. Mansoor Rahman in the paper tried to begin with the larger framework of economy and service sector development in India.

Providing the historical background of service sector revolution leading higher and professional education sector, the authors situated the knowledge and economy as a complementary to national development. Different waves of economic development leading to knowledge revolution supplemented by Information and communication technology and industrial growth have uplifted the entire education sector in India. This paper deals with economic perspective of education in India. Lastly, Dr Fayaz Ahmad Bhat in his paper "Higher Education and its Labour Market Aspects" has placed the major research questions and methodological paradigms which had showed linkage between levels of higher education and its labour market aspects. The linkages between globalisation, requirement of skilled manpower relating with its historical growth of higher education have also been considered in the paper. Quantitative data support with locating higher education in the contemporary developmental scenario has further strengthened the paper.

Excellence in Higher Education

In this sub-theme, few papers have been included largely on quality and excellence issue in higher education sector. It begins with the paper of Dr Tanu Shukla on "Professional Ethics in Higher Education" which is the foremost need of the hour in present context of higher education. It largely deals with the need of code of professional ethics as a core component of any organisation in order to maintain its values and quality as well. The dire need of professional code of conducts in institutions of general higher learning especially in teaching profession. Whereas, Dr Shazli and Mr Shaik in their paper "Assuring Quality and Excellence in Higher Education Institutions" exposed that the Quality assurance is a key factor which is to be seriously applied to the system of higher education. Accreditation and assessment are continuous process to be implemented properly in all the higher learning institutions to draw the line of standard through NAAC. Establishment of an Internal Quality Assurance Cell (IQAC) is mandatory task that should be undertaken by all the institutions on an urgent basis. The focus of the present research paper is to highlight the need to maintain and assure quality in Higher Educational Institutes of India. The authors have investigated the role of "principal accreditating agency"- the NAAC and establishment of "Internal Quality Assurance Cell" in assuring sustained quality in institutes of higher learning-with reference to a case study of Maulana Azad National Urdu University (MANUU). In a nutshell, it can be said that sustaining and nurturing a quality and a continuous quality culture holds the key to growth and development of an institution and a Nation as a whole. Lastly Dr Gajendra Singh Chauhan in his paper "Cognizance of Media Literacy in Higher Education" discusses about the increasing role of massive media industry and establishment of media education for developmental agenda of the country. Further it also states that the multicultural India and increasing globalisation and Internalis ation of cultural fabric can be maintained with reorienting media education in higher education.

Social Concerns in Higher Education

This unit has been fabricated with two articles; first of Dr Tanu Shukla in "Discussuing Gender in Higher Education" raised the growing issues of gender concerns capability issue in higher education sector. It portrays marginalisation, discrimination and inequality experienced by women, especially belonging to minority sections. It vanquishes the goal of women's social and economic status over the past few years in developing world. The overriding discourses claimed that women's priority must be families which affect their professional lives. There is a strong interaction amongst various factors which leads to differences in academic output of women, thus, the present study would focus on different aspects related to social and psychological barriers faced by women in the developing world. The study is empirical in nature and employs a qualitative method to identify the factors accountable for the aforesaid issue. It focuses on marginalisation, hereafter researcher would contribute in the area of inclusive education. Whereas, Dr Arifa Makandar in "Inclusive Growth and Public Expenditure" opines the importance of huge economic fluctuations in the form of reforms. The focus of the government in recent years is towards building Inclusive India. Inclusive growth basically means "broad-based growth and pro-poor growth". The objectives of an inclusive growth agenda is to reduce poverty, improve quality of life, and ensure to the extent possible, that all segments of society benefit from the economic growth of the country. Education especially higher education is an important tool to attain the objectives of Inclusive Growth. The Present research paper highlights the current structure of higher education in India. The states approach towards the higher education is to be change. The paper highlights the views of experts on the problems of higher education in India and suggest policy measure to improve the same.

Global Perspectives in Indian Higher Education

Bhanu Pratap Pritam in his paper "Internationalization of Higher Education" discusses that, as a result of LPG movement, the mobility of students, being a potential manpower, to the international Universities and also the international students' mobility to the Indian Universities appeared at great extent in recent decades. The outward and inward student mobility has also mobilised the teaching manpower nationally as well as internationally. Students and teachers exchange programme with different international Universities, as a policy of bond of cultural relation between two or more nations, and vice-versa also registered at great extent in recent past. Therefore, the most obvious manifestation of internationalisation of higher education in India has become the increasing presence of international students in Indian university campus. But India, for a long time, has been slow in reacting to the wave of internationalisation and Indian Universities have not been able to take advantages of the possibilities that internationalisation offers for improving the quality of education, for promoting Indian culture worldwide, deriving political and economic benefits. Diversity increases quality in higher education, the most known and discussed issue, furthermore, leads to rethink about the diversity coming from international students to Indian Universities needs to be tackled through competent and professionally equipped teaching manpower. Here comes the issue of needs of professional development of teachers, who can carry forward international brains, considering them as international knowledge resource and produce such kind of manpower from Indian higher education institutions who can compete in global market of knowledge economy. The paper discusses such issues and concerns related to internationalisation of higher education and how this can lead to the professional development of teachers in higher education institutions? Here, internationalisation of higher education is considered as a tool for professional development of teachers. Whereas, Prof P F Rahman and Bhanu Pratap Pritam in their paper "World University Rankings: Status of Indian Universities" have tried to describe the concept and derives that Quality is a process whereas excellence can be attributed as an indicator for outcomes. The thrust of knowledge and achievement has always been central force to receive attention of mankind since inception. Education has become the latest addition among all the sectors of governance in society with increasing importance of knowledge economy in recent past of modern history. This paper makes an attempt to show the global scenario in which world university ranking system emerged along with its methodological concerns consequently at global, continental as well as national level. Further it also describes the efforts of Asian and Indian institutions to come up with their pursuit of excellence in order to queue up in global rankings. Finally, a critical outlook of some of the efforts of Indian agencies and government in the wake of world university ranking system have also been included for future plan of action in higher education sector.

Conclusively, Dr Khwaja M Shahid and Bhanu Pratap Pritam in their final word critically debated the contemporary concerns of Indian higher education and its way forward in the paper "Indian Higher Education: A Way Forward". It further describes the suggestive direction to integrate the Information and Communication Technologies in higher education along with role of skilled based education as the need of the hour. Nonetheless, the increasing complicated role of leadership and management of higher education furthers the quality maintenance in this sector. The demographic dividend management, quality concerns, globalisation & privatisation issues, qualitative growth of institutions, etc are some of the area of great concerns on the present time.

Prof Khwaja M Shahid
Pro. Vice Chancellor
Bhanu Pratap Pritam
Assistant Professor of Education
Maulana Azad National Urdu University, Hyderabad

Development of Indian Higher Education

1

Historical Development of Higher Education in India

Prof Khwaja M Shahid,

"Education is the manifestation of the perfection already in Man"

- Swami Vivekananda

3rd March 1894

India's rich cultural and philosophical account of heritage is enormous and, at times, unfathomable. The education history of India is also very rich and interesting. It has been served by sages, saints, clerics, feudal lords, rulers and common men simultaneously resulting in a very fascinating history. The history of education in India can be traced back to 5000 years old and may be divided into following eras for the sake of convenience of understanding.

Vedic Era	3000 B C - 500 B C
Buddhist Era	500 B C – 1200 A D
Muslim Era	1200 A D – 1700 A D
British Era (the pre-Independence period)	1800 A D – 1947 (Post-independence era) 1947 onwards

It is said that in ancient times the education was imparted orally to transfer knowledge from generation to generation. The recorded history of education in ancient India can be traced back to the third century BC which involved elements of religious education and training in warfare. After the development of language the use of palm leaves and barks of trees came into existence for writing and providing education that led to spreading of written tradition of education.

Around 500 BC, Upanishads also became part of Hindu scriptures and its teaching method of reasoning and questioning became popular in the educational system. Later, Mahabharata and Ramayana, the two famous epics with rich content of discourse on human relationship and philosophy of existence evolved the concept of Dharma. This ancient system of education is considered one of the most effective systems of learning.

The Vedas which is considered as the oldest among the known literature of the world, was a part of education system in ancient India. The Vedas were considered not only as books of religion but also the books of knowledge and life. During the Vedic period 5000-500 BC the education was mainly confined to Vedas which included philosophy of life and skills. The Vedas also included subjects like herbal medicines like medicine for snake bites etc. The main aim of education during Vedic period was to ensure preservation of knowledge and wisdom and to transmit it to the next generation.

The education system during Vedic period was based on *'Gurukuls'* as centers of learning. During this and subsequent ancient Indian period education was imparted through the institution of *'Gurukuls' nor 'Patshalas'* which were residential schools in the form of either a monastery or Ashram or householding of the Gurus. All *'Shishyas'* (Students), rich or poor, used to live in the same *'Gurukul'* or *'Ashram'* and the edu-cation was free except donations of voluntary *Gurudakshina* or support from the kings. It has been noted that the education on religion, scripture, literature, warfare, astrology, medicine and governance was imparted. The students were also required to follow the *Brahmacharyam* to devote fulltime to education and to avoid luxuries and pleasures of life leading to self-discipline and self-control. The *'Shishyas'* and gurus lived an austere life at isolated places away from their homes and towns in residential centres of learning where rich and poor enjoyed same type of brahmacharism. Education was free but supported by Rajas or '*Gurudakshinas*'. The methods of teaching were oral discourses, memorization and *'chintan'*. There was no fixed period or curriculum of education. The guru had the final verdict on the completion of education of a student.

During the Buddhist period the monasteries became the centre of learning where students were called *'bhikshus'* and they use to live a simple life and go out for collection of bhiksha. The main aim of education in these monasteries was to achieve moksha through spiritual and religious studies of Buddha.

The historical record of education in India informs us that around the beginning of AD period there were many centres of higher education at Nalanda, Taxila, Ujjain and Vikramshila where architect, painting, logic, grammar, philosophy, astronomy, literature, Buddhism and other Indian religious literarture, astrology and medicine etc. were taught. The Taxila University was famous for Medicine while, Ujjain specialised in Astronomy. The Nalanda was the biggest centre of learning with around 10,000 students and imparting knowledge in all branches of education.

The acquaintance of India with Muslims started in 712 AD with the arrival of army of Mohammad Bin Qasim up to Sindh. However, Muslims started entering into India and setting up empires at the beginning of the of 11th century. The new rulers also brought with them an education system which was based on Madrasas and Maktabs; secondary schools were called *Madrasas nor* primary schools were known as *Maktabs*. During this period, a large number of such schools of Muslim elementary and secondary learning were established in India. "There is no record of what the maktabs used to teach. It is, however, definite that they catered to the needs of the masses. The elites taught their sons and daughters at home at the elementary stage. Maktabs probably taught memorization of some paras of the Quran, basic rules regarding preparing for and performing *namaz*, and possibly basic reading and writing of Arabic and elementary arithmetic. The same curriculum continues even now, almost nine or ten centuries later." (Page No. 128 – *Madrasa Education in Modern India by Saral Jhingran).* This period also initiated the promotion of urban centres of education. The Students from these Madrasas were eligible for appointment by the court as Qazi and administrators. These Madrasas were set up by Kings, Nobles, and Feudal Lords and even by influential and rich ladies. A large number of such centres of high repute of Islamic learning were set up at Delhi, Lucknow, Allahabad, Ujjain, Gulbarga, Bidar, Rampur, Lahore, Hyderabad, Ahmadabad and Jaunpur etc. There has been mention of calling Jaunpur as 'Sheraz-e-Hind'due to the educational importance of the city. (Education in Emerging India by R.P. Pathak, published by Atlantic publishers and distributors Pvt Ltd)

Emperor Akbar's time saw an important development of introduction and popularisation of "various rational sciences *(ma'qulat)* which became a major part of madrasa curriculum." Though eduation was free, only the sons of the elite went to madrasas because they were expected to become *qazis*, *muftis* and other government officers after completing their education.

In addition to madarasa education system, there was another independent system of learning from Islamic scholars of very high repute specialising in one or more than one disciplines and subjects. Those who want to acquire knowledge in their area of specialisation would go to their seat of learning. In this way seekers of knowledge would travel from city to city who taught students at their homes. Students who were really desirous of knowledge went to more than one teacher, as each scholar's specialisation was different. In addition, there were Sufi Khanqahs (a form of monastery) where traditional Islamic teaching was imparted, in addition to their own mystical knowledge (tasawwuf). As in the rest of the Islamic world, there was no arrangement for higher education of masses or of women. Women of higher classes took their education at home under a Maulavi, and some of them excelled in literature and the arts.

Arabic language including *sarf* (etymology) and *nahw* (conjugation) i.e. grammar were most important subjects taught in madarsas. The *tafsirs* (commentaries on the Quran), m*antiq* (Logic), *falsafa* (philosophy) were also taught. These subjects are still an integral part of curriculum in Madarsas. As a matter of fact, there have not been any major changes in the madrasa curriculum, as far as these subjects and education system is concerned. Ilm e *kalam* (discourse on Quran), *tasawwuf* (mysticism), *tibb* (medicine), *riyazi* (mathematics), *Hindsa* (engineering) and *haiyat* (astronomy) were other important subjects in Madarsa curriculum.

With the Muslim rulers, nobility, rich and clerics establishing mosques, madrasas and khankas to impart education, the old system of gurukuls and ashrams slowly went into background and the new system of maktabs and madrasas came into being. The language of instructions changed from Sanskrit and Pali to Persian as it has then became the language of the court and literature.

II

Later, the fading Moghul Empire due to political and near anarchy administrative situation provided the British a historical opportunity to fill in the space vacated by the Moghul Empire. And they did it smartly and correctly using all means of political machavilliaism and technological and warfare superiority. The present system of modern education came into existence in India with the arrival of Britishers in the country. The introduction of modern Western education by Britishers gave a serious setback to traditional vernacular system of learning, which was prevalent in the ancient and medieval period of history.

The East India Company founded on 31st December, 1600 with the objective to trade with the Eastern countries, "undertook no educational activity worth the name in India during the first 100 years of its existence". The company which was to periodically renew its Charter from the

Government of Her Majesty was directed in the Charter of 1698 to maintain the school wherever necessary. This resulted in the setting up of St. Mary's Charity School in Madras in 1715; another school in 1718 in Bombay and in Calcutta in 1731. "Throughout the 18th Century, therefore, the encouragement of these similar charity schools was the main educational activity of the East India Company". It catered to the needs of a very small section of the society mostly comprising the children of company's employees. Later, by some efforts of individuals many other educational institutions were set up including Calcutta Madarasa by Waren Hastings in 1781 and Sanskrit College at Banaras in 1791 by Johanthen Duncan. The main objective of Calcutta Madarasa was to provide qualified Indians as clerks and petty administrators to implement the dictates of the company or to communicate in vernacular languages with native states. The first and foremost objective of these institutions was "to train Indian Assistants to Indian Judges in order to explain the principles of Muslim and Hindu laws".

The aim of establishing the Calcutta Madarasa was stated to be the desire "to conciliate the Mahomedans of Calcutta to qualify the sons of Mahomedan gentlemen for responsible and lucrative offices in the State, and to produce competent officers for Courts of Justice to which students of the Madrassah on the production of certificates of qualification were to be drafted as vacancies occurred."

In the same way, Jonathan Duncan wrote, as under, to Lord Cornwallis regarding the Benaras Sanskrit College:-

"*Two important advantages seemed derivable from such an establishment, the first to the British name and nation in its tendency towards endearing our Government to the native Hindus; by our exceeding in our attention towards them and their systems, the care shown even by their own native princes..............The second Principal advantage that may be derived from this institution will be felt in its effect upon the natives....... by preserving and disseminating a knowledge of the Hindu law, and proving a nursery of future doctors and expounders thereof, to assist European judges in the due regular, and uniform administration of its genuine letter and spirit to the body of the people*" (Selections from Educational Records, Volume I, pp. 10-11).

The above were considered as efforts by individuals as exception to the general observation that during the initial years of its dominion, the East India Company did not take any interest in the promotion of education in India. It is said that Britishers were reluctant to provide education to individuals of India because of their bitter experience in America. However, we do find that in 1770s the question of providing higher education to the people of British India was debated in the British Parliament. When the Charter of company was renewed in the year 1773, following resolution was passed in the House of Commons:

"*That it is the peculiar and bounden duty of the British Legislature to promote by all just and prudent means the interest and happiness of the inhabitants of the British Dominions in India; and that for these ends such measures ought to be adopted as may gradually tend to their advancement in useful knowledge and to their religious and moral improvement*".

In 1784, the Asian Society of Bengal was founded by Sir William Johns; the society also started many English schools and colleges. However, the British gradually felt the need to educate the natives to provide qualified educated subordinates to assist them in the governance of the country. Indians like Raja Rammohan Roy and Sir Syed Ahmed Khan strongly supported the propagation of western English education in India.

One of the important turning point in the history of modern education in India is said to be the book of Charles Grant — *'Observations'* of 1772. This book had "tremendous effect on the future development of education in India". Charles Grant (1746-1823) had been to India on different occasions - first in the Military in 1767 and then as a Factor in 1773. In 1802 Charles Grant became a Member of Parliament and later, in 1805 Chairman of the East India Company. In this famous book, *"Observations"* he presented a very "decadent conditions of Indian Society" and therefore argued to sent missionaries to India. He argued for reform in India and said as following:

"*The true cure of darkness is the introduction of light. The Hindus err. Because they are ignorant; and their errors have never fairly been laid before them. The communication of our light and knowledge to them, would prove the best remedy for their disorders; and this remedy is proposed, from a full conviction that if judiciously and patiently applied, it would have great and happy effects upon them, effects honourable and advantageous for us.*"

"*There are two ways of making this communication: the one is, by the medium of the languages of those countries; the other is by the medium of our own. In general when foreign teachers have proposed to instruct the inhabitants of any country, they have used the vernacular tongue of that people, for a natural and necessary reason, that they could not hope to make any other means of communication intelligible to them. This is not our case in respect of our eastern dependencies. They are our own, we have possessed them long, many Englishmen reside among the natives, our language is not unknown there, and it is practicable to diffuse it more widely. The choice, therefore, of either mode, lies open to us; and we are at liberty to consider which is entitled to a preference.*

The acquisition of a foreign language is, to men of cultivated minds, a matter of no great difficulty. English teachers could, therefore, be sooner qualified to offer instruction in the native languages than the Indians would be prepared to receive it in ours."

The introduction of English in the administration of the revenue, in judicial proceedings, and in other business of Government, wherein Person is now use, and the establishment of free-schools for instruction in this language, would ensure its diffusion over the country, for the reason already suggested, that the interest of the natives would induce them to acquire it."

This led to introduction of following clause in the Charter of the Company, 1793:

"That it is the peculiar and bounden duty of the British Legislature to promote by all just and prudent means the interest and happiness of the inhabitants of the British Dominions in India; and that for these ends such measures ought to be adopted as may gradually tend to their advancement in useful knowledge and to their religious and moral improvement."

East India Company, however, was reportedly inclined to neutrality in religious matters. They perhaps feared that the missionaries' zeal for conversion might invite trouble.

Again in 1813, the question of education in India was debated in British Parliament when Charter Act of East India Company was renewed. At the time of this renewal of the Charter the debate was around two main groups. One was of the opinion that English should be taught and the propitiation should be left to the missionaries. The other group was of the opinion that the education of India classics should be liberally taught; and missionaries should not be encouraged to practice the religious neutrality. The Charter Act 1813 resolved the issue by stating that "*It is the duty of this country to promote the interest and happiness of the native inhabitants of the British dominions in India, and that measures ought to be adopted as may tend to the introduction among them of useful knowledge and moral improvement. That in furtherance of the above objects sufficient facilities shall be afforded by law to persons desirous of going to, or remaining in India for the purpose of accomplishing those benevolent designs'. That meant that the missionaries were to be allowed to enter India and to reside there; they might preach, found churches, and discharge all spiritual duties; in a word, they might fulfil their missionary calling in its completest and widest sense."*

But, one more Section was also adopted in the Charter which read as follows:

"A sum of not less than one lac of rupees in each year shall be set apart and applied to the revival and improvement of literature and the encouragement of the learned natives of India, and for the introduction and promotion of a knowledge of the sciences among the inhabitants of the British territories in India."

The fact that Charter Act 1813 became an important turning point by compelling the East India Company to provide one lakh rupees per year for education in India. Simultaneously, missionaries also supported opening of English schools in different parts of the country.

The Governor General of India subsequently in 1823 appointed a "General Committee of Public Instruction". The amount of rupees one lac was also placed at the disposal of this Committee for taking up educational activities. The Committee during 1823-1833 encouraged oriental studies of Sanskrit and Arabic; established new oriental colleges at Agra and Delhi and initiated the work of translation and publication of oriental work. Interestingly, Indians, particularly in Bengal led by Raja Rammohan Roy apposed establishment of Sanskrit colleges and wanted to promote liberal and modern education like Mathematics, Philosophy, Chemistry, Anatomy and other sciences. Raja Rammohan Roy pleaded that India should read English and acquire knowledge of the west and modern sciences. On the whole, there was a division of educational policy regarding medium of instruction, study of modern and western subjects and promotion of oriental literature. It is stated that by 1834 the General Committee of Public Instruction was evenly divided on these issues with fivemembers each on either side. Lord Macaulay, who was the law member of the Executive Council of the Governor General was also the President of the 'Committee of Public Instruction'.

Macaulay supported English as medium of instruction, desired closure of oriental learning and opposed spending company's budget on printing and publishing of Arabic and Sanskrit books. But he also supported religious neutrality of the Company. The final seal was put on the controversy by the 7th March, 1835 resolution of the Governor General of India. It is read as follows:

"The Governor-General of India in Council has attentively considered the two letters from the Secretary to the Committee of Public Instruction, dated the 21st and 22nd January last, and the papers referred to in them.

First, His Lordship in Council is of opinion that the great object of the British Government ought to be the promotion of European literature and science among the natives of India; and that all the funds appropriated for the purpose of education would be best employed on English education alone.

Second, But it is not the intention of His Lordship in Council to abolish any College or school of native learning, while the native population shall appear to be inclined to avail themselves of the advantages which it affords, and His Lordship in Council directs that all the existing professors and students at all the institutions under the superintendence of the Committee shall continue to receive their stipends. But His Lordship in Council decidedly objects to the practice which has hitherto prevailed of supporting the students during the period of their education. He conceives that the only effect of such a system can be to give artificial encouragement to branches of learning which, in the natural course of things, would be superseded by more useful studies; and he directs that no stipend shall be given to any student that my hereafter enter at any of these institutions and that when any professor of Oriental learning shall vacate his situation, the Committee shall report to the Government the number and state of the class in order that the Government may be able to decide upon the expediency of appointing a successor.

Third, It has come to the knowledge of the Governor-General in Council that a large sum has been expended by the Committee on the printing of Oriental works; His Lordship in Council directs that no portion of the funds shall hereafter be so employed.

Fourth, His Lordship in Council directs that all the funds which these reforms will leave at the disposal of the Committee be henceforth employed in imparting to the native population a knowledge of English literature and science through the medium of the English language; and His Lordship in Council requests the Committee to submit to Government, with all expedition, a plan for the accomplishment of this purpose".

The immediate impact of the Resolution dated 7th March, 1853 was the loss of Persian which loss its position as official language. The English replaced Persian as the official language of the Govt. Lord Macaulay is considered by his admirers as "torch bearer in the path of progress". Others, who opposed Lord Macaulay, considered him as the cause of all troubles in India. He is also severely criticised due to his ignorance and condemnation of India Literature, Language and culture. Apparently either view is exaggerated in its crucification or admiration of Lord Macaulay. If one tries to take balanced view it will not be inappropriate to state that Lord Macaulay was vigorously arguing to bring modern education, sciences and governance to India and he believed that it could be possible by imparting western education in the medium of English. He can be summed up by quoting his speech in the House of Commons in 1833.

"I have no fears. The path of duty is before us; and it is also the path of wisdom, of national prosperity, of national honour. The destinies of our Indian Empire are covered with thick darkness. It is difficult to form any conjecture as to the fate reserved for a state which resembles no other in history, and which forms by itself a separate class of political phenomena. The laws which regulate its growth and its decay are still unknown to us. It may be that the public mind of India may expand under our system until it has outgrown that system, that by good government we may educate our subjects into a capacity for better government; that having become instructed in European knowledge, they may, in some future age, demand European Institutions. Whether such a day will ever come I know not. But never will I attempt to avert or retard it. Whenever it comes, it will be the proudest day in English History.

Meghna Carta of modern education in India is considered to be the Wood's Education Despatch of 1854. Charles Wood was the Chairman of Board of Control of Company and at his instances" the Education despatch of Court of Directors dated 19th July, 1854 was written. This detailed document dealt with many important instances of Education system in India. The document analysed the controversy between Anglisists and Classicists dealt with question of medium of instruction, explained the objects of the educational policies. The document laid down the new scheme of education which was later implemented in India. The Woods' despatch established Department of Public Instruction in each province (i.e. Education Department); proposed establishment of Universities; established schools all over India; suggested Grant-in-aid to educational institutions; and training of teachers. The Wood's Despatch also gave strong suggestion relating to necessity of female education, vocational instruction and vocational colleges. But the fact remains that many of the schemes of Wood's Despatch were not achieved to the fullest extent. It was desired in the Despatch that the idea of management of education in the private hands through maintenance of grant-in-aid could not be achieved as at that point of time the private education was by and large in the hands of Christian missionaries. The political revolt of 1857 adversely affected some of the schemes of the Despatch.

As far as higher education is concerned many new Universities were established after Despatch, 1854. It may be worth mentioning here that before establishment of Universities in India, some very famous colleges were started including Madrasa Alia by Waren Hestings in, Calcutta and Banaras Sanskrit College (now Sampurnananda University of Sanskrit) by Duncan in 17, Hindu Vidyalaya of Calcutta by Raja Rammohan Roy 1817, Elphinstone institute, Bombay, Delhi College and College at Agra.

Some very famous colleges were set up after Woods' Despatch including Canning College, Lucknow in 1864, Mohammedian Anglo-Oriental College 1875, at Aligarh by Sir Syed Ahmed Khan and Oriental College at Lahore in 1870. Interestingly, at initial stages most of these colleges have both English and oriental sections. But the data reveals that lesser number of students was enrolling themselves in the oriental section than English section. The demand for English medium of education was obviously more than the oriental medium of education. However, more and more colleges started functioning after 1857 when new Universities were established on the lines of London University which was mainly an examining university. In 1857, Govt. of India incorporated three Universities at Calcutta, Bombay and Madras. These Universities were established "for the purpose of ascertaining, by means of examination, the persons who have acquired proficiency in different branches of Literature, Sciences and Art and of rewarding them by Academic Degrees as evidence of their respective attainments and marks of honour proportioned thereunto" (Bombay University Act, 1857). In other words these Universities were mainly to conduct examinations and to award degrees. The Punjab University was established in 1882. The 5th Indian University was established in 1887 at Allahabad. They were affiliating Universities which led to rapid growth of college education from 1857 onwards.

Later on, the Government set up Indian Education Commission in 1902 which gave landmark recommendations for development of education, relating to grant-in-aid to colleges for their maintenance and development, provision to encourage diversity in culture, morality in text books, insistence on duties of citizens, rationalisation of fee, disbursement of scholarships etc.

There was growing demand whether the University should also start teaching in addition to merely taking examinations and awarding degrees. In fact the University of London was also transformed from the examining university to a teaching university by an Act of Parliament in 1898. The then Govt. of India appointed the Indian Universities Commission in 1902. The main objective of this Commission was to examine the conditions of the Universities and make recommendations to improve their constitution and functioning and also to improve the standards of teaching in these Universities. Based on the recommendations of the Education Commission, 1902, the Indian Universities Act 1904 was enacted. This Act provides that the University shall now make provision for instruction of the students and appoint Professors, Lecturers etc. Universities became teaching Universities instead of only examining Universities. The Act also provided the provision of elected members in the managing bodies like Senate and Syndicate, laid down conditions for affiliation of colleges and gave powers to senate to frame Regulations.

A large number of new Universities were established during 1917 to 1922 as no new university was established since 1887 when Allahabad University was last established. Mysore University (1916), Patna University (1917), Banaras Hindu University (1915), Aligarh Muslim University (1920), Dhaka University (1920), Lucknow University (1920) were added. During 1921 to 1937 Universities were established at Delhi, Nagpur, Andhra and Agra. Annamalai University was also established during this period.

One of the important events of this period was to establish the Inter-University Board to coordinate the activities of the Universities. The main functions of the Board were:

(i) To act as an inter-university organisation and bureau of information;

(ii) To facilitate the exchange of professors;

(iii) To serve as an authorised channel of communication and facilitate the co-ordination of university work;

(iv) To assist Indian Universities in obtaining recognition for their degrees, diplomas, and examinations in other countries;

(v) To appoint or recommend where necessary a common representative or representatives of India at Imperial or International conferences on higher education;

(vi) To act as an appointment bureau for Indian Universities; and

(vii) To fulfil such other duties as may be assigned to it from time to time by the Indian Universities.

Simultaneously, some very famous institutions of higher learning were established though they were not Universities.They include Oriental Research Institute - Pune, the Bose Research Institute - Calcutta, the Harecourt Buttler Institute- Kanpur, Agriculture Institute - New Delhi, Indian Institute of Science – Banglore, Indian Institute of Mines – Dhanbad, Indian Women University – Bombay and Viswa Bharati etc. In 1920 non-cooperation under the leadership of Mahatma Gandhi gave a call to students to bycott the Universities manage and run on the British system. The national leaders simultaneously undertook the task set up the national Universities therefore Rastriya Vidya Peet, JMI and Gujarat Vidya Peet came into existence, which were the babies of the freedom movement and probably propagated and practiced Gandhian principles of education and nationalism.

The history of modern higher education in India since the East India Company taking the responsibility of education shows that the education remains the responsibility of Central and provincial Governments and the presence of private participation in higher education was negligible. Although initial discussion about the medium of instruction, teaching oriental and classic subjects and languages and propagation of religion was settled with Lord Maculay's note and decision of the 7th March, 1854 of the Governor General, which has been briefly discussed in earlier paragraphs.

III

Post-independence history of higher education in India is disclosing history of an educational system which we inherited from colonial rulers which had been structured on the educational system prevalent in the British Empire.

Some new Universities established after Independence did not correspond to any traditional pattern of Universities viz. the Gujarat Ayurvedic University (1966) at Jamnagar and the Indira Kala Sangeet Vishwavidyala (1956) at Khairagar in Madhya Pradesh. The former, as the name implies, is limited to the study of Ayurveda, while the latter, and teaches only music and dance. The University of Roorkee and the University of Jadavpur were primarily established as technical Universities. On the other hand, the five institutes of technology (IITs), though not called Universities but have been given the power to grant degrees. There are many institutions of national importance which have been given the status of 'deemed to be Universities'.

Committees/Commission After Independence

After Independence, the Government of India appointed various

Committees on higher education to improve the quality of education at this level and to remove the administrative problems of the institutions of higher learning since the time of Sadler Commission's report of 1917. A University Commission was appointed in 1948 under the Chairmanship of Dr S. Radhakrishnan. Thereafter in 1952 the Secondary Education Commission was appointed under the chairmanship of Dr A. Lakshmanaswami Mudaliar to look into the problems of secondary education. The report of the Education Commission (1964-66) also dealt with the Higher Education as a part of total educational system. Beside, the University Grants Commission appointed many committees to look into the problems/issues related to various fields of higher education. National policy of Education (1986) as modified by the Programme of Action in 1992. Some of important Committees/Commissions and their recommendations are briefly discussed below:

(i) Committee on Model Act

In December 1961, the Ministry of Education of the Government of India appointed a Committee under the Chairmanship of Dr D. S. Khotari, the then Chairman of UGC to consider broadly the organisational structure of Universities and to prepare the outline of a 'Model Act' suited to their role and functions in the present context of fast developing society. The Committee opined that a certain amount of variation in the pattern and organisation of Universities might be desirable in the interest of development and progress of higher education in a large country like India. Taking into consideration the need for frequent changes in academic life due to rapid expansion of knowledge especially in Science and Technology, the committee further stipulated that the main Acts of the Universities should lay down the structure and organisation in broad terms and relevant detail may be prescribed by Statutes and Ordinances. The Committee further state that the function of the university is not only to preserve, disseminate, and advance knowledge but also to furnish intellectual leadership and moral tone to the society. The Universities are also to provide trained personnel to advance the country's prosperity by making full use of modern knowledge. The organisational pattern must enable the Universities to achieve these objectives. Unfortunately the recommendations of this committee were, by and large, not implemented.

A phenomenal growth of the University system in India has been witnessed with the number of Universities increasing from 18 in the year 1947 to nearly 300 in 2002. Traditionally, Universities have been established as major institutions for providing higher education and research opportunities to the youth for shaping their future, and recognised as the most important indicator of a Country's future. More recently, the UNESCO World Conference on Higher Education has observed that higher education and research act as essential components of culture, socioeconomic and environmentally sustainable development of individuals, communities and nations, since the society is now becoming increasingly knowledge based.

Thus, in the 21st, century Universities are becoming complex institution with many distinctive features that set them apart from other social and business institution.

While, Universities funding by Center/ State Governments has been a well established tradition in the country, this practice is steadily declining nowadays. The setting up of professional Universities and deemed Universities is relatively new in the country, with the latter category expending rapidly in recent years.

More often, the Universities have a culture that is a mix of academic and bureaucratic cultures, while the academic units like faculties departments, colleges, schools are generally academic in their approach; the central administration manned by officials may not be so. And, it is often likely to be of the bureaucratic type. Sometimes this can result in difficulties, as academic decision being based on committee's deliberations may not be always easy and practical for implementation by the concerned officials. In such situations, it is only the wisdom and positive approach of senior academics in the University hierarchy that can come to the rescue to the system. The Universities now also have commercial culture and corporate culture. The former culture is useful to support activities like continuing education, testing and consultancy, distance education and publication/ distribution of course material, which are important for revenue generation and time bound work. On the other hand, the latter culture emphasises the leadership role provided by senior academics/ officials and the top-down planning and monitoring practices which may be introduced by them in the functioning of the University.

It may be noted that learning is a personalised process not dependent on technology, whereas educating is a social process dependent on interactivities between learners and teachers which may make use of tools and technologies. The on-going globalisation in the higher education sector, the steady reduction in Government-funding of the Universities, the increase influence of Information and Communication Technology (ICT) on education is rapidly shrinking the time scale of change in these institutions. It is observed that a generalised University of the 21st century in the country has to perform multiple functions like, educational, sponsored research and consultancy, continuing education and extension, development and services and management.

This calls for the adoption of an appropriate strategy for their governance, organisation and management. The Conference of Governors held on January, 11-12, 2003 recommended that a model Act governing the State Universities should be formulated with the intention to lay down safeguards against curtailing the power and position of the Chancellors and to protect the autonomy of the Universities. The University Grants Commission has appointed a Committee to consider these and related aspects of Universities and formulate a Model Act.

It has been well brought out in the Reports of these Committees that the success of a University depends not only on the Act, but also on its personnel, their sense of dedication, discipline and responsibility and the traditions/conventions they establish.

The committee has already circulated the draft Model Act to Universities and other relevant organisations for their comments and views. Thereafter the committee will give its recommendation.

(ii) Education Commission

Another event of great importance and significance for the future of university education was appointment of a commission in 1964 under the Chairmanship of Dr D. S. Kothari. The main objectives of the Commission were "to survey and examine the entire field of education in order to realise within the shortest possible time a balance integrated and adequate system of national life". The Commission submitted its report on 1966. Amongst its many invaluable recommendations the Commission suggested that without a suitable administrative structure, no university could achieve its objectives. Kothari Commission had taken up issues related to Universities such as university autonomy, academic freedom and administrative structure of the Universities. It said that the university autonomy properly lies in (a) the selection of students (b) the appointment and promotion teachers (c) the determination of courses of students (d) methods of teaching (e) areas of study and (h) problems of research. It further mentioned that the university autonomy functions at four levels namely (i) within the university (ii) interaction between Universities (iii) autonomy in relation to the university and the association of Indian Universities and the UGC and (iv) interaction between the university and the Central and State Governments and other external agencies.

The Kothari Commission opined that Universities autonomy cannot become real and effective unless adequate provisions are made to meet the financial requirement of Universities and colleges. It also recommended that the membership of court/ senate should not be more that 100, while that of Syndicate/Executive Council should be 15-20, half of which should be external members in both the cases. The Commission also recommended the constitutions of an Academic Planning Board in each university, for planning evaluation, detached from day to day administration. Supporting the recommendation of Model Act Committee, the Commission endorsed the view that university constitutions should be formulated in sufficiently general terms as to leave room for promoting innovation and experimentation.

(iii) Committee on Governance of Universities

The UGC appointed two committees in June, 1969 to consider the issues relating to the Governance of Universities and colleges respectively. The committee constituted under the Chairmanship of Dr P. B. Gajendergadkar, the then Vice-Chancellor of Bombay University, was concerned with the Governance of Universities. Simultaneously another committee constituted under the Chairmanship of Rev. P. T. Chandi, the then Vice-Chancellor of Gorakhpur University, was requested to deal with governance of colleges. Later, both the committees were amalgamated into one committee under the Chairmanship of Dr. Gajendragadkar. The committee on Governance of Universities for the first time in India reviewed the situation existing in Universities in-depth particularly matters relating to statutes, ordinances and regulations, visitors and the Universities, authorities and bodies of these organizations, teaching departments, university administration, student participation, and such other relevant matters. The recommendations of the committee relating to the constitutions and functions of the Court Executive Council, Academic Council, Finance Committee, faculties, student council and various other committees including finance, teaching staff selection, student administration, affiliated colleges, buildings, grievances of employees other than teachers, grievances of students are briefly given below: -

(i) Introduce autonomy in Universities to encourage innovations, experimentation and change.

(ii) Promote and strengthen student participation in the administrative and academic affairs of Universities.

(iii) Leave the administration of extracurricular activities entirely to students.

(iv) Provide adequate financial support and financial autonomy.

(v) Introduce adequate machinery to deal with the grievances of students, teachers and administrative staff.

(vi) Ensure that the constituent unit of the university have a sense of belonging to the university and thereby ensure their participation in all facets of university life and;

(vii) Ensure that the channel of communication remain alive and are never allowed to be blocked.

(iv) Committee on the Working of Central Universities

UGC appointed a committee under the Chairmanship of Dr (Mrs) Madhuri B. Shah, to enquire into the working of Central Universities. The major objectives of the committee were:

(a) To examine whether Central Universities are fulfilling the objectives set for them in their Acts and Statutes.

(b) To examine the general state of discipline in the central Universities causes of periodic disturbances in the campuses and remedial action thereof.

(c) To examine the adequacy of the machinery in the central Universities to deal with the grievances of students, teachers and administrative staff and suggest measures for strengthening corporate life in these Universities.

(d) To examine the desirability of evolving a code of conduct for political parties and to set limits to their involvement in the university affairs and;

(e) To Suggest such other measures of reform as are necessary for the efficient functioning of central Universities and promoting an academic atmosphere conductive to study and scholarship on the campuses.

The recommendations of the committee include amendment to Acts, composition, powers and functions of the authorities and officers, revision of pay scales, provision of amenities and promotion to teaching and non-teaching staff, hostel and campus management, administrative decentralisation and provision for grants etc.

Towards New Educational Management

UGC appointed a committee in 1987 under the Chairmanship of Prof A. Gnanam the then Vice-Chancellor, University of Madras: The committee submitted its report on January 1990. The Committee discussed the issues of Autonomy, Participation, Decentralisation, Accountability, Planning Monitoring and Co-ordination, Funds University and Govt. relationship, Role of Central Govt. Aware of the many administrative constraints along the way to total reform of university governance, the committee presented separate strategies for each of the university related constituencies i.e. the Government of India, the University Grants Commission, the State Government, the Governing bodies of the Universities, and the Management of the Colleges. These strategies were in addition to recommendations, suggesting specific course of action in the directions of realising the organisational objectives. Union Legislation in this regard needs to take the lead to set in motion the strategies for implementation by the different constituencies of the systems. Summary of important recommendations are given below:

(1) It is necessary that each university clearly spells out the objectives which it intends to pursue.

(2) The role of the university as a centre of creation and dissemination of knowledge must be preserved and protected.

(3) It is to be ensured that only people of the highest level of competence, integrity, morals and self-respect are appointed as Vice-Chancellor and that conditions are created so that once appointed they receive cooperation of all including the Government/Chancellor to discharge their duties satisfactorily until the end of their full tenure.

(4) It must be ensured that appropriate modalities and norms are developed by the Central and State Governments, the UGC and other funding agencies so that adequate funds are allocated to the Universities, colleges, and that they are also released in time.

(5) Suitable procedures and norms must be evolved to overcome delays in decision-making by the Central and State Governments, the University Grants Commission and other concerned agencies.

(6) The Ministries, Department of Education, the UGC, other parallel bodies and the university system must enable the teachers and students to play a meaningful and constructive role in planning and implementation of 'Making the System Work Better' by setting up consultative forums at various levels.

(7) Appropriate machinery for quick redress of grievances of teachers, students and non-teaching staff must be created/ improved in all Universities and colleges.

(8) The administration of Universities needs to be modernised and the procedures rationalised so as to ensure that delay in admission, conduct of examinations and declaration of results etc. are totally eliminated.

(9) 'Performance Audit' within the institution must be instituted forthwith, to apprise the institution of its own shortcomings and possibilities of its improvement.

Higher education in India during British period remained an Urban phenomenon and a large number of Indian population remained outside the ambit of modern higher education. These Universities produced intellectual persons who were well conversant with western thoughts of liberty, human rights, democracy etc.

There has been a general feeling that although, great quantitative increase in higher education has taken place in India after Independence, but quality of education has not improved much. Several Committees and Commission appointed by the Government have expressed concerned at the law academic standards of many colleges and Universities, the lack of significant research, the tendency to concentrate on passing examination rather than acquisition of knowledge and skill. As a consequence, the emphasis remains on memorizing the text and not on understanding by the learning process. Therefore, the emphasis of the programmes and strategies for implementing the educational policy of 1986 (as revised in 1992) is on consolidation along with the expansion of institutions development of autonomous colleges and departments, redesigning of courses, training of teachers, strengthening of research, improvements in efficiency, mobility of teachers, coordination at the State and Centre level and review and monitoring. One of the most important landmark observed in Indian education system was the National Policy on Education of 1986 and its follow up POA 1992 which are discussed below.

1986 National Policy on Education mainly emphasised on removing disparity and equalising educational opportunities for all the sections of Indian society based on the principle of equity and equality. Some of the main features of NPE 1986 were; National system of education; reorganization of education at different levels; common educational structure; development of manpower; focus on environmental education and science and technology education; restructuring and reorganising of teacher education and technical education in India; remphasising distance education also by establishing Indira Gandhi National Open University as a centre of higher advanced learning through distance mode; special focus on vocationalization of education and conceptual change in renaming Ministry of Education to Ministry of Human Resource Development in India. Most importantly, NPE 1986 highly emphasised on inclusive development of education in general and higher education in particular by providing special provisions for the upliftment and financial support for the marginalised sections of the society i.e. SC, ST, OBC, Minority and female education.

Followed by NPE 1986, a review committee chaired by Acharya Ramamurthy constituted in order to revisit and review the implementation challenges and strategies. Based on the recommendations of this committee a Programme of Action was prepared to reorient entire education system in the year 1992. Some of the salient features of POA were; the Policy and Programme laid importance on higher education and research work; Vocational education was given importance by the POA to increase individual competency and national productivity; It emphasised that teacher training facilities should be provided to eligible candidates in the teaching profession. It also suggested that the service conditions and salaries of teachers should be improved; It also directed to establish regulatory institutions to monitor quality in Higher Education. Finally it can be briefed that POA as a follow policy of NPE 1986 and also an immediate need of the hour due to the new economic reform of 1991 proved as significant policy milestone in Indian education system.

Maintaining Standards in Higher Education

There are a number of organisations in India which are entrusted with the responsibility of coordinating the efforts of various agencies of higher education and monitoring and controlling the standards of higher education. In the following section a brief sketch of these organisations/ apex bodies is given:

(i) Central Advisory Board of Education

The Central Advisory Board of Education (CABE) has emerged as a very effective instrument of meaningful partnership between the States and Centre particularly at evolving a consensus on major policy issues in the field of Human Resource Development. The CABE established in 1920 is the oldest and most important advisory body of the Government of India on all aspects of education. Calcutta University Commission (1917-19) suggested for the first time, the need for such an advisory body. This was abolished in 1923 for want of financial resources. However, it was revived in 1935. The present composition of the board is as follows:

1. The Union Minister of Human Resource Development is the Chairman.
2. Representatives of the Government of India. (All other Ministers in HRD).
3. Representative of State Governments. It includes ministers of education of each state and representatives of all Union Territories.
4. Six members of Parliament (two from Rajya Sabha and four from Lok Sabha)
5. Two members of Inter-University Board.
6. Two members of All India Technical Education.
7. One representative of Indian Council of Agricultural Research and one representative of the Medical Council of India.
8. Chairman of University Grants Commission, Education Member of Planning Commission, Education Secretary, and Govt. of India.

Major functions of CABE are to advise on any educational question which may be referred to it by the Government of India or by any State Government, to call for information and advice regarding educational development of special value to India and to examine the information and circulate it with recommendations to the Government of India and to State Governments.

The Board has been passing resolutions in various educational development areas e.g. spread of universal elementary education for the age group of 6-14, removal of 'adult illiteracy', women education, vocationalisation of higher education etc. Resolution and recommendations made in the meetings serve as guidelines for policy-makers, planners and administrators in education; such resolutions provide considered opinion and thinking of experts on various topics. Mohanty rightly sums up its role as "On the whole the Board provides a common platform for a nation-wide cross-section representatives hailing from various sectors of education whose deliberation and decisions emerge out of the cross fertilisation of rich ideas and long experiences. This helps immensely in the formulation of sound educational policies and programmes keeping aloof from hot bed of politics and partisan verbal fights."

To quote National Policy of Education (1986), "The CABE will play a pivotal role in reviewing educational development, determining the changes required to improve the system and monitoring implementation. It will function through appropriate committees and other mechanism and has been created to ensure contact with and co-ordinate among the various areas of Human Resource Development. The departments of education at the Centre and the States will be strengthened through the involvement of professionals."

(ii) Association of Indian University

The Government of India constituted Inter-University board 1924 (now Association of Indian Universities) on the basis of recommendation of Lytton Committee relating to Indian students in England. The Committee had noticed that the standards of Indian Universities varied greatly and recommended that Indian Universities should secure uniformity and coordination of standards by constituting an Inter-University Organisation. The functions of Association of Indian Universities are to:

(i) Act as an Inter-University Organisation and bureau of information.

(ii) Facilitate the exchange of Professors.

(iii) Serve as an authorised channel of communication and facilitate the co-ordination of university work.

(iv) Assist Indian Universities to get recognition for their degrees and diplomas in other countries, and

(v) Represent as a common representative of Indian higher education.

The Association provides a forum for discussing the problems of university. It also acts as an advisory body.

(iii) University Grants Commission

The University Grants Commission was set up in 1945 in response to the recommendations contained in the Sargent Report. Its main functions were recommendatory i.e. recommending grants for Central Universities to the Ministry of Education. The University Education Commission (1948-49) recommended the creation of UGC with funds of its own. The Committee suggested that "the first and most essential change is that the Committee shall have power to allocate grants with in total limits set by the Government instead of merely recommending their allocation to the Finance Ministry which may or may not agree. In a democratic country the decision of how much public money shall be allocated for a Sector can be made and ought to be made only by the Government; it is a political decision and a part of their yearly budgetary proposals. But once decision is taken, then the detailed allocation of the money must be left to an expert body not merely non-political, but as rigidly protected from political or personal lobbying and pressures as the Constitution of the country can make them".

From a Committee, it become a Commission in 1953 through an executive order of the Government of India based upon the recommendation of the University Education Commission for the purpose of allocation and disbursement of grants to the Universities as well as for the purpose of coordination and maintenance of standards of higher education in India. With the passage of University Grants Commission Bill 1956 by the Parliament, the UGC became a statutory body.

UGC Act 1956 provided for a Chairman and nine members. The nine members should include not more than three from amongst the Vice-Chancellor of the Universities, two members from amongst the officers of the Union Government to represent the Central Government; the remaining members were to be eminent educationist.

The Sapru Committee has suggested strength of 15 members of whom at least five members should be full time. The serving Vice-Chancellor should not be the members of the UGC. The UGC Act was amended in 1968 and then in 1972. According to the amended Act, UGC consists of 12 members excluding a Chairman. The other members are (a) officers of the Central Government, (b) teachers of the Universities and (c) experts in the areas of agricultural, industry, medical, commerce etc.

The National Policy of Education Review Committee in line with the Sapru Committee suggested the creation of full time members. In the opinion of the Committee, the commission should consist of at least five full time members apart from the Chairman and Vice-Chairman, with specialisation in specific areas of teaching, research, extension, management and finance. On this recommendation, the UGC expressed its views: "The UGC Act was indeed amended in 1971 to provide for three full time members the amendment was later repeated as it was felt that it would not be desirable to have two categories of members, viz. full time members and part time members, with the latter having by implication, lower role and status as compared to full time members. We appreciated this point of view and felt that there is no need for appointment of full time members".

Both CABE and National Policy on Education Review Committee (NPERC) suggested the setting up of regional offices. The CABE observed that "the NPERC suggested the opening of regional office with adequate decentralisation of authority and functions. We were informed that the UGC had accepted the need for establishment of some regional offices and also received a report of the Administrative Staff College, Hyderabad. We strongly recommend that regional offices should be set up at the earliest with adequate authority and functions."

The main functions assigned to the UGC are (1) to advise the Central Government on problems connected with the co-ordination of facilities and the maintenance of standards in Universities and to take such executive actions as may be necessary in that behalf; (2) to enquire into the financial needs of Universities and to advise the Central Government on the allocation of funds for grants-in-aid to them; (3) to take all necessary executive actions in the matter of deciding on the grants to the Universities and in disbursing them out of funds placed at the disposal of the Commission; (4) to advise any authority, if such advise is asked for, on the establishment of new university or on proposal connected with the expansion of the activities of any existing university; (5) to advise the Central Government or any university on any question which may be referred to the Commission by the Government or the University as the case may be; (6) to advise the Central Government or State Governments in regard to the recognition of any degree conferred or granted by a University for the purpose of employment under the Central Government or the State Government and (7) to advise Universities on measures necessary for the reform and improvement of university education; and (8) to undertake such other duties and functions as may be prescribed or deemed necessary by the Government of India for advancing the cause of higher education in India or as may be incidental or conducive to the attainment of the above functions.

The UGC has been helping the higher-education through various activities aimed at raising the Standard of Education in Universities and Colleges. The UGC has been meeting the development needs of the Universities. It has helped in raising the academic/ educational expertise of teachers. Many programmes have been initiated for the betterment of the students. It has helped the mobility of teachers through the funding of conferences, seminars and cultural exchange programmes. Some of the current activities of UGC are as follows: -

(i) *Promotion and Support of Autonomous Colleges:* Under this scheme a college is declared autonomous by its affiliating university. Such college is responsible for conduct of examination and quality of education. Till May 2003, 135 colleges were granted autonomous status.

(ii) *Re-designing of Courses:* The UGC has designed the scheme of restructuring of undergraduate courses in general education with a view to make the degree courses relevant to environmental needs.

(iii) *Improving the Standard of Education:* UGC is providing assistance for the College Science Education Improvement Programme (COSIP) and College Humanities and Social Science Improvement Programme (COHSSIP).

(iv) *Special Assistance Programme:* The Commission provides assistance and special assistance to the university departments to upgrade their status as advanced Centres. 'Centre of Advanced Study' and 'Departments of Special Assistance' in science, engineering and technology have been created and provided assistance.

(v) *Scholarships and Fellowships for Development of Research in Universities and Colleges:* The Commission provides junior research fellowships in various subjects. These fellowships are awarded only to those research scholars who have qualified in national level tests conducted by the UGC, CSIR, GATE, etc. Teachers of outstanding eminence are awarded national fellowships for a specified period to devote themselves exclusively to research and writing. Under the scheme of 'Visiting Professors/ Fellows', assistance is provided to Universities for the appointment of Visiting Professors/ Fellows.

(vi) *Media and Educational Technology:* The UGC has taken the initiative to utilise the time slot given for higher education and televising the programmes in higher education entitled "Countywide Classroom".

(vii) *Adult, Continuing and Extension Education Programmes:* The Commission is providing assistance to Universities for promotion programmes of adult education and extension, eradication of illiteracy, continuing education, population education and planning forums.

(iii) State Council of Higher Education

The State Council for Higher Education acts as a link between the Universities and colleges and the State Governments and to work closely with the UGC in view of its statutory responsibility for the maintenance and coordination of standards of higher education at all India level. In order to achieve the objectives set out above, the Central Government may advice State Governments for enacting legislation for setting up of

State Councils of Higher Education in the States. In an Indian state where the numbers of Universities are too few, an advisory body may be set up to fulfil the above objectives.

A State Council of Higher Education may consist of 10-13 members as follows:-

(i) A Chairman

(ii) Not less than two and not more than four members drawn on all-India basis from the following:

(a)Persons who have obtained high academic distinction in teaching, engineering, medicine, agricultural science or law;

(b) Who are industrialists or educationists of high repute.

(iii) Not more than two from amongst the Vice-Chancellors of the Universities in the area including Vice-Chancellors of Central Universities, if any

(iv) Not more than two from amongst the teachers of Universities colleges in the state.

(v) Secretary, UGC or an officer of the UGC not below the rank of Joint Secretary nominated by the Chairman, UGC.

(vi) Education Secretary of the State Government (Ex-Officio).

(vii) Finance Secretary of the State Government (Ex-Officio)

If any State so desires it may include the Director of Higher Education as an ex-officio member.

The terms and conditions of service of Chairman and Members are:

(i) The chairman shall hold office for a term of five years and other members shall hold office for a term of three years.

(ii) The office of the chairman shall be a whole-time and salaried one and subject to the terms and conditions of service as prescribed.

(iii) The salary of the chairman shall not be less than that of a vice-chancellor of a university.

(iv) A person who has not attained the age of 65 years shall be eligible for appointment as a Chairman.

The council shall appoint a Secretary and such other employee as it may think necessary for the efficient performance of its functions. The Secretary shall be a whole time functionary. The terms and conditions of service of the employees shall be determined by the council.

The Council may associate with itself in such a manner and for such a purpose, any person whose assistance or advice it may desire in carrying out its work. A person associated with the Council for any purpose shall have a right to take part in the discussions relevant to that purpose but shall not have a right to vote at a meeting of the Council and shall not be a member for any other purpose. The Council may associate with its members of Medical, Engineering and Agricultural Universities with a view of developing co-ordination amongst Universities.

The Council shall meet at such time and places and shall observe such rules of procedures in regard to the transaction of business at its meetings as may be provided by regulations.

The Council shall functions for co-ordination and determination of standards in institutions for higher education or research and scientific and technical institution in accordance with the guidelines issued by the UGC from time to time. The main functions of State Councils of Higher education are summarised below:

(a) Planning and Co-ordination

(i) To prepare consolidated programmes in the sphere of higher education in the state in accordance with the guidelines that may be issued by the UGC from time to time, and to assist in their implementation.

(ii) To forward the development programms of Universities and colleges in the state to UGC along with its comments and recommendations.

(iii) To assist UGC in respect of determination and maintenance of standards and suggest remedial action wherever necessary in accordance with the guidelines.

(iv) To evolve perspective plans for development of higher education in the State.

(v) To monitor the progress of implementation of such development programmes.

(b) Academic Functions

(i) To encourage and promote innovations in curricular development, restructuring of course and updating of syllabi in the Universities/colleges.

(ii) To promote and co-ordinate the programmes of autonomous colleges and to monitor its implementation.

(iii) To devise steps to improve the standards of examinations conducted by the Universities and suggest necessary reforms.

(iv) To facilitate, training of teachers in colleges/ Universities.

(v) To promote publication of quality text books, monographs and reference books.

(vi) To develop programmes for greater academic co-operation and interaction between university teachers and college teachers and to facilitate mobility of students and teachers within and outside the state.

(vii) To regulate admission on the basis of physical facilities and to develop entrance examination for admission to institution of higher education.

(viii) To encourage sports, games, physical education and cultural activities in the Universities and colleges.

(ix) To encourage extension activities and promote interaction with agencies concerned with regional planning and development.

(x) To prepare an overview report on the working of the Universities in the State. A copy of this report should be sent to the UGC.

(c) Advisory Functions

(i) To advise State Government into determining the block maintenance grants and to lay down the basis for such grants.

(ii) To set up a State Research Board so as to link educational institutions research with that of the research agencies and also with research needs of the state.

(iii) To examine the statutes and ordinances in various Universities in the State (excluding Central Universities) and suggest modification wherever required.

(iv) To advise State Government regarding the Statutes proposed by the Universities in the State.

(v) To perform any other function necessary for furtherance of higher education in the State.

(d) Administrative Functions

To administer and release grant-in-aid from State Government to Universities and colleges in the State. For this purpose, the State Government should place the grant meant for the Universities and colleges at the disposal of the Council.

National Assessment and Accreditation Council

The University Grants Commission (UGC) has established the National Assessment and Accreditation Council (NAAC) in September

1994 at Bangalore, in pursuance of the National Policy on Education and the Programme of Action (POA), 1986. NAAC has been entrusted with the task of performance evaluation, assessment and accreditation of Universities and colleges in the country. The approach of NAAC in its assessment is objective analysis and continuous improvement instead of being punitive or judgmental. It will help institutions of higher learning to maximize their resources, opportunities and capabilities with the objective of continuous improvement in the quality of education.

Assessment is a performance evaluation of an institution and its units. It is accomplished through a process of self-study and peer review using well defined criteria. The process of assessment is in accordance with internationally accepted practices and norms which are suitably modified to meet the Indian requirements. Accreditation is granted through a certificate given by NAAC which is valid for a period of five years.

NAAC draws its expertise from senior academics from all over India. Vice-Chancellors of Universities, Directors of Higher Education and Science and Technology Institutes, Deans, Principals of Colleges, Heads of Departments drawn from all disciplines, as well as educational administrators, lend their valuable time, expertise and leadership for the academic activities of NAC. Its National Consultative Committees in various areas provide necessary inputs for establishing and strengthening process of assessment. In addition, NAAC is also generating a large pool of experts/ assessors in all subjects by periodically conducting orientation programmes across the country.

An objective, fair and independent assessment followed by accreditation enable an institution to know its strengths, weaknesses and opportunities trough an informed review process. It also helps us proper planning and allocation of scare resources. The assessment also provides funding agencies a very dependable and objective data about performance of the institution and helps in getting funds. This process also leads to innovation and a new sense of direction and identity. The credibility of the institution before the society with reliable information on quality of education is establishment by the certification of NAAC. It enables institutions initiate innovative and modern methods of pedagogy. It is an established fact that the higher quality of education promotes intra and inter-institutional interactions and linkages.

The NAAC regularly interacts with its stakeholders through regular correspondence with the institutions, awareness programmes, newsletter, press and NAAC, Press conferences and press release, special articles in newspapers and magazine on NAAC, TV coverage, publishing a directory of accredited Institution, a directory of assessors and networking of Accredited Institutions. The NAAC also regularly refines its methodology through scientific feedback obtained by Met-evaluation, Case studies, Impact analysis, In-house deliberations, Feedback from Peer Team visits and Seminars. In this direction, NAAC has so far, sponsored five regional workshops on "Capacity Building of Women Managers in Higher Education' in North, North-East, East, West and Southern regions covering all the States. One of the positive initiative in academic institutions identified in these workshop was to give adequate representation of women in decision making bodies like, management council, academic council senate, board of studies, selection committees, admission committees, student welfare council, finance committee, housing committee etc.

NAAC functions through its General Council (GC), Executive Committee (EC) and other academic, advisory and administrative subcommittees.

The General Council is headed by the Chairperson of Universities Grants Commission as its president and it includes all members of the Executive Committee, the Secretary, Department of Education, Ministry of Human Resource and Development, Government of India, the Secretary General of Association of Indian Universities and four Vice-Chancellors and Principals.

The Executive Committee manages the affairs of the NAAC. It includes Vice-Chairperson of the University Gants Commission, Secretary, Ministry of Human Resource and Development, Department of Education, Chairperson of AICTE, DEC, NCTE, AIU by rotation and Secretary, University Grants Commission. The representation of academics, Vice-Chancellor is also proved in the Executive Committee.

Present Scenario of Higher Education

Indian Higher Education has manifested the most volatile development in last one decade due to several policy initiatives on one hand and due to the consequences of such initiatives on other hand. The liberalisation, privatization and globalisation have affected all the areas of education especially the higher and professional education in India. Post 1991 has constructed the formation of several professional bodies to maintain quality and standard in higher education whereas many existing bodies were strengthened as well for the similar purposes. The unprecedented growth in school education sector through DPEP, SSA and

RMSA have pushed the higher education sector at great level apart from the larger phenomenon of privatization. The private University/Deemed University growth since 2005 along the directive lines of National Knowledge Commission 2005/06 preceded by mushrooming growth in private medical, engineering, management and teacher education colleges have contributed optimally in quantitative growth of higher education at one side whereas deteriorated quality of education on the other side. Quantitative growth of higher education institutions and enrolments were some of the main features of National Knowledge Commission. The previous government also tried to actualise the vision of NKC by increasing budgetary allocations to education sector upto 20 per cent of the total budget. With the increasing potential of demographic dividend and its optimal utilisation, Rashtriya Uchchtar Shiksha Abhiyan (RUSA) was launched in 2013 in order to achieve 30 per cent GER in higher education by 2020 along with several provisions of quality maintenance in this sector.

Nonetheless, merely discussing the developmental aspects of Indian higher education institutions and its different agencies will not provide the complete understanding of this sector unless the nature and complexities are also extensively discussed. In order to comprehend the entire gamut of higher education, the following chapters gradually discussed about the related sub-sectors of higher education in India.

References

- Ahmad, M.A. (1985). Traditional Education among Muslims. Delhi: R.K. Publishing Corporation.
- Jhingran, S. (2012). *Madrasa Education in Modern India — A study.* New Delhi: Manohar Publishers and Distributors.
- Darul Uloom, Deoband's website: http//www.darululoom-deoband.com/English syst-_of_edu/index.htm, ' The system of Education'.)
- Khan, I. A. (2013). Sir Syed Aur Jadidiyat. Delhi: Educational Publication House.
- Hundastani Madaris ka Talımi Nizam Isme Islah ki Zaroorat : Ek Jaiza published by Global Media Publications, New Delhi.
- Pathak, R.P. (2007). Education in Emerging India. New Delhi: Atlantic Publishers and Distributors Pvt Ltd.
- Richter, J (2010). A History of Missions in India. BiblioBazaar.
- Shahid, K. M. (2004). Management of Higher Education: A Comparative Study of State and Central Universities. An unpublished Ph.D. thesis. New Delhi: Jamia Milia Islamia.

- Govt of India (1992). National Policy on Education: Programme of Action. Ministry of Human Resource Development. Government of India.
- Raza, M. (1991). Status and Prospects in Higher Education in India. New Delhi: Association of Indian University.

2

Issues in Managing Indian Higher Education

Prof Khwaja M. Shahid,

"By education I mean an all round drawing of the best in the child and man —— body, mind and spirit"

Mahatma Gandhi,

Harijan 31 July 1937

The complexity of the management and administration of Indian institutions of higher learning have been increasing with the advent of globalisation and its enhancing arena. In order to understand the issues and concerns of higher education in India, let one should first understand the complex nature of Indian Universities through types of institutions.

(i) Types of Universities

At present, the following six main types of Universities/ institutions of higher learning are in existence in India:

(1) Affiliating Universities
(2) Unitary Universities
(3) Federative Universities
(4) Deemed to be Universities
(5) Open and Distance Learning Universities
(6) Private Universities
(7) Other Institutions of Higher Education

Affiliating Universities: The affiliating type of Universities are once which exercise control in varying measures over the large number of affiliated colleges, which are scattered over a particular specified area to secure certain minimum conditions; but the main service they renders is still that of providing syllabi departments as well as research centres. Several of the Universities in India are established as affiliating Universities. For example, Osmania University, Andhra University, Mysore University, etc. are some of the Universities that come under this category. In fact most of state government Universities are affiliating Universities.

Unitary Universities: In a unitary university almost the entire teaching is done by the university in its own departments and as far as possible students reside on the campus. This type of Universities is generally restricted to a single town or its immediate neighbourhood. But the catchment area of the students is entire country and abroad. Aligarh Muslim University, Jawaharlal Nehru University and Banaras Hindu University are examples of this type of University.

Federative Universities: The federative university is a variation from the above. While the campus of such Universities is also restricted to a town or a geographical area, there are a number of colleges which generally work under the direction of, and in cooperation with, the university. The University of Delhi and agricultural Universities are examples of this type.

Deemed to be Universities: Some of the prestigious institutions have been established in India as educational institutions with private as well as government management. They include Tata Institute of Social Science Research, Bombay; Satya Sai Institute of Higher Learning, Andhra Pradesh; Indian Institute of Science, Bangalore; School of Planning and Architect. These institutes are full-fledged educational institutions and they provide teaching as well as research facilities. They satisfy the conditions laid down by the UGC for reorganisations as deemed to be university. The UGC, after assessing the standard of education, capabilities of awarding degrees, expertise in specialised subjects, management of examination etc. have recognised such institutions as 'Deemed to be University' under power delegated to it in the UGC Act. Such deemed to be Universities are generally unitary and federative in nature.

Open Universities: Such Universities do not impart education/ teaching through traditional system of class room or face to face teaching. The students are also not required to come to the campuses of such Universities, but lessons are imparted to students through the medium of electronic communications, satellite, TV, Videos, CD, etc. The hard copies of course material, assignments, evaluation material is posted. The Open Universities set up the regional resource Centres and Regional Offices for contact programme. The concept is to take out the education from the four walls of a class rooms in a campus to the door steps of students by using modern means of communications which could be fast and live. The administrative arrangement and management issues are different in such Universities. The example of such Universities in India are Indira Gandhi National Open University, Dr Bhim Rao Ambedkar Open University, Vardhman Mahavir Open University, Nalanda Open University, Yashwantrao Chavan Maharashtra Open University, Madhya Pradesh Bhoj Open University, Dr. Babasaheb Ambedkar Open University, Karnataka State Open University, Netaji Subhas Open University, UP Rajarshi Tando Open University, Tamil Nadu Open University etc.

Organisational structure is not same in all distance and open learning institutes. The organisation of a small scale distance and open learning operations is different from large institution. For example, Indira Gandhi National Open University, Vice-Chancellor is the Chief Executive Officer of the University. He/she is assisted by Pro Vice-Chancellors. The overall functioning of the university is managed by various statutory authorities like the board of management, planning board, academic council, finance committee, distance education council and the school of studies. There are schools of studies which are responsible for the design and development of academic programme. On the other hand, Maulana Azad National Urdu University which is also mandated by the Act of Parliament to impart "education through conventional teaching and distance education system" has a full fledged Directorate of Distance Education headed by a Director, who along with faculty members of different subjects looks after all the operations of distance and open learning under the overall supervision of the regular university management. In the case of regular Universities offer very few distance learning courses, the administrative structure is still very small consisting of a Director and few supporting staff.

Private Universities: These are not very old institutions of higher education in India. Many state governments are permitting private individuals or societies / Trusts to establish a university. The funding and management of such private Universities are hundred per cent by private organisations or individuals. These Universities came into existence by the mandate of a specific Private University Act passed by the Legislative Assembly of the state. The management structure is by and large same as that of any other regular Central or state university.

Other Institutions of Higher Education: Government of India has set up many specialised institutions of Higher learning for example, All

India Institute of Medical Sciences; Indian Institutes of Technology; Indian Institutes of Management; National Institutes of Fashion Technology; National Institute of Design etc. They are subject specific teaching and research institutions with legal power to award degrees though they are not Universities in traditional sense. They are not headed by a Vice Chancellor; instead by a Director. They do not have a Chancellor or authorities like Senate or Court. They are directly funded by the Government of India and not by University Grants Commission.

The above brief presentation of different categories and type of Universities and institutions of higher education will show that India has the experience of all types of educational system which is very diversified in its nature, systems and consequently management. Hence, the Management of Universities is a complex issue and no single approach can be worked out as a role model.

(ii) Organisational Structure of Universities

The university system can be seen from the point of view of its structure as well as its dynamics. Irrespective of the type of the university, the internal systems for the purpose of administration is more or less same in all the Universities. Within the overall system of institutions of higher education, there are four following main subsystems, namely:

1. Governance System;
2. Administrative System;
3. Academic Affairs System; and
4. Student Affairs System.

These systems are governed with the help of specific committees to carry out specific tasks assigned to such committees. The three main authorities of a university are the Court or Senate, the Executive Council or Syndicate and the Academic Council. Their composition, powers and functions are laid down by the Act under which a university has been established, and statutes framed under the Act. Basically the governance of the university follows the principle of Collective Management. The Court or Senate is a large body with a membership of about hundred or more. It includes representatives of the teachers of the University and its colleges, the general community, ex-graduates of the university, the donor if any, and other group relevant to the university. It is basically a deliberative body and it generally meets once a year. It is presided over by the Chancellor, and in his absence, by the Pro-Chancellor or the Vice-Chancellor. It provides a forum where the university teachers together with other groups interested in the university discuss and review the broad policies and programmes of the university, suggest measures for improvement and development of the institution and express view on its annual report and annual accounts. The court was conceived and created to enable the university to know the need and requirements of the public and to try to meet them, on the one hand and to explain its problems to the public.

The Executive Council or Syndicate is the principal executive body of the university in the hierarchical sense; it is a powerful authority which provides sanction/ approvals to the actions of Vice-Chancellor. It is small body with and Vice-Chancellor – as chairman and Pro Vice-Chancellor (one or more) as ex-officio member. Other members include Deans of the faculties (by rotations in case their number is large), and few members elected by the Court and a few persons nominated by the Visitor and/or the Chancellor of the university. In some Universities Dean Student Welfare or Proctor is also the ex-officio member of the Executive Council. The Council/ syndicate normally meet periodically and also on specific occasion if the Vice-Chancellor feels the need for it on any particular issue(s). Apart from considering and deciding matters relating to day-to-day administration of the university, the Executive Council is also authorised to frame new statutes and ordinances and amend existing one. But no statues can be made operative unless it has been duly approved by the Visitor or the Chancellor of the University.

The Academic Council is the principal academic body of the university. Briefly speaking it lays down the academic policies of the university co-ordinates them and exercise general supervision over them. The Vice-Chancellor is the Chairman of this body too. The members include the Pro Vice-Chancellor or Rector, if any, Deans, Librarian, Heads of the Departments of Studies, Principals of colleges and some other functionaries. The Academic Council has also generally been meeting once a year, but now it meets more often.

There are some other important bodies also in the university organization. These include the Finance Committee, Faculty Committee, Examination Committee, Sports Committee, Library Committee, Planning Boards and the Building Committee etc. The Vice-Chancellor or his nominee is generally the Chairman of these committees and bodies. Each of them has specified assignments as indicated by their name. The Finance Committee for example, is concerned with screening of the budget of the university and all major proposals with budgetary/ financial implications. The decision of each of these bodies are generally subject to the approval of the Executive Council/ Syndicate of the university.

The Court, Executive Council, Academic Council, Faculty Committee, Board of Studies etc. are various important authorities of the university. The function of university administration is greatly influence by these authorities. These authorities take various decisions which have considerable implications on the finance and administrative aspects of the Universities. Although the Vice Chancellor or Director is the chief executive and academic officer and it is his duty to ensure that the provisions of the Act and all relevant laws and rules are implemented, he has to exercise his authority in collaboration and consultation with various committees mentioned above.

(iii) The Main Administrative Functionaries

The Central Universities have at the apex level the President of India as their Visitor. In the case of other Universities, the Governor of the State is the Chancellor. The Visitor or Chancellor is not assigned any administrative responsibility in day to day affairs of the university. The Chancellor is an officer of the university and he has right to preside over the convocation and meetings of the Court/ Senate. The Visitor or Chancellor is responsible for approving or not any new amendment in the statute. He may also be concerned with very serious matters like the appointment of a committee of enquiry on university.

The Vice-Chancellor is the principal executive and academic officer of the university. He exercises general supervision and control over the affairs of university and ensure implementation of the decisions of the Executive Council/ Syndicate and other authorities. He has also to see that the university functions in accordance with its Act, Statutes, Ordinance and Regulations. According to the model Act Committee for Universities The Vice Chancellor is the most important functionary in a university. Not only on the administrative side but also for securing the right atmosphere for the teachers and students to do their work effectively and with right spirit.

Some Indian Universities, particularly if they are large have one or more Pro Vice-Chancellor. He is invariably a person of the Vice-Chancellor's choice and normally appointed from amongst the Dean or Professors of the university. He functions like deputy to the Vice-Chancellor and helps him in the discharge of his duties, under specific authority delegated to him or otherwise.

There is a Dean of each faculty, appointed by rotation from amongst the university professors in various departments of the faculty. He presides over meetings of the faculty and speaks whenever needed, on behalf of the faculty. He is also concerned with the implementation of decisions affecting the whole faculty.

Each teaching Department of the university has a Head or Chairperson. They are appointed in the department by rotation from among the senior teachers of the concerned departments. The head of the department has the right to speak for the whole department on its behalf in certain matters, but it is desirable that in academic matters, he respects the equality of all professors and the autonomy of all teachers of the department.

The Registrar of the university supervises the work of the secretariat of the University. He is the Head of the administration of the university. He has important duties to perform as he assists the Vice-Chancellor in all administrative, academic, legal and developmental functions. He is also the secretary of almost all o the statutory bodies. He assists the Vice Chancellor in meetings of the main authorities of the university. There is then the Finance Officer of the University. He is responsible for looking after finance. More specifically, it is his responsibility to properly invest university funds match the expenditure, and deal generally with all matters connected with the finances of the university.

The Court, Executive Council, Academic Council, Faculty Committee, Board of Studies etc. are various authorities of the university. The function of university administration is greatly influenced by these authorities. These authorities take various decisions which have considerable implications on the finance and administrative aspects of the Universities.

(iv) Issues Relating to Higher Education Institutions

The institutions of higher learning/Universities are not meant only for pursuing higher education and research but they also have very wide ranging social responsibilities. These responsibilities are toward the societies where they are situated and the humanity at large. The main purpose of setting up of Universities is development of human resources. They are not supposed to only impart knowledge and skill to students but also to train and develop their personalities. These human resources when ready, after acquiring necessary knowledge and skill, are sent out to the society for the growth and development of the country and the humanity. The type of knowledge and values imparted to students will determine the conscious of the nation. Hence, the Universities are termed as conscious keepers of the nation. These values should include: (a) to live like a good human being in a society; (b) how to respect basic human values; (c) to preserve and promote secular values and peaceful co-existence, (d) mutual respect for different groups and individuals, (e) to work for justice and fundamental rights of the people and to preach and practice non violence in dealing individual and social issues.. The Universities are also supposed to promote scientific temperament. Scientific temperament demands working against superstition and other social biases, prejudices and discrimination of any kind. It should result that reason, logical thinking and experimentation should be part of life. The Universities should also work against prevalent social evils like dowry, atrocities against women and weaker sections, child marriage, corruption etc. The overall aim should be to improve the quality of life and dignity of human being, both in terms of physical comforts and moral and ethical values. As Mahatma Gandhi said, "real education consists in drawing the best out of yourself. What better book can there be than the book of humanity".

The present status of the Universities as being observed/ seen by its stakeholders is not quite satisfactory. The university system is not in the desired shape and under great pressures from many directions. There are various challenges in running the system of higher education and many issues arising there from. We know that different Universities have different organizational structures, funding patterns, nature of education imparted, types of students and faculty, socio-cultural set up, political atmosphere, style of administration and management. Consequently issues and challenges faced by the University are as diversified and of different nature as types of Universities and organisational and funding systems prevalent in India. Such challenges and issues are required to be handled in a particular manner which is specific to each university. It may perhaps not to be possible and advisable to identify such issues and challenges which may be applicable equally to all Universities and institutions in India. However, on the basis of functioning of Universities in India, following areas may be identified where new challenges are faced by them:

(a) Decision- making process
(b) Academic Administration
(c) Financial Management
(d) Human Resource Management
(e) Municipal function
(f) Welfare function

(g) Modernisation and Development
(h) Technological upgradation

The University System is a dynamic system and the milieus in which it is working have also been changing very rapidly. There can be a long list of large number of complex issues which are unique to university system. Some of the major concerns of institutions of higher education which are directly related to the administration of higher education and affecting its functioning can be as follows.

Explosion in the Number of Students

There was rapid expansion in fifties and sixties. The growth rate came down in seventies. Further the eighties made an upward trend. Thus, the phenomenal growth in the field of higher education and the extraordinary increase in the volume and diversity of education efforts at various levels have imposed heavy strain on the existing administrative structure and organisation in Universities. The National Policy on Education, 1986 recommended that the number of full time students enrolled in university should be limited on the basis of physical facilities and staff. In spite of all these recommendations/ concerns and administrative problems, there appears to be no check in this regard.

Students Unrest and Indiscipline

Nowadays, indiscipline is a general rule. The adherence to rules, code of conduct or values is more by an exception than as a rule. Quite a large number of working or teaching days are lost because of strikes, bunks, elections and other agitations. It is unfortunate in most institutions that punctuality in offices and class-rooms is missing. Less said about the discipline of students is better. The reasons for this may perhaps be more stress or increasing student population. The number of students going to Universities and colleges has been increasing every year as higher education is open to all irrespective of available facilities. Students have no bright future in terms of employment. Some recent newspaper reports suggested that employability of passing out professionals is only 25 per cent.Teachers do not have time to cope with the ever increasing student population. All these are putting stress on the university system which ultimately affects the discipline on the campus.

Student agitations have now become a common feature of the Universities. In some of the campuses of the Universities the atmosphere is so explosive that any cause or pretext is good enough to lead to a disturbance. Over the decades along with the unrest in society, due to political developments, students have become more vociferous perhaps because of mounting unemployment or under employment. This has several manifestations e.g. student disrupting classes, interfering with management functions, indulging in violence during elections or otherwise and engaging in unfair practices in examinations. Observations have pointed out existence of some neglected underlying local grievances or general lack of motivation for studies or lack of respect toward authority in general, including teaching and university functionaries behind such instances.

Professional Competencies of the Staff

The recruitment processes as prescribed in Act or Statutes of Universities are well-defined for higher statutory posts and members of the faculty. The system is broadly based upon the open selection process on all India basis. Although now a degree of doctorate or successfully passing of National Eligibility Test (NET) is made compulsory, however, many studies have shown that the Universities are providing employments to its own products which is leading to inbreeding. The situation in the case of non-teaching staff is much worst. In most of the cases regular appointments are preceded by daily wage appointments and ad hoc appointments. Incumbents are selected on the basis of personal choice without going through prescribed procedure of selection. Daily wage or ad hoc appointments continue for a number of years. These employees are ultimately given permanent appointments and they in turn get promoted without much scrutiny. Promotion is practically on the basis of seniority without any process of performance evaluation. In the whole process merit is sacrificed. There is also no effective mechanism or avenues for in-service training or skill development programmes. The quality of faculty and Karamcharies, therefore, on the whole has lowered. These very people are required to manage the university system.

If persons with inadequate academic expertise with no spirit of dedication and inferior qualifications are appointed to the faculty positions, such persons often resort to favouritism in student evaluations and encourage factionalism etc. By virtue of the system of getting confirmation after one year of probation, every employee gets a fixed tenure of service till superannuation. It can be stated with a great deal of personal experience that staff gets promotional increments regularly almost independent of meaningful assessment of performance. Mostly, promotions are given by seniority and not by merit/ selection.

Unionisation of Teaching and Non-Teaching Staff

Another problem of the higher education in India, at present, is that of unionisation of teaching and non-teaching staff. So far as unionisation of non-teaching staff is concerned, it is spill over of the general spread of the trade unionism from the industrial sector to the service sector and from the public sector to public supported institutions. The disturbances created by the non-teaching staff in the Universities are no less in their intensity than those which originate from the student.

The trade unionism among teachers, however, is of more ominous significance. Teachers are regarded as the pillars of the academic structure and traditionally they have been objects of respect. Teachers are also expected to set examples not only of learning but also of character and moral values. The unionisation of teacher represents, therefore, very serious break with traditional norms. No doubt teachers are also suffering from inflationary pressure but there could be other conceivable methods of redress of their serious grievances. Teachers also resort to strikes, *dharnas* and at times, resort to violence, which is unbecoming of a teacher.

Proliferation of Higher Education

The post-Independence period witnessed an enormous expansion of colleges and Universities by private agencies as well as Government and these colleges were established for reasons or consideration other than quality of education. The State Governments also become active in establishing more and more Universities with criteria other than academic criteria. Political expediency to satisfy regional demands has been solely responsible for the multiplicity of Universities. Presently there are 325 state Universities, 45 central Universities, 128 deemed Universities, 195 private Universities and more than 38 thousand colleges in the country making the second largest number of institutions in the world. Altogether in 693 Universities and 38 thousand plus colleges/institutes, 8.33 lakh plus teachers are providing education at higher education level. The current gross enrolment ratio at higher education is 22 per cent (appox.) wherein, central Universities have merely 2.3 per cent enrolment, state Universities have 38.6 per cent enrolment and the highest segment of student enrolment are with private institutions/universities which is about 58 per cent. However, the course structure continues to remain unaltered even in the older Universities and the newly established Universities have not shown any creativity or innovation.

Inadequate Funding

Inadequate funding is another major problem due to which Universities are facing severe financial crisis. Problem is more severe in the case of State Universities. The various State Governments and University Grants Commission which are the major sources of finance of Universities in India, seems to be interested to get out of this sector. The funding for maintenance is slowly getting confined to salary of staff; while support for other maintenance of infrastructure or operational expenses is progressively getting reduced. As a consequence, the financial position of Universities is far from satisfactory. Many Universities are facing this problem and are struggling a lot in managing their own finances. They are operating with heavy deficit. Sometimes it is difficult to pay salaries to the staff and meet other day-to-day expenses, particularly in state Universities. This position is causing deep concern to the academician as well as the administrators of the Universities in India.

Of late, the changes brought in the economic policies of the Government have caused a situation where Universities have been asked to meet more and more of their financial requirements. The system of 100 per cent funding or matching grants to meet the total expenses of the Universities are being replaced by block grants or part funding. As a matter of fact during the decade of nineties the grants of the Universities from the Central Government was fixed at the 91-92 level without taking into account rate of inflation or any other increase in the cost of education. The Universities are asked to raise internal resources or generate alternative resources to meet their growing demands of growth and development. The situation in the State Universities is very bad and some of the Universities have been compelled to mortgage their property to meet urgent financial requirement of payment of salaries and other normal maintenance expenses. Although, there is a need to control the avoidable expenses but increasing financial crunch adversely affect various academic and development programmes relating to research, interfacing, growth and development leading to new challenges before University administration.

The students also individually benefit from the higher education. The rate of return at the individual level is more than rate of return at social level particularly in professional courses like Engineering, Medicine and Management. The cost of education can be provided by students themselves. Therefore, there is strong case to share the cost by students in the form of increased fees or in the form of student loans.

The industry is the biggest beneficiary as trained manpower/human resource is a capital for the industry. The industry should, therefore, come forward to meet substantial cost of higher education, particularly for the development of technical skill and research. At times it is suggested to levy taxes on industry for utilising trained manpower.

The society is the major beneficiaries of the higher education and the investment in education is for the betterment of society. Therefore, the taxpayer through the Government should continue to provide funds for higher education. Education Cess has recently been removed in the budget of 2015 – 16. Government should find some other mechanism to divert funds from corporate or other beneficiary sectors to education sector. How much should be this contribution? It can be discussed and worked out. The Government should not, in any case, stagnate its funding at any specific level or confine it to the maintenance of institutions in terms of salary and other office expenses.

Autonomy and Accountability

Most of our Universities are either set up by the Central government or by the State Governments or funded by them. The appointment of Vice-Chancellor or other senior functionaries are also controlled by the Government. The Parliament and the Parliamentary Committees directly or indirectly supervise the functions of these Universities. This has led to a situation where Universities, particularly State Universities have practically become one of the departments of the Government. The autonomy and freedom which are expected to be enjoyed by these institutions of higher education are missing. There are a large number of instances of direct political interference, clashes within the management board which are dominated by the different political parties or their representatives. Political parties' interference through students for their vested interest adversely affects the administration of the Universities. All this leads to group politics on the campus among teachers, *karamcharies*, students and administration. These external situations are beyond the control of the university management. However university management is left to face these situations and find solution which requires special skills.

Autonomy to sub-units, groups/individuals is also not at the desired level. Mostly decisions are taken at the level of Vice-Chancellor or Registrar. No powers are delegated to the Department of Studies or other functionaries mentioned in above paragraphs. Therefore, there is no effective system of performance evaluation or accountability. Concentration of powers with the Vice-Chancellor leads to a situation where decisions are unnecessarily delayed and affect the efficiency of the Administration viz. Financial, administrative and academic. So far as administrative autonomy is concerned, it may be stated that its preservation depends largely on the independence and the integrity of the higher management of University.

Criteria for Assessment of Performance of Educational Institutions

It is very difficult to assess the quality of education on the basis of identifiable tangible parameters/ indices. While conceding that the quality of education cannot be measured as it can be done in case of other products, but the human resources who are being developed in these Universities are not equipped with the expected level of knowledge and skills. There may be isolated instances of excellence. However, a large number of Universities are suffering due to bad quality of education being imparted to students. There have been no serious and meaningful efforts to improve and update the knowledge of teachers and their art of teaching. Moreover, most of these Universities are not equipped with modern teaching facilities and they are still using out-dated methods.

Another difficulty in assessing the performance of Universities is that the goals or objectives of the Universities are not very tangible. The end products are human being. While other organisation, say, companies, government, banks etc. use the skill and capability of these manpower. But the Universities produce this very manpower; the quality or benefits of their products are reaped by other organisations and systems. One of the most common criteria of judging the performance of an educational institution is the employment and pay packages obtained by its products. It is debateable that how absolute is this parameter. The better students normally leave the university system and join other services/ organization or even go to a developed country to work. The Universities are left with those who perhaps have no option to go elsewhere. The achievement and success of the Universities cannot be seen within the Universities in tangible terms. The recent activities of strengthening the role of National Assessment and Accreditation Council (NACC) is a welcome step to improve the quality in higher education and its assessment.

Vested Interest in Decision Making

According to the prescribed university system, decision making process is based upon collective wisdom. The Vice-Chancellors are supposed to perform his/ her duties on the basis of collective wisdom. There are bodies like Executive Council, Academic Council, Court, Finance Committee, Planning Board, Examination Committee, Library Committee, House-Allotment Committee etc. Although, the Vice-Chancellor is the chief of the University, all decisions are to be taken or endorsed by these bodies. These Committees and Council, largely consist of internal members like Deans, Heads of Departments, senior faculty members, Karamcharies and other ex-officio members. Therefore, they are themselves the decision makers and beneficiaries also. The situation gets more aggravated if the quality of persons constituting these bodies is not up to the mark. The decisions which may lead to adverse reaction from students and *karamcharies* are often avoided or altered. It is a common scene in a university when examination schedules are changed very frequently in view of student's demand. It is daunting task to take just decision according to rules in such a decision-making process where vested interests are represented and quality of decision makers is also not up to the mark.

The hierarchy in the organisational setup of Universities is also quite loose as the Universities are organized rather on horizontal instead of vertical hierarchy. The system of rotation of Chairman and Deans do not provide permanency to the incumbents to these offices. The same person may be an officer at a particular point of time but also becomes a subordinate when he is not holding the office due to rotation and his subordinate man becomes either Dean or Chairman. Mostly, Vice-Chancellors have no choice in appointment of these academic functionaries as they are appointed on rotation by seniority. Therefore, the university system does not allow following a strict hierarchy system which is normally prevalent in other organisations. This system also adversely affects effective and proper decision-making.

Composition of University Community

The working atmosphere of Universities is very different from any other organisations. It's clientele consists of educated people like teachers, *karamcharies* and students. They are more conscious of their rights than other social groups. This group is trained in not accepting anything without questioning. Clients of University are hard-task masters. They are not only beneficiaries but also the decision-makers.

The composition of student community is not permanent and it is an ever changing sub-group of the Universities. On an average, students stay in the university for five to six years. There is induction of fresh students every year. The student community is generally the largest group on the campus. In fact the whole organisation is set up with the intention of providing knowledge, training and skills to students. The position of this group is not static; it is rather dynamic. This dynamism brings changes in the aspirations, expectations, qualities and performance of the student community. The administration has to be responsive to meet the challenges of ever-changing position of student community. It requires unique skills ever evolving new technique and methods to handle this particular group of the University Community.

Politicisation of Campuses

The interfering role of political parties in the functioning of Universities is at many levels. It starts with appointment of Vice-Chancellors to other appointments, transfers, use of students and teaching and other staff for political goals. It is well reflected in student's union elections as noted in the report of the Lyngdoh Committee appointed by the Supreme Court on elections of students in Universities. The student union election in some of famous Universities like Delhi University on the basis of affiliation to political parties' is well established. It is more than common that a Vice-chancellor or registrar gets telephone calls from ministers or MPs offices for various recommendations in matters of day to day administration. A very strict code of conduct should be put in place to protect functionaries from undue political interference.

The above list is not exhaustive but only illustrative to some of the important concerns of management of higher education. However, due to large number of complex issues internal, external, functional, organisational and historical, the present situation of Universities is not very happy as the internal systems of Universities are not functioning properly. In fact the systems were designed for a different situation; whereas the present situation is very different from what they used to be say, fifty years back. There is groupism, politics, corruption and moral degradation within the Universities. The associations of students and teachers and *karamcharies*, have turned into trade unions of a factory. These Universities are now affected by regionalism, casteism and communalism. The commitment and involvement by top official and administrators of the Universities is lacking. It has been observed that the teachers, *karamcharies* and the students get involved in activities and business which are not part of their primary duties. Their involvement in national politics and political activities is rampant. They actively pursue private business like manpower export, tuitions, coaching centres, publications of low standard literature for students, property/ assets business, translation, interpreter work etc. The list is endless. It is seen that large number of teachers and *karamcharies* get involved in side business, so in order to supplement their income. However, not only does it violate the conduct rules, but very adversely affect the moral and academic authority of these teachers and functionaries.

The Universities perform within the overall atmosphere of the society. They are as much part of the society as any other organisation and they are directly affected by the atmosphere in which they perform. If bigger systems like politics, social system, economic system are plagued with corruption, communalism, casteism, violation of human rights, misuse of power, criminalisation etc. It is very difficult for the university to remain unaffected.The Government appointed various Commissions and Committees on higher education before and after the Independence to improve the quality of education and to remove administrative problems of the institutions of higher learning. The recommendations of various Commissions include amendment of Acts and Statues, Constitution, power and functions of the authorities and offices, revision of pay scale, administrative decentralisation, provision of grants etc. There are some constraints in implementation of these recommendations, i.e. lack of proper planning, lack of funds, lack of control and co-ordination and the likes. Keeping in view these constraints one would imagine that governance of Central and State Government run Universities is becoming more and more different and difficult. It requires specialised skills and tools.

References

- Nururllah, S and Naik, J.P (1943) *History of Education in India: During the British Period.* Delhi: Macmillan.
- R.P. Pathak (2007) *Education in Emerging India.* New Delhi: Atlantic Publishers Pvt. Limited.
- *Education Development in India* after 1813 by Puja Mondal. Accessed through http://www.yourarticle library.com/history/educational-development-in-india-after-1813/23718/
- Shahid, K. M. (2004) *Management of Higher Education:* A Comparative Study of State and Central Universities. An unpublished Ph.D. thesis. New Delhi: Jamia Milia Islamia.
- Govt of India (1992) National Policy on Education: Programme of Action. Ministry of Human Resource Development. Government of India.

Policy Issues in Higher Education

3

Management of Higher Education in India: Problems and Prospects

Prof. Faizan Mustafa

Education is powerful and pervasive agent for all round development of individual. The cherished goal of education is the development and enhancement of the seeker's knowledge through the process of enquiry. But if the curiosity or quest for knowledge is to be fruitful, it must be associated with most modern techniques of acquisition of knowledge. The father of nation has said that the true meaning of education is harmonious development of head, heart and hand, i.e. enlightenment of mind, compassion and dignity of labour. Swami Vivekanand has also shown us a way as to the goal of education when he said: "We must have life building, man building and character building education". Thus, as education administrators we must keep in mind that education we impart in our Universities and institutions of higher education must aim at the development of moral, spiritual and ethical values.

Education basically stands for the development of mind and for liberation from ignorance of our interaction with nature. It stands for innovation and adventure of ideas. Science and technology have always been recognised as most basic fundamental prescription for prosperity, prestige and status which a common man aims to enjoy. The countries which

---

- The paper is based on the speech delivered at National Seminar on the "Management of Higher Education- Perspectives, Challenges and Strategies", 6th March, 2014, Maulana Azad National Urdu University's seminar on Higher Education.

have implemented this basic formula do enjoy a very high standard of living because standard of living in any country is directly proportional to the educational levels of its masses. It is an old saying "to build a better nation, build better individuals". Perceptive education is indeed sovereign remedy for all economic ills. Martin Carnoy rightly observed that "because knowledge is the most highly valued commodity in the global economy, nations have little choice but to increase their investment in education".

Progressive nations continue to invest heavily in order to be at the forefront. Sweden leads with an investment of 8.2 per cent of its GDP on its education. In contrast we spend just about three per cent of our GDP on education. Our investment in education is not only lower than the global average of 4.8 per cent but it is also below several low income and least developing countries whose average is approximately 3.3 per cent . The situation is indeed quite alarming as we spend just 1.0 per cent of our GDP on higher education.

India has certainly come a long way from 28 Universities and 578 colleges at the commencement of the constitution to over 677 Universities and more than 35,539 colleges today. The country has the largest number of higher education institutions in the world and some 20 million students are enrolled with the institutions of higher education in the country. The higher education sector has witnessed a tremendous growth since independence as number of Universities has jumped 23 times and number of colleges has registered an impressive increase of over 66 times. Similarly the student enrollment of 3,97,000 (Girls 43,000) in 1950 has surged to 1,69,75,000 (Girls 70,49,000), the number of graduates coming out of technical colleges was slightly over 7,00,000 in 2011-12. However, it is disgusting to note that as per Mackinsey report 75 per cent of our technical graduates and more than 85 per cent of general graduates are unemployable.

The Indian higher education system is plagued with outdated curricula and ill-equipped libraries (average 9 books per person). In 2011 FICCI Higher Education Survey, 48 per cent of Universities and 69 per cent of colleges were lacking infrastructure. Similarly there is acute shortage of faculties 45 per cent of positions of Professors, 51 per cent of positions of Associate Professors and 52 per cent positions of Assistant Professors are vacant in Indian Universities. Even in our institutions of excellence such as IITs, IIMs, NLS etc. 40 per cent faculty positions are vacant. It is also shocking to note that as many as 57 per cent of our college teachers do not have either a Master or Ph.D. degree. Our educational system completely lacks innovation and creativity and we continue to have examinations which are memory based which merely test student's mugging up abilities.

There was a time when Indian Universities like Nalanda, Vikram and Takshila were widely known for their rigorous academic curricula and excellence. Chinese Traveller Huen Tsang and Moorish Traveller Ibn Batutah visited these temples of learning to study our education system. These Universities produced some of the finest minds. The Holy Vedas and philosophical Upanishads too were the scholarly works of people who graduated from our gurukuls. It is a matter of grave concern that today we do not have any world class university in India. In fact Philip G. Altbach had observed that India is a world class country without a world class university. Today there are serious concerns as to our quality of our Universities. Latest Times Higher Education Survey has shown that in global assessment none of our Universities figure in top 200 Universities of the world. As many as seven Chinese Universities did make to the elitists club. In fact amongst the BRICS nations, we are the only one who do not have a university in this list even though countries like Hong Kong and Singapore do have Universities making it to the top 100 Universities.

The phenomenal increase in the student strength has resulted in high requirements of infrastructure facilities and finances. But one is at pains to say that while the student population of the country did increase in geometrical proportion, the financial allocations by the government have increased, at best, in arithmetical progression, causing havoc with the quality of our education. No one can dispute much greater allocation and new sources for generation of resources are vital to ensure the quality of higher education. Public funding alone would not be adequate to meet this challenge. Economic liberalisation and globalisation have imposed certain additional obligations on the higher education sector. A massive training of manpower is urgently needed to keep pace with the newer technologies and fast-changing global market. This would necessitate expansion of specialised institutions in the subsectors of higher and technical education and vocationalisation of education at secondary stages. Most Universities are struggling to survive in the face of increasing enrollment and growing complexities of new types of academic programmes. In our cultural traditions, teaching or educating has always been considered as a sacred task and service to humanity. In fact Kabir has given teacher a place higher than even God and since God is the giver and not taker, the education should also come for free. It was during the British period that the government funding of education started and by and large we continue to follow the same model. But today because of new socio-economic realities of globalisation, it has become difficult for governments throughout the globe to continue to provide liberal financial support to higher education sector. In fact governments in all countries of the world including developed world are finding it difficult to sustain public educational institutions. As a matter of fact the size of the higher education sector has outgrown the capacity of the governments to finance it. In our country recognition of larger social benefits which primary and elementary education brings in comparison to higher education was the other reason because of which government shifted its focus to invest more in these sectors rather than higher education. This situation has led to privatisation of higher education. We have no choice but to privatize and globalize higher education by forging partnership with big business houses to produce employable skilled graduates. It is unfortunate that many of us continue to look down at private Universities. We must know that the best Universities of United States are private Universities and in any case even in India most of us have been educated in the so called "Public Schools" which indeed is a misnomer as we were educated in private English medium schools. The country has seen establishment of large number of Deemed Universities under Section 3 of the U.G.C. Act, 1956 or Private Universities through State enactments. The National Knowledge Commission has suggested that we should have 1500 more Universities and with government not having enough resources we have no option but to establish these Universities in the private sector. Private presence in higher education did get a flip in the last two decades. In 2001 private unaided institutions made up to 42.6 per cent of all higher education institutions and 32.8 per cent of students received education in these private institutions of higher education. But by 2006, the share of private institutions went up to 51.5 per cent. Today it must be in the range of 65-70 per cent . In legal parlance we have a concept called i.e. *res ipsa loqotiur* which means facts are speaking for themselves and in such a situation no evidence is required to be adduced. Today it is a well-recognized fact that it has been private sector that has really driven capacity creation in higher education. We need to encourage more and more private investments in the higher education and find a solution to the debate 'for profit or not for profit'. The apex court has held that education including higher education is a 'non-profit' activity. The court has also held that the right to establish and administer educational institutions under Art. 19 and 30 is not a trade/

business or profession but indeed an 'occupation'. Thus no 'profiteering or capitation fee' can be allowed but the court has permitted that unaided private institutions may devise their own fee structure so that they can efficiently run these institutions. They are also allowed reasonable surplus for future expansion. This reasonable surplus has to be ploughed back into the institution, while keeping intact the overall non-profit nature of educational institution. We need to do more to attract private investments in the higher education. The Planning Commission Working Group Report on Public Private Partnership in higher education has suggested at stepping up budgetary outlays and creating Public Private Partnerships to enhance the number of higher education institutions. The approach document of 12th plan says that higher education accounts for 18 per cent of public spending on education or 1.12 per cent of GDP which should ideally be raised to 25 per cent. This translates into an additional allocation of Rs.25,000 crores to higher education. Public Private Partnership would be an improvement over an exclusively private institutions as many of them indeed do have profit motives. There can be number of models for Public Private Partnership such as where private sector invests in infrastructure and runs the place while the government pays for it, where private sector makes investment in infrastructure but the government runs the institutions, or where investments are shared by the government and private sectors but operations are handed over to the private sector and finally where the government invests in infrastructure but private sector is entrusted with the responsibility to run the operations.

The new Companies Act has now mandated two per cent allocation for Corporate Social Responsibility which can easily be used for higher education. We must establish National Education Finance Corporation and National Educational Loan Fund. We need to give permission to private institutions to raise funds through public offering of bonds and shares. We need to allow these private institutions to convert themselves into Sec. 25 companies under the Companies Act and finally we need to designate these private institutions of higher education as "infrastructure" to allow them legal and tax benefits which are available to other big infrastructure projects. At the same time these private institutions should not become mere degree selling shops. Many private Universities today make tall claims in respect of their flexible academic system, choice-based credit policy and industry relevant curricula. But I am sorry to say that in many cases these claims are not visible on their campuses but exist only in their admission advertisements, websites and brochures. Many Universities in the private sector simply copy the academic structure and course outlines from the leading Universities of the world but they fail to deliver as necessary operational procedures to implement these ambitious courses and adequate and latest teaching methodology have not been put in place. The other flip side of some of our private institutions of higher education is that they misuse or abuse their autonomy and initiate courses in niche areas without adequate planning, proper infrastructure facilities or necessary faculty recruitment. Similarly many Universities have stereotyped vision and mission statements and their vision does not show any innovation or creativity. Many institutions in fact have plagiarised mission statements which have been copied from other institutions. Moreover private institutions should understand that big and attractive buildings do not make a university. It is the academics, and academics alone which matter most. Similarly if they want to make something of themselves then the management should not interfere in the day to day operations of the university. Most Vice-Chancellors of private Universities feel uncomfortable and are in fact caged parrots in the hands of management of these institutions. Ideally, the administration of the university should be left in the hands of academics and investors should stay away from the day-to-day administration. In a shocking revelation, a review committee set-up by the Ministry of Human Resources Development, Government of India in 2009 found that 88 of the 130 Deemed Universities were of poor quality. Supreme Court's intervention saved the day for these institutions. We need to remedy this situation.

Returning to the goal of our education system, we may recall that the National Policy on Education, 1986 explicitly lays down: "In our culturally plural society, education should foster universal and eternal values, unity and integration of our people. Such value education should help eliminate obscurantism, religious fanatism, violence, superstitions and fatalism". No one can deny that lack of values eventually leads to corruption due to unnecessary greed for quick success in purely materialistic terms and eventually to the total degradation of the society as a whole. The Education Commissions headed by Dr D.S.Kothari and Dr. S. Radha Krishnan did recommend that eternal values such as truth, peace, right conduct, non-violence and love for everyone be made an integral part of core values of our educational system. It is indeed painful that with the advent of globalization these values have been given a quite burial in our education system. We observe today that sense of service, responsibility and duty has completely evaporated from our Universities. We have become a right-based society and have completely given up classical duty based (*Kartvya*) character of our society. Everyone is simply demanding rights and no one bothers any more about the fundamental duties which our constitution expects from us.

Though we have become more materialistic today but we are definitely less happy, a far more knowledgeable but less wise and more educated and certainly much less learned. Contentment has become a rare commodity and in spite of all the bounties of life the satisfaction level is at all times low. We have indeed degenerated from the high pedestal of moral rectitude. Our education is neither liberating nor enlightening nor empowering us. It is also sad to note that it is no more vehicle of equitable growth as disparities and inequities continue to rise. It is not re-engineering the intended social transformation and the goals of inclusive growth and equitable development continue to remain a distant dream. We certainly need an education system which creates better human beings. To be a good human being one needs to inculcate in himself our traditional moral values and self-discipline. Today's divisions and hatred in the society can easily be attributed to our bad education. According to Prof. D.S.Kothari: "Bad education is bad because it breeds intolerance towards fellow beings and is fraught with danger to cause great and lasting harm to the community, nation and humanity at large". The basic aim of education is to promote power of mind, acquisition of special skills and advancement of knowledge. But above all to generate in the young generation a sense of purposefulness and mission, dedication, confidence in themselves and faith in the country's future. The report of Human Resource Development Ministry, Government of India also favours the same idea: : "Truth (*satya*), Righteous Conduct (*Dharma*), Peace (*Shanti*), Love (*Prema*), and non-violence (Ahimsa) are the core universal values which can be identified as the foundation-stone on which the value-based education programme can be built. These five values are indeed universal values and respectively represent the five domains of human personality; intellectual, physical, emotional, psychological and spiritual. They also are correspondingly corelated with five major objectives of education, namely, knowledge, skill, balance, vision and identity.

The architect of modern India Pandit Jawaharlal Nehru has said: "university stands for humanism, for tolerance, for reason, for the adventure of ideas, and for the march of the human race towards even higher objectives." What is the ultimate purpose of university education is the moot question. John Stewart Mill rightly answered way back in 1867: "Universities are not intended to teach the knowledge required to fit men for some special mode of giving their livelihood. Their object is not to make skillful lawyers or physicians or engineers but capable and cultivated human beings. Men are men before they are lawyers, or physicians or merchants, or manufacturers; if you make them capable and sensible men, they will make themselves capable and sensible lawyers or physicians". These words of wisdom from one of the most influential political thinker of 19th Century are relevant for all of us as we should not view Universities merely as a way to securing a job and for the administrators of the Universities to understand that educational institutions are not supposed to produce just competent professionals. We need to produce not only competent professionals but socially sensitive professionals.

We recently celebrated the 60th anniversary of Martin Luther King Jr.'s famous speech 'I have a dream'. The great visionary has said that "our scientific power has out burned our spiritual power. We have guided missiles and unguided men". To know so much and have control over nothing is the greatest tragedy of our times. We have failed to regulate an atrocity of knowledge, money, polity and technology through the well-tested and long experimented power of ethics and spirituality. This is an alarming sign for our higher education.

4

Reforms in Higher Education: Facts and Impacts

-K. Sudha Rao[1]

Note: (This paper is a part of Prof Dolarrai Mankad Annual Lecture of Saurashtra University, Gujarat)

My fascination to Gujarat and its people goes back to early seventies while I was a student in Rajasthan University. If I saw everything beautiful in one place it is Gujarat and its people. Be it human beings and their behaviour, culture and tradition, appreciation of colours and its depiction in textiles, Arts and Crafts, Festival Celebrations and above all, their concern and commitment to the people in general, their business acumen and business ethics, and of course, last but not the least, the security that they have provided to women are only a few examples. I can go on and on, but this is not the occasion. It is time that education in general and higher education in particular takes over in this part of the country.

Today, education has occupied a core position in the march towards development of nations and higher education is in the epicenter of this core. Probably it is the only field which teaches students at the right age to be open to reason and argument, and to be fearless and lucid in the expression of one's own thoughts which is the core character of this discipline. These virtues if coupled with relentless desire to pursue intellectual truth at this young age country is bound to be in success path.

When I entered the field of Higher Education, I was fascinated by its aura which facilitated questioning, counter-questioning, arguing, searching and researching, and finally approving, disapproving, and coming to the judgment with regard to right and wrong based on authentic

---

[1] Chief Executive Officer, SDM Education Society. Bangalore. Former Vice Chancellor KSOU Mysore, Senior advisor AICTE and Head, Higher Education Dept, NUEPA New Delhi.

knowledge and evidence base is a quality inherent to this discipline. I was all the more overwhelmed, by its atmosphere, where in the juniors and seniors, powerful and powerless, youngsters and experienced could equally brainstorm on issues and remain restless till the solutions are found. It is this aura and the atmosphere enabled young minds to get sharpened through questions and answers, feeling for the issues, and direct the minds to serve for the cause in the interest of the community and the nation. Present time is the right time where opportunities are in abundance. Every problem is a challenge and every solution is a credit earned? Globalisation, privatisation, liberalization are the policies in favour of this.

I remember the days when I was doing my PhD, computer had just arrived in India and was occupying a whole room in Delhi University, with all restrictions posed on though students for its touch and usage. There use to be a small window thru which we use to submit the punched cards and wait for hours and at times days to receive analysed data. It always left us out of reach for touch and feel, leave alone to play and try new things. But it was an era of hope and there was great optimism about the prospect and development. Today it is a toy in the hands of every person to make use, experiment, keep pace with, and face challenges and grab opportunities.

We are proud to announce that higher education system in India is one amongst the largest in the world, may stand next only to China and the United States in terms of number of institutions, number of students and the number of employees employed in these institutions. Centre's budgetary allocation is up by six times in 11th Plan period. 1986 policy, the Knowledge Commission, Yeshpal Committee and the 11th Plan all together gave greater focus and determination to the Center and the States that have started implementing the innovations on the ground by getting the needed clearances, be it passing of the various Bills or needed regulations etc. Reforms in higher education became one of the priority agenda. We can already see s6me of them in terms of new IIITs, IIMs, Central Universities, State Universities, Govt. colleges, Autonomy to the existing colleges, Accreditations of colleges and Universities, increase in intake in the existing institutions are evidences to this. Further manifestations of globalisations, liberalisation, industrialisation, technology advancements etc can be seen in terms of diversification of programmes, administration and managements within the institutions and between the institutions- local, regional, national and international; Strategies evolved for mobilisation of resources, increase in intake, collaborations and co-operations within and outside the country are all though encouraging somewhere a sense of uncertainties haunts with regard to quality.

Ever since the economic reforms began in India, economy has been growing more than Seven per cent per annum even when the economies of several developed countries were going through recession. With the result, today, opportunities for Indians are unlimited. India will need a huge talent pool to keep its growth curve rising all through. Increased age group population of 15 to 35 ages will continue to rise and is considered to be greatest advantage in favour of the country. Study by Boston Consulting Group declared that there will be a global workforce shortage in the order of 46 million by 2020. And over 60 per cent of its one billion people are part of a potential labour pool (between the ages of 15 and 64) and are seen as country's economic potential. India's own estimation is 47 million surpluses of young work force by then. As of now, the intake capacity is 12.4 per cent of age group of population (18-23) which is enrolled and out of these only five are graduates. As per National Knowledge Commission, we need to reach minimum of 15 per cent GER in high education by 2015 and as per MHRD 30 per cent by 2020.That by 2020, the average age of an India will be 29 years, compared to 37 for China and 48 for Japan further encourages to believe that being young is a huge advantage for our nation. All of us in the world of higher education business have been excited about *India's demographic advantage.* But the real challenge is to skill them on the one hand and also to consider the sociological challenges confronting our youth.

All these have raised the common man's expectations from this sector. Gone are the days when people use to look for access and certificate. Today an aware person looks for quality higher education. Demand for world class education in both conventional and non-conventional streams has increased. Obvious it is, that converting this 'mere youth' to a 'resourceful youth' and enabling them to contribute to the country's economic advantage and in turn expect them to contribute to global economy needs a massive quality education both in terms of knowledge, skill and the needed behaviour. Planning for this, and putting in place the needed infrastructure, and the resources in terms of men, money, material is a major challenge. More important is, the task of putting in place the process aspect. Expectations from India have risen amongst the developed, underdeveloped and developing countries. If the developed and developing countries are looking for outsourcing and hiring qualified youth, underdeveloped countries are looking for leadership and support.

Higher education was considered as an important stage for developing creative and critical minds, training individuals to be good citizens and for allround development of an individual. Hence, it was considered as the responsibility of the state. Today, higher education is seen as an investment in human capital drawn into the market and is viewed as a commodity Commoditisation of education. It is viewed in terms of costs, benefits and returns. This understanding has been strengthened by the entry of World Bank and the global market which supported the LPG policy. Higher education is diverted towards producing global citizens who may be comfortable visiting, working and living in diverse conditions and countries.

This change in understanding has given rise to: Changes in the perception, attitude and the very thinking of the policy-makers, planners and administrators at all levels-students, parents and teachers etc. in other words total clientele group. The resultant outcome has been gearing policies, plans, and programmes towards the changed perceptions. Thus the focus of the XI Plan is for opening of large number of new and different types of institutions such as deemed, private, Interdiscipline, multidiscipline, multilingual etc. Admission and selection of students have been designed to take through national, state, university level entrance tests in addition to the donation, management and self-financing modes. Institutions have been empowered to recruit teachers on hire and fire basis, on contract, adhoc, per-session, and even per hour basis in addition to permanent employment. There have been variations in academic content as well in terms of discipline wise, area wise, programme wise, course wise, subject wise and audit and credit courses. All these compromises that the institutions are making to meet the stakeholders demands have its own impact on the system, institutions, programmes and the product quality in terms of erosion in culture, tradition, values and ethics. It is these confusions, apprehensions and fears have reflected in Supreme Court judgments.

Five Year Plan Projects that growth of higher education needed per year is at the @ 37, Increase per year is at the @11, Demand increase per year is at the @20 and the Human resource demand is increasing per year at @ 18. Bridging the gap between the aspiration and the availability, finding quality and qualified faculty to fill the vacant positions; Attracting brilliance to science based careers. Increasing and improving "Supply Slide" of scientific and technological manpower.

By investing Rs 40,000 crores only for 2.5 age group is provided - not going to solve the problem of HE Foreign Education Providers Act as it may not be the right catalyst What is more important is skilling the unskilled and making them employable,. diverting teachers/students interest from unwanted politics, stress, value, Conflicts and corruption. Filling the gap between the skills that are in demand, and that which is imparted. Streamlining the regulatory and legal hurdles, Removal of disparities across different states/regions and sectors. Increasing access in an inclusive manner to ensure equity, quality and relevance. Creation of multiple autonomous accreditation agencies - Govt, region wise, profession-wise etc., Ensure parity in quality and standards among different institutions to facilitate mobility of students. Granting autonomy to all colleges. Arresting affiliation system completely. Research Emphasis in the PG colleges. Quality teaching and accountability of employees in permanent employment structure.

More than 80 of the HE is in its affiliated colleges that are regulated by the university. but hardly take any responsibility for their performance - Major hurdle to the quality, Converting three year UG program to four year to enable global requirements, Introduction of credit system to facilitate credit transfer, Curriculum renovation and Autonomy of academic institutions, Maintenance of Indian culture, tradition and values, Professional ethics in teaching and research.

For achieving this goal, Yashpal Committee and Knowledge Commission Recommended 1500 Universities to be opened, IRAHE to be established, reform existing Universities, introduce transparency of information at all level, Provide scholarships/freeships to those who cannot afford, Support and encourage Affirmative Action, Ensure English education in all government schools at primary level, Certification to be permitted only after accreditation and assessment.

Some of the crucial issues that needs our focused attention are: disparity in access and unplanned expansion, quality and standard equity and Inclusive Education, and affordable quality and relevant higher education. To overcome the shortcomings in these areas and to ensure comparable quality of higher education, that is comparable with higher education provided by the developed countries sufficient initiatives have been taken by the centre in the recent past. Most important amongst these are: the reforms in Regulations, Governance, Administration and Transparency. Regulatory bodies' reorganisation became essential to enable them to act as a true facilitator, and an enabler. In doing so, there have been recent initiatives initiated by MHRD in Higher Education. Some of them are:

National Commission for Higher Education and Research (NCHER) Bill 2010 to set up an autonomous overarching regulatory authority for Higher Education and Research.

National Authority for Regulation in Accreditation of Higher Educational Institutions Bill, 2009 to create a law for mandatory assessment and accreditation in higher education through an independent regulatory authority. Foreign Education Providers (Regulation) Bill, 2010 a law to regulate entry and operation of Foreign Educational Providers. A law to establish a Tribunal for fast-track adjudication of disputes concerning stakeholders set up a mechanism for speedy redressal of disputes Laws to prevent prohibit and punish educational malpractices to penalize institutions indulging in unfair practices)

Each of the bills is addressing a particular need and is a clear step towards an effective regulatory framework. People are really excited, energized and enthusiastic to see that actually something is beginning to take place on the ground - the reform in Indian higher education which is long overdue. The reform that is being proposed, as it is now, is expected to promote autonomy and innovation in the true sense of the term and is welcomed. Obvious it is that such regulatory system is expected to be transparent and accountable.

To sum up, education sector is witnessing an exponential growth and we have to synchronise our processes to meet the growth. The greatest challenge, which is beyond doubt, is that higher education will be a huge market in the coming decade, with competition becoming intense. But, like in any other growth industry, the biggest challenge is to execute growth plans and building information systems that can scale with business growth. With total 179 million students and 888,000 educational institutions, modernising India's education system is a huge challenge. The shifting structure of our society from an industrial economy to a knowledge economy offers us both a threat and an opportunity as we seek to modernise our education system. There is a need to evolve an appropriate policy framework for facilitating greater flow of private investment in education sector including removal of entry barriers, simplified procedures for affiliations etc., without elements of commercialisation and profiteering.

Listing reforms, challenges and opportunities are easier than implementing the reforms. It is the effort of one and all in the higher education sector that makes it easier to implement and take the country to the greater heights.

5

Challenges to Higher Education in India

Prof Dr DN Reddy

I would like to briefly touch upon the points of what are the challenges faced by the higher education in our country, particularly the impact of globalisation on higher education, how it effects the country's higher education as well, because many foreign Universities are coming in India. Due to globalisation more opportunities are available to our Indian students who are to peruse higher education in various countries across the globe. But the major difference in overseas Universities is the flexibility in the courses, whereas flexibility is not built in Indian system. We need to note further ahead because overseas education system like British they have structured courses like two years, four years, three years structured courses and flexibility not much brought in except in Universities. I think we need to do that, with regard to quality and relevance. Government of India policies are based on access, inclusion and quality. Relevance of higher education could also exist apart from access to education to all the needy. We have 55 million youngsters in this country only 15 % are coming to higher education; we need to promote it to 30%. Our average is 23% and we are lagging behind, so access is important but at the same time mushrooming of institutions without quality is not desirable. Whatever education is given should be relevant to the society at large. It is the most important challenge because quality and relevant teaching-learning process will drive to improve the quality. Teaching methodologies beyond the practice of black board and chalk piece method should be innovated. ICT greatly helps, particularly teaching faculty to make the students learn faster and also understand. We have to use information and communication technology in teaching learning process.

Education is a luxury for the elite and necessity for all others, it is necessary for everyone in this country. But the question arises, why education and what for education? Education gives us competence, education gives us confidence, education gives us creativity. The uneducated person works hard and sleeps without any worry, educated person is a worried lot; he wants so many things in life. Today a student should not necessarily come to the class room; he remains digitally mobile. Students whether in a classroom inside library, cafeteria or lawn, can access to the teaching learning processes by new teaching learning methodology. They can access content while remaining digitally mobile. It is possible because of internet.

The new world believes in human capital; that is why the world is looking at India and China because these countries have large human capital base, a large number of youngsters are there who are English speaking and hard working and sincere. They can adopt any culture and they are able to work in any situation. That is why the world is looking at Indian and Chinese students as human capital in a new world where new technology is internet tools. Internet technology gave an impetus to all of us to access the information in every way. Earlier, there was no calculator there was no computer and only library sources for students. Today library sources are available at door steps; students can access it. Now the students do not depend more on the teachers while, earlier students were dependent only on teachers. Now more information is available for students to pursue better understanding. Millions of youngsters today access to the information through Google which gives a lot of information. The difference now is that we need to have an interface with the technology to imbibe higher level of understanding.

Education imperative is our concern. We have skills and knowledge as institution is meant for creating knowledge; whereas industry is meant for creating prosperity. We require both prosperity and knowledge. As Universities are meant for creating knowledge, therefore Universities and industry should join hands together, so that knowledge and prosperity both are available to us. That is the idea of interface with Universities with industry. Skills are important, Indian students are theoretically very good, highly qualified but when coming to practical knowledge, they are not comparable to other overseas students. Skills are still more important if our students go to foreign countries like Singapore, Malaysia, Taiwan, Korea, Japan. Their students are not much educated but their skills are very good. Today we are buying Samsung television or mobile phones which are coming from these foreign countries. When India is a large human resource base; why we are not able to make electronic and digital mobile phones? Because, our skill base is not there. Indian skill base is only 15 per cent to 20 per cent whereas skill base in Singapore, Malaysia, Japan is 85 per cent.There is educational employment gap due to skill gap. We need to fill this gap. It is very important as skills and knowledge go a long way, particularly bridging the much talked about educational employment gap. There is UNESCO report and another NASSCOM report; they all mentioned that only 23per cent of Indian students are employable; majority are not able to take job readily because they are not able to get employed for organisations who are looking for some skills whether one joins a tourism industry or hospitality industry or they join management or any other corporate sector. They want that students should be able to fulfill the need of the organisation which students have to do. Skills could be in many forms say technical skills, analytical skills, communication skills and personal skills, which are most important, communication skills are also important. Communication does not mean one should speak English or Urdu or Telugu or any language. Whatever one speaks other person should understand that is communication in true sense of the word. We should be able to convey better. Soft skills and analytical skills both are most important. It is not enough to become a graduate and get an employment and then get married, it is one part of life but also service to the society. It is important how we are useful to the society at large.

Development of key behaviour skills, behaviour attitude and behaviour are very important in this world. People are looking at outcome based education, which means, what a student is doing after graduating from Universities. Outcome is measured in three forms.

1. Knowledge
2. Skill and
3. Behaviour attitude

There should be behavioural difference between an uneducated fellow and an educated fellow. Behaviour skills and attitude play a vital role in our society, cultural and even corporate system.

It is very important to effectively apply the concepts whatever one learns here in Universities otherwise there is no use. Somebody works hard for four years for Ph D, ultimately the knowledge acquired should be translated into technology or drugs discovery or something useful to society. It should be the aim of getting Ph D not of getting personal benefit of getting promotion or job. It must be seen as how society is benefited because country is spending huge amount of money on a graduate. It is an obligation on each student to repay to the society.

Imbibing higher level of understanding in the class room is important. Normally a bright student in a classroom can absorb only 25 per cent and not more than that rest of knowledge comes by discussing with colleagues and with the teachers. We are using technology and using access to information and while working with all these technologies one tries to acquire knowledge, but acquiring higher level of understanding should be more important. Our education system in the class room in the Universities is such that we have to force the students learn by taking attendance. 10 to 15 minutes go, waste on taking attendance in the period of a teacher. One part of course is that attendance is required, interest should come among students community and they should be willing to come, we cannot force them all the time.

Learning approach: Earlier, we had a teacher centric or student centric learning methodology. Now-a-days we have learning centric. It means teacher has to learn and student has to learn, that is why now it is a learning centric environment. In this approach we have to follow the instruction methodology in the Universities.

Innovation is the key, as far as innovation ability is concerned we stand 45th rank in the world. There are several countries whose innovative ability is very good. It means their basis is knowledge and skill. Their mind set is that whatever research we do it should translate into innovation and also translate into products.

Excellence, knowledge and innovation are the key words in entire process in this way excellence will come.

Sustainable Development

Sustainable development is very important. Development is required but should be sustained for a longer time frame work. Economy goes down because GDP growth rate is coming down. India is aiming for nine per cent economic growth but we are now as low as five per cent, it means something is going wrong in the country. We need to act and economic slowdown should not be allowed.

Dramatic Change in Demography

Today there are no geographical boundaries, now students can go anywhere in the world to pursue higher education, therefore, demographic situation is ever changing. Similarly, Cultural Boundaries are being drawn.

Major Shift in Higher Education

A major shift is taking place and taking place in higher education. India now has different kinds of Universities like Central Universities, State Universities, deemed to be Universities, Private Universities, Institutions of National Importance, IITs, NITs, IIITs. This shift is taking place in higher education because the government alone cannot provide higher education to the needy people. Today 80 per cent education is given by private sector. We have to ensure that they also provide quality education, in fact quality education should be ensured at central level, state level as well as at the private level.

Intense Completion Among Universities:

Now we have a central university, MANUU, Manlana Azad National Urdu Unversity B.R Ambedkar Open University, Osmania University are there. Professional competition among University can lead to uality education. Similarly, Corporate Universities are also coming.

Corporate Universities are coming to exist. They provide by campuses say 600 acres campus, they provide all AC rooms, AC dining hall. The corporate culture is coming in education, whereas a central or state university cannot afford to provide good infrastructure. The tendency of students is to go to these corporate Universities leading to competition with corporate world.

Virtual Universities

Many Universities in the world are going in virtual environment role, virtual classroom, in virtual Universities students need not come to campus, they can learn from home or work place. It is also happening by using modern technology.

63 per cent workforce in India is literate but young population of 18 to 24 years age group is only coming to 12 per cent to 15 per cent higher education. Large youngsters basis is there, but we don't find many youngsters in European countries. India's asset is that we are young population. 55 million youngsters in IT in the age group are there, as said 12 per cent to 15 per cent are only coming to the higher education.

There are 4000 Universities in Japan, 3015 Universities in USA and 600+ Universities in India provide as more than one billion 1.4:1.45 billion as a youngsters are given education and gross enrollment ratio we want to move from 15 per cent to 30 per cent in fact our distinguish Prof Ramaswami also highlighted, so increase gross enrollment they should development countries 55 per cent more than that only average is 23 per cent as mentioned.

- To achieve and measure greater increase education inclusion
- High quality learning
- Better attainment rates, attainments is important
- Prepare for change
- Development expertise
- Lead in the knowledge economy
- Societal needs, social needs are important so what is the focus is quality
- Relevance
- Employability
- Citizenship
- Social

These are important factors which one must apply in the university system, this focus should be there on entire education system.

Universities should have a

- Networking
- Benchmarking
- Knowledge sharing
- Advocacy
- ICT Technology
- Distance/Vocational Education

Distance and vocational and skill base uppgradation courses and form. Face to face learning is important but apart from that we also require open and online learning.

Mentoring Concept: American Universities introduce a concept called mentoring. They will maintain every 10 students, but we are already short of faculty we have not been able to put mentors. We need to have a ratio of 1:10 i.e. every 10 students should have one mentor. Educational resources should be packaged so that all contents of the courses should be made available to students, not only in the classroom but also can be accessed from home. Virtual learning by using cutting edge technology is available today in the world, we need to adopt it.

Some of the areas which Universities can introduce formal structured courses, job oriented courses (Diploma/certificate), integrated dual degree programs, twinning programmes, exchange programs, joint degree programs (National/ International), distance education, off line/on line, industry sponsored programs in India.

The government support right now for education is 5 per cent. We need to increase it 1.5 per cent to 2 per cent of GDP, then only Universities can perform better. It is extremely difficult to impart quality education as more funding is required whereas state Universities are starving of funds. They get one-fourth or one-third of the cost which they incur. There is an upper limit of Tuition fee by the government. We cannot charge more than 20 per cent by the Universities, thus maximum 20 per cent we can get from the students.

- UGC plan/non plan grants,
- Consultancy services

Funding for university, Industry is not coming is a big way in our country, whereas in an American University large funding grants come from industry. In India they don't have confidence in the university. University also does not go to industry. Somehow something lacks in India in this aspect. In Germany, a Vice-Chancellor of the university will go to and grow as Managing Director next day and Managing Director of the industry can become Vice Chancellor. It is not happening in India. Both are shy of sharing with each other.

1. Self-finance courses.
2. Distance education and training programmes can generate more income for Universities. That is the only way to fill up the gap.
3. Research support from funding agencies.
4. Other sources of revenue generation.

Technology enabled learning is now used as one of the best practices. We have to bring improvement in the university. Some institutions have adopted best practice technology enabled learning not simply because we have used the technology in one classroom. Digital classroom is required everywhere BITS has experimented digital classroom in Dubai campus. They impart education from which are four campuses are digitally connected and lectures are to be accessed by others everywhere.

Innovative approaches for evaluation and assessment. Normally we recommend 25 per cent to 50 per cent internal assessment. The university declared calendar degrading of year and stick to several problems so we have not able to common calendar.

1. Introduction of professional and multi disciplinary curricula.
2. Developing lateral entry in higher education.
3. Flexibility in higher education system like Arts, Science and Engineering. But in engineering we are not studying economics, accountancy, business practices, English literature, heritage culture. Engineering students do not know about all these subjects like Arts, similarly social science student should know technology i.e. how to use the computer technology. These interdisciplinary approaches are needed in the educational system.
4. Testing systems measurement of skills and application testing.
5. Acceptable accreditation system. Every institution should go for accreditation.
6. Attracting international students.
7. High quality research.
8. Society upliftment.

6

Taking Higher Education in India to the Future – Some Thoughts

Prof Sunaina Singh

"Several reports in the past few months point out to a serious lacuna between the capabilities of our university students and the needs of their employers."

"More worrying, not a single Indian university figures among the top hundred Universities globally."

"India has perhaps the most number of Universities and institutions of higher learning anywhere in the world."

Juxtaposed, these three important pieces of information are alarming to those who are interested in the future of higher education in India. People, like you and me, whose existence has been education and for which we have spent the greater part of our lives and efforts. Where do we look for a course correction in order to ensure that not only is our education top-notch, but more importantly, the next generation are truly prepared as GLOBAL leaders in our Universities?

This talk/paper lays out a few steps to help us get on track, if not to the goal itself drawing on my experience as an administrator and my experiments as an academic. We must first agree that for higher education to achieve its end there needs to be a regular looking within, an introspection. A periodic reassessment of goals is the first aspect that I will stress upon. Our students, on an average, spend five years in a university and when they step out of the portal of the university they are still not able to fetch a job for themselves. We have over 600 Universities in this country, the highest number of educational institutions, and consequently a lot of 'well-qualified' youngsters looking for a job. And, when s/he does get a job, we hear complaints about how it was a disappointment. A disappointment for both the fresh employee and quite often for the employer too. It is evident that the link is missing somewhere. When this happens once too often, then we know it is time for us to question, to reassess the role of Universities and the contributions they make.

Let me be clear here: reassessment of the goals of education is not the prerogative of the governments alone. Academics have an equally significant role to play. Furthering knowledge is an important strategy in making education relevant to the future. This is why I stress that research needs to be disseminated not just in conferences and seminars – but in our very classrooms too. It is certainly important that the outcome of conferences are put together not just in the form of a book but also as suggestions for the growth and development of the country to be sent to policy-makers and nation builders. Otherwise you lose significance of conferences and research; what I am also suggesting is that the spirit of inquiry pervades our classrooms as well. Surely all Universities participate in innovative research that throw light into new areas of knowledge, that make productive suggestions leading to the expansion and creation of the body of knowledge. This must be shared. Shared with policy- makers and the industry. Which brings me to another significant step we need to take as educators and administrators – shifting from the age-old paradigm of linear, top-down functioning to networking and collaboration.

Is the role that of dissemination of knowledge or is it knowledge transfer, or is it production of knowledge? I firmly believe that Universities must produce knowledge - they must help create new knowledge. For this we must prepare minds to ask questions that have never been asked before, enable them to look for answers and assist them find the answers. We need to explore the research capabilities of students. Hence, an ideal university must train students not merely to study and prepare for an exam and pass with a distinction, but enable holistic development with an eye on the future. If we look at some statistics of the spending patterns of Universities outside India, we may perhaps, get to understand what ails our education system. As per a recent study, China spends US $ 296 billion on research and development; the USA has an outlay of $405 billion for the same India spends only $36 million, which is less than one per cent of its GDP on research. This is perhaps a significant reason why Indian education has a long way to go. We need to start thinking that even undergraduate level is not too early to start research training.

One step forward I think is that at the national level we need to have debates on what is the purpose of higher education. RUSA is a noble policy and I must congratulate the government for thinking of such a comprehensive scheme. But as Universities we need to study the outcome ensured by the Scheme closely – access, equity and quality. While government initiatives can ensure the first two, and I appreciate the fact that they have been well-addressed, quality is an issue. Setting parameters for quality is something that we need to assure as education providers. Unless we focus on quality assurance, India cannot figure on any global competitive radar. If access and equity are norms of social justice, it is important for us as Educators to build in to system quality for national growth. This is also where research can come in. This is why there needs to be constant debates and discussions with all stakeholders to set goals and chart paths unique and distinct to the Indian education scene, paths that do not let us lose focus on our Indianness.

Transferable skills are as essential as, or perhaps more important than the knowledge that is transmitted in our Universities. I remember reading somewhere that an average employee today stays at each of his or her jobs for less than three or four years. This means that a university graduate on an average will change around 15 – 20 jobs over their working tenure span. Yet another striking aspect of 21st century workplace is that many of the jobs our students get into are/were unheard of five years ago. For instance, I hear my students, my children, and their friends discussing career options like nano medic, motion designer, body parts engineer, life coach, social media manager, waste data handler, child designer, vertical farmer, etc. So what is it that we can do in higher education to prepare our youngsters to succeed in a world that is fundamentally different from what they saw as children and young adults, to thrive in a constantly changing global workplace, flourish in a job that they have not received training in? This is where transferable skills play a vital role. A survey by the European University Association (EUA), lists the core transferable skills that a student should have are management skills, life skills, creative thinking skills, social and communication skills, ideating and innovating skills, the capacity of dealing with complex and multidisciplinary work and team working skills.

It is high time higher education tuned itself to the requirements of the constantly changing global workplace and the needs of our nation by forming linkages with the industry. We find that traditionally, we have been training students to get good marks and then acquire a job. What happens 10 years down the line once the student does get that job? Does it sustain her/him? Does the job satisfy? Does it contribute to the development of the nation? These are questions that we need to ask and can be answered if we keep our fingers on the pulse of the nation's development needs. Academic auditing for quality assurance, reassessing the syllabi for ensuring continued relevance and networking with industry are all essential factors for higher education retaining relevance within the larger scope of what the student is preparing for; and it is certainly not just a degree.

TS Eliot had asked, "Where is the wisdom we have lost in knowledge? Where is the knowledge we have lost in information?" We also need to reflect on this. Does the road to education end with the quest for information? What we need to ask, and find out is whether we are carrying the sagacity within us, the wisdom within us to know the purpose of education. Education should be defined by what man can gift to life. Noble achievers like Einstein, Newton, Ramanujan, C V Raman, Tagore and others have contributed to life. This is also where culture of diligence and discipline comes in. In India we call it *shram*, where the *tahzeeb* and *Sanskriti* also plays an important role.

Our youngsters rush abroad when the rest of the world looks towards us. What is this paradox? What is the attraction that India offers? Is it our culture, our values, our beliefs, our policies, our systems? The attraction of India is its soft power, a combination of all these. This has to be imbibed by our youngsters who need to be led to the right values that need to be upheld and nurtured, and hence the significance of value based education. India has a lot to give in terms of culture and values. The whole world would like to learn from us but before that I think we need to study our own culture to be able to carry forward our value system.

We are in a time where we talk about and assess human growth patterns. Growth and development need to be holistic in order for one to be a better human being. Discipline and diligence are two values I would like to see more in our students, (and also in some teachers!). Determined dedication to the goal at hand is what has to be instilled and ensured. As an administrator I find myself wasting a lot of time answering ubiquitous enquiries under RTIs seeking to know number of cups of tea consumed or served, location of my accommodation, travel details, etc. Well, our resources and energies could be put to better use. Some laws need to be amended, so that every Head builds a vision and works towards translating the vision in to reality. Let us assess our growth pattern by results.

When youngsters move into the second phase of their lives I would expect them to take their values too, forward. That is very important. As Martin Luther King Junior said it is character plus knowledge which makes education. If we do not have values, no amount of knowledge is ever going to help us. I think that is what higher education should give our youngsters along with imparting knowledge and developing competence.

We need to set a benchmark for ourselves, focus on a goal which is of the highest order, and not to be satisfied with mediocrity. Because when we compete, we must compete with only the best. Regular reassessment of higher education helps set clear cut goals both for our teachers and students. Universities are the seed-bed for new ideas, new thoughts – they need to be actively encouraged. The world outside, and the places that the students intend to go and work are excellent places to look for guidelines for our curriculum and such linkages with the industry will help students be relevant long after they have passed out with their degrees.

Contemporary Higher and Professional Education

7

Growth and Development of Engineering Education in India

Dr Pradeep Kumar Choudhury

1. Introduction

The Indian higher education sector has undergone massive expansion, though not uniformly, during the six and half decades following independence. There were only 0.26 million students in higher education in 750 colleges and 30 Universities in India in 1950-51. This has increased to about 20.29 million students in 35.5 thousand colleges and 700 Universities in 2012-13. The gross enrolment rate has increased almost fifty times from 0.4 per cent to 19 per cent between 1950-51 to 2012-13 (UGC, 2013). With this, India has grown into one of the largest systems of higher education in the world. Among those enrolled in higher education, about 80 percent students belong to three disciplines, namely arts (42 per cent), science (19 per cent) and commerce (18 per cent) and the remaining 20 per cent are in the professional courses like education, engineering and technology, medicine, agriculture, veterinary sciences, law etc. Of the 20 per cent enrolment in professional courses engineering and technology accounted for ten per cent in 2009-10 (UGC, 2010). Furthermore, during the last two decades (1991-2011), the number of institutions of higher education (including all disciplines) in India has increased at the rate of eight per cent, whereas in engineering education it has gone up at the rate of fifteen per cent (Government of India, 1991, 2011). Similarly, enrolment in engineering colleges increased sevenfold, whereas it increased only threefold in overall higher education during the same period (UGC, 1991, 2010).

The larger demand for engineering education in India supports the widely argued fact that it is one of the most crucial components of human resource development and for economic well-being of a nation and also considered as a basic and essential input for national development and for strengthening the industry, economy and the quality of life of India. Further, the importance laid down in the post-independent India on industrialization and building of infrastructure has put pressure for the greater demand of graduates in the engineering and technical education. With the significant growth of graduates in this discipline, India is considered as the third largest reservoir of scientific and technical manpower in the world that helped the nation in achieving a reasonably high and sustainable rate of economic growth and in the realisation of the national goal of self reliance in various sectors. From the global point of view it has also been well recognised that India supplies highly skilled scientific and technical manpower to the world market produced at a relatively lower cost (Tilak, 2004, p. 2159). However, there is hardly any attempt to analyse and discuss the growth of engineering education in terms of institutional expansion and enrolment capacity, required to get an overall picture of this discipline. Also, within the last six and half decades of expansion of engineering education in India, a number of issues like regional disparities in the growth of institutions, uneven access by gender and social groups, public financing of engineering and technical education etc. have come up in a serious way and demands for a detail discussion.

In this context, this paper has analysed the growth and status of engineering education in India using the data collected from the publications of the Ministry of Human Resource Development (MHRD) (Selected Educational Statistics, Statistics of Higher and Technical Education in India); University Grants Commission (Higher Education in India at a Glance, Annual Reports); and the publications of All India Council for Technical Education (AICTE).

2. Growth of Engineering Institutions and Enrolments in India: Issues and Challenges

In 1847, the first engineering college was established in Roorkee named as Thomson Engineering College to train civil engineers. However, the first formal school for engineering was setup in Guindy, Madras, in 1842, which was attached to the Gun carriage factory. At the end of nineteenth century the technical education in India was consisted of only four engineering colleges at degree level, about 20 survey and technical institutes, and about 50 industrial schools (Government of India, 2004).

The Sarkar Committee, appointed by Government of India in 1945 recommended the establishment of higher technical institutes based on the Massachusetts Institute of Technology in the four regions of India which has resulted in the setting up of the five Indian Institutes of Technology (MIT) at Kharagpur (1950), Bombay (1958), Kanpur (1959), Madras (1960) and Delhi (1961) (Delhi was added on to the original four). Afterwards, the increasing demand for engineering education has resulted in the establishment of a large number of institutions in India. There were only 44 degree level engineering institutions in the country at the time of independence with a total intake capacity of 2570 which increased to 2894 institutions with more than 1.92 million intakes in the year 2009-10. Higher education institutions in India increased from 5726 in 1985-86 to 26334 in 2009-10, which arises to six per cent growth rate while engineering education institutions increased from 242 to 2894 in the same period, leading to ten per cent rate of growth. Also, within two and a half decades, the share of engineering institutions and enrolment to total higher education institutions in India increased from six to eleven per cent (Table 1).

Table 1. Growth of Engineering Institutions and Enrolment in India

w	Institutions			Enrolment		
	Higher Education	Engineering Education	Share (%)	Higher Education	Engineering Education	Share (%)
1985-86	5427	242	4.46	36,05,029	1,76,540	3.42
1990-91	6323	277	4.38	49,24,868	2,16,837	3.30
1995-96	8188	355	4.34	65,74,005	3,15,720	2.84
2000-01	11568	678	5.86	83,99,443	5,29,469	3.05
2005-06	20769	1562	7.52	1,10,28,020	7,95,120	7.20
2009-10	26334	2894	10.99	1,72,95,086	2,00,5,563	11.59
Growth rate (1985-86 to 2009-10)	6.52	10.44	-	6.47	10.21	-

Source: Selected Educational Statistics (various years) and Statistics of Higher and Technical Education (2009-10), MHRD, Government of India.

Note: Total higher education institutions include colleges for general education, colleges for professional education (Engineering, Technical, Architecture, Medical, Education and other colleges), central and state Universities, deemed to be Universities and institutions of national importance.

The overwhelming increase in the higher education institutions (particularly after the post-liberalisation period) is mainly due to the intervention of private sector (Agarwal, 2006). Considering the inability of the government to invest further in technical education, and given the growing demand for engineering graduates, opening up of institutions became an inevitable choice. After 1980s, many state governments encouraged private entrepreneurs to set up self-financed professional colleges, without any financial support, except providing land and other infrastructural supports at subsidised rates (Blom and Cheong, 2010). Though the private partnership in technical education in India began with the establishment of the Indian Institute of Science (IISc) at Bangalore in 1906 and later Birla Institute of Technology (BIT) Ranchi (1955), Birla Institute of Technology and Sciences (BITS), Pilani (1964), the rapid expansion took place soon after the advent of liberalisation of Indian economy in 1991 (Chopra and Sharma, 2010). The enrolment in undergraduate programmes of self-financing private institutions was 90 per cent while it is less than four percent in premier technical institutions like Indian Institutes of Technology and National Institutes of Technology in 2007. During 1997-2007, the students intake has increased with the growth rate of 19 per cent which is mainly due to the setting up of new institutions in the private sector; as the growth rate of private engineering institutions was 13 per cent during this period (Banerjee and Muley, 2008). Intersetingly, more than half of the total private engineering institutions (51.17 per cent) in the country are in the southern region alone, with an inatek capacity of 53.5 per cent (Table 2). On the other hand, only about six per cent of the total private institutions and their intakes of India are in eastern region. Similarly, out of the total institutions in this region more than 95 per cent are self-finaced with the intake capacity of 97.4 per cent. Thus, the expansion of private sector in engineering education is largely concentrated in the southern region. Several national level studies in India (Kumar et al, 2005; Rao, 2006; Biswas et al, 2010) have established that the larger partcipation of private sector in the engineering education has resulted the decline in the quality teaching imparted in these institutions.

The regional imbalance continues to be a major issue despite expansion of higher education in India in recent years even though it was seriously undertaken in the National Policy on Education (1986, p. 6), which states that "steps will be taken to facilitate inter-regional mobility by providing equal access to every Indian of requisite merit, regardless of his origins as per the higher and technical education is concerned". Around

Table 2. Region and Management Wise Number of Techinical Institutions and Intakes in India (2006-07)

	Institutions				Intake			
Regions	*Govern ment*	*Private*	*Govern ment*	*Private*	*Govern ment*	*Private*	*Govern ment*	*Pri vate*
Southern	4.60	95.40	30.30	51.17	2.60	97.40	24.91	53.50
Northern	10.37	89.63	15.15	10.29	6.64	93.36	11.93	9.63
Eastern	15.28	84.72	13.33	5.81	7.99	92.01	9.14	6.04
Western	5.68	94.32	7.88	10.29	5.85	94.15	10.43	9.62
Central	12.90	87.10	19.39	10.29	10.95	89.05	21.15	9.87
North	8.27	91.73	13.94	12.15	10.19	89.81	22.43	11.34
India	7.29	92.71	100	100	5.43	94.57	100	100

Source: *Author's Calculation from the available information from AICTE Website (Accessed on 13th December 2011).*

two-third of India's engineering institutions at undergraduate level are located in the states of Tamil Nadu, Karnataka, Andhra Pradesh and Maharashtra even though they account for less than one-third of the total population of the country. The southren region is having almost half of the total enineering institutions whereas eastern region is having only about seven per cent.[1] There are around 1418 degree level engineering institutions in the southern region where as it is only 208 institutions in the eastern region. At the extreme end of the spectrum, Mizoram, Nagaland, and Daman and Diu have no engineering institutions at all. Similarly, the state of Tamil Nadu has the highest sanctioned intake of 19 per 10 thousand of its population, while the large states like Uttar Pradesh and Madhya Pradesh have three and six intakes per 10 thousand population respectively (Chopra and Sharma, 2010). Five southern states, namely Andhra Pradesh, Karnataka, Kerala, Pondicherry, and Tamil Nadu account for 39 per cent of the total intake in engineering education while the other four regions (northern, western, central, north west) have less than 10 percent of the total intake. Nationally, an average of 350 students per million people enter into technical degree programmes; in the South, the figure is 1,047; South-West (689); West (486); East (131); and in the North, just 102. The lack of regulation and planning by the AICTE has allowed for geographical pockets of oversupply and undersupply in technical manpower in different regions of the country (WENR, 2007).

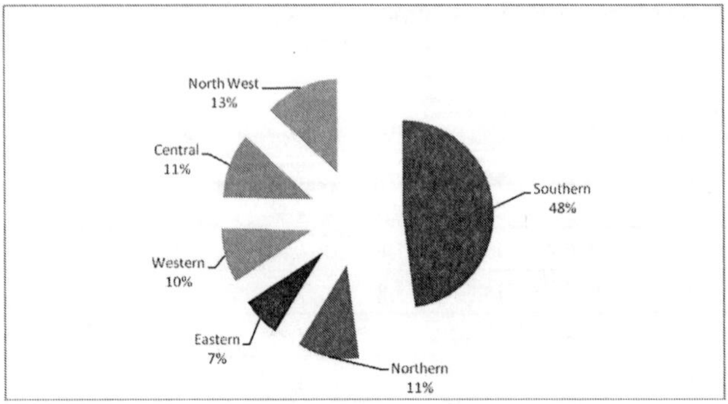

Figure 1. Region-wise distributions of degree level engineering institutions in India (2009-10).

Source: Author's estimation from the Annual report 2009-10, AICTE

Engineering and technical education in India has been highly selective in terms of providing social access to the disadvantaged sections of the society such as scheduled castes, scheduled tribes and women (Rao, 2006). Though there has been a phenomenal growth in the enrolment of female students in higher education in India, their share to total enrolment still lags behind that of their male counterpart. The gross enrolment ratio in higher education among girls was 12.7 per cent as against of 17 per cent for males in 2009-10 (Government of India, 2010). Of the total enrolment of 170 million students in higher education in India in 2009-10, 40.2 per cent are women and their share is 28.7 per cent in engineering education (Table 3). Gender-wise enrolment in different disciplines of higher education in India provides some useful insights. In arts discipline (particularly in the subject of 'education'), there is heaviest concentration of women, whereas in some other disciplines like engineering and technology the share has been simply marginal. The Gender Parity Index[2] (GPI) in engineering education was 0.3 which is much less than the higher education, i.e., 0.7 in 2009-10. Good number of research studies have found that professional education is, by and large, dominated by males than general education in which females constitute a larger proportion (Salim, 2008; Ghuman et al, 2009). Often, it is argued that engineering and technical education is a masculine domain and hence out of reach for women. Those who support this line of argument point to the perseverance of certain social myths like 'women are emotional, while technology is strictly logical and hence, both do not go together'. There is also view that men are good at mathematics and machines, while women have no clue about these (Rao 2007, p.187). The improvement in the participation of women in engineering education (3.8 per cent in 1980-81 to 28.7 per cent in 2009-10) perhaps reveals the gradual interest of women in this discipline.

Table 3. Women Enrolment in Higher and Engineering Education in India

	Higher Education		*Engineering Education*	
Year	*Total*	*% Share*	*Total*	*% Share*
1980-81	748525	14.35	4949	3.83
1985-86	1067484	24.53	12182	6.90
1990-91	1436887	27.19	17130	7.89
1995-96	2191138	29.61	26368	8.35
2000-01	3012367	32.47	109069	20.59
2005-06	4466348	34.10	185800	23.36
2009-10	6969850	40.29	576851	28.70
CAGR 1980-81 to 2009-10	7.99	-	17.83	-

Source: Selected Educational Statistics (Various Years) and Statistics of Higher and Technical Education (2009-10), MHRD, Government of India.

There exists a wide disparity in the access to higher education by different social groups in India. In 2009-10, the GER in higher education is about 15 per cent at the overall levels while it is nine per cent among SCs and 10.3 per cent among STs (Government of India, 2011). Engineering and technical education in India has been highly selective in terms of providing access to these disadvantaged groups. The percentage of SC enrolment in the engineering education is 16.1 per cent in 2006-07 which was merely 3.6 percent in 1985-86. Similarly, the enrolment share of STs in engineering education in India has increased from less than one per cent to 5.6 per cent in the period of 20 years (Table 4). The study by Ghuman et al (2009) using the primary survey data of 2,085 students in rural Punjab found that as high as three-fourth of total students from rural set-up studying in different professional education programmes belonged to forward castes. Professional education in India is nearly inaccessible to the students belonging to backward social groups. Furthermore, the access to higher education among females belonging to different disadvantaged social groups (doubly disadvantaged- being women and belonging to SC/ST) appeared to be worse than that of the females belonging to forward castes. For example, women enrolment constituted 36 percent in the total enrolment in higher education among SCs and STs, whereas it was 40 percent among the general population in 2009-10 (Government of India, 2010). Also, the representation of female in engineering education from these two social groups are quite low. Only about 4 percent of SC-female and 1.5 percent of ST-female are accessing engineering education (Table 4). Therefore, even after six and half decades of independence equitable access to educational opportunities in general and higher professional education in particular has remained a major challenge in India.

Table 4. SC and ST Enrolment in Engineering Education in India

Year	SC	SC Female	ST	ST Female
1985-86	3.68	0.21	0.98	0.03
1990-91	6.36	0.67	1.19	0.08
1995-96	6.68	1.14	1.79	0.18
2000-01	6.90	1.67	2.59	0.33
2006-07	16.18	4.23	5.64	1.58

Source: Selected Educational Statistics (Various Years), MHRD, Government of India.

Conclusion

There has been a massive expansion of both institutions and enrolment in engineering education in India during the post-liberalisation period. The share of engineering enrolment to total enrolment in higher education in India increased from five per cent in 1985-86 to 10 per cent in 2009-10. The enrolment in higher education in India went up by four times whereas in engineering education it increased by nine times during this period. The statistics show that the expansion of the number of institutions in engineering education has apparently taken place in the private sector, as their share is more than 90 per cent in the year 2006-07. The advent of liberalisation and privatisation of the economy provided increased growth for nation's economy and thus prompted private initiative to accelerate the pace of engineering education in India.

Even with an overwhelming growth of engineering education in recent years, there however, exist, glaring regional imbalances. Around two-third of India's engineering institutions at undergraduate level are located in the states of Tamil Nadu, Karnataka, Andhra Pradesh and Maharashtra even though they account for less than one-third of the total population of the country. The southren region is having almost half of the of the total enineering institutons whereas eastern region is having less than ten per cent. The regional dispatity in the educational opportunities would not get removed if left entirely to the market forces, and therefore there is an urgent need for state interventions to promote location of new institutions in educationally deprived regions. Also, there is unequal access of engineering education to the different disadvantaged groups namely to women, scheduled castes and scheduled tribes. The exclusion of these groups is creating inequity in the growth and development of engineering and technical education of our country.

This study is an important contribution to our understanding of the growth of engineering education in India in post-1990s. The issues and concerns discussed in the paper have brought-up some promising avenues for future research in this endeavour. These may include, among others, examining the regional pattern of the growth of private engineering institutions in India, and its further consequences on access, equity, and quality. Although we have a common understanding that "the phenomenal growth in the intake and in number of institutions in the private sector has resulted the degradation of quality " there is a need to study these in detail. There is also a need for comparative studies to find out if these results can be generalized in other fields of technical and professional education such as management, law, and medicine, as the present study is only limited to engineering education.

Notes

1 AICTE has classified all the states into seven regions, where central region consist of Madhya Pradesh, Chhattisgarh and Gujarat; Eastern region consists of Mizoram, Sikkim, Orissa, West Bengal, Tripura, Meghalaya, Arunachal Pradesh, Andaman and Nicobar, Assam, Manipur, Nagaland and Jharkhand; Northern region includes Bihar, Uttar Pradesh and Uttaranchal; North-West region includes Chandigarh, Haryana, Jammu and Kashmir, New Delhi, Punjab, Rajasthan and Himachal Pradesh; Southern region includes Andhra Pradesh, Pondicherry and Tamil Nadu; South West region includes Karnataka and Kerala; Western region includes Maharashtra, Goa, Daman and Diu and Dadar Nagar Heveli. The southern and south-west regions together considered as southern region here.

2 Gender parity index (GPI) (as defined by the UNESCO Institute for Statistics) refers to the ratio of female to male values of a given indicator. A GPI equal to one indicates parity between females and males. In general, a value less than one indicates disparity in favour

of boys/men and a value greater than one indicates disparity in favour of girls/women. However, the interpretation should be the other way round for indicators that should ideally approach 0 per cent (e.g., repetition, dropout, illiteracy rates, etc). In these cases, a GPI of less than one indicates a disparity in favour of girls/women and a value greater than one indicates a disparity in favour of boys/men.

References

- AICTE: All India Council of Technical Education. (1994). *Report of the High Power Committee for Mobilisation of Additional Resources for Technical Education*, AICTE, New Delhi.
- AICTE: All India Council for Technical Education. (2010). *Annual Report 2009-10*, AICTE, New Delhi.
- Agarwal, P. (2006). *Higher Education in India: The Need for Change*, Working Paper No. 180, Indian Council for Research on International Economic Relations (ICRIER), New Delhi.
- Banerjee, R. and Muley V.P. (2008). *Engineering Education in India*. Draft Report, Observer Research Foundation, Mumbai.
- Biswas, G., Chopra K. L., Jha C. S. and Singh D.V. (2010). *Profile of Engineering Education in India: Status, Concerns and Recommendations*. New Delhi: Norosa Publishing House.
- *Blom, A. and Cheong, J. (2010)*. Governance of Technical Education in India : Key Issues, Principles, and Case Studies, *Working paper no. 190, Washington D.C., World Bank.*
- Chopra, K.L. and Sharma, P.B. (2009). *Higher Technical Education in India – Profile of Growth and Future Perspectives*, Asian Development Bank Regional Technical Assistance Project. Retrieved10 April, 2013 from http://www.namstct.org/ADB_RETA_Report/Prof_KL_ Chopra_Prof_PB_Sharma.pdf
- Ghuman, R. S., Singh, S. and Brar J.S. (2009). *Professional Education in Punjab: Exclusion of Rural Students*. Patiala: Publication Bureau, Punjabi University.
- Government of India (1945). Report of the Committee Appointed to Consider the Development of Higher Technical Institutions in India (Sarkar Committee Report), Department of Education, Health and Agriculture, Government of India, New Delhi.
- Government of India (1986). *National Policy on Education*, Ministry of Human Resources Development, Government of India, New Delhi.
- Government of India (1991). *Selected Educational Statistics*, Ministry of Human Resources Development, Government of India, New Delhi.

- Government of India. (2004). Committee to Review working of the Indian Institutes of Technology (Rao Committee Report), Ministry of Human Resources Development, Government of India, New Delhi.
- Government of India. (2009). *National Knowledge Commission Report to the Nation 2007*, Government of India, New Delhi.
- Government of India. (2011). *Statistics of Higher and Technical Education*, Ministry of Human Resources Development, Government of India, New Delhi.
- Kumar A., Sengupta, S. K. and Vij, S. (2005). "Educational and Employment Scenario in Electrical Engineering at Degree and Diploma Levels," *Journal of Educational Planning and Administration* 19 (1): 31-48.
- MHRD: Ministry of Human Resources Development, Government of India, New Delhi, *Selected Educational Statistics* (various years).
- Rao, S. S. (2006). Engineering and Technology Education in India: Uneven Spread, Quality and Social Coverage. *Journal of Educational Planning and Administration*, 20(2), 205-225.
- Rao, S. S. (2007). Neglected Terrain in the Quest for Equality: Women in Elite Engineering and Technology Education. In Jandhyala B G Tilak (Ed), *Women's Education and Development* (pp. 187-212). New Delhi: Gyan Publishing House.
- Salim, A. A. (2008). Opportunities for Higher Education: An Enquiry into Entry Barriers. In K.N. Nair and P.R. Gopinathan Nair (Eds), *Higher Education in Kerala: Micro Level Perspective* (pp. 49-88). Delhi: Danish Books.
- Tilak, J. B. G. (2004). Absence of Policy and Perspective in Higher Education. *Economic and Political weekly*, 39(21), 357-377.
- UGC: University Grants Commission. (1991). *Annual Report 1990-91*, University Grants Commission, New Delhi.
- UGC: University Grants Commission. (2010). *Annual Report 2009-10*, University Grants Commission, New Delhi.
- UGC: University Grants Commission. (2013). *Higher Education in India at a Glance*, University Grants Commission, New Delhi.
- WENR: World Education News and Reviews. (2007). Engineering Education in India: A Story of Contrasts. Retrieved 25 August, 2008 from http://www.wes.org/ewenr/07 jan/ feature.htm

8

Teacher Education at a Cross Roads: Critical Reflections from Justice Verma Commission Report

Bhanu Pratap Pritam

The Liberalisation, Privatisation and Globalisation in post-1991 pushed several obligatory reforms in terms of standards and excellence across the sectors in India including education in general and higher education in particular. Quality of education has direct relation with economic productivity and development of the nation. Quality of teacher education is one of the factors affecting the over all education of the country. Teacher education in turn depends on higher education for its standard as it is nurtured by higher education. Thus, the impact of teacher education which falls under the ambit of higher education is reflected on school education, making it as a catalysing factor. Last decade has manifested an unprecedented growth in teacher education leading to quality degradation in this sector including unplanned mushroomed institutional growth, undersupplied institutions for teacher educators, lowering criteria for teacher educators and uncontrolled indulgence of local market forces.

Some of the reformist approaches initiated by the NCTE in the recent past have proved as landmarks in Indian Teacher Education system. The first initiative was to take forward the wisdom of National Curriculum Framework (NCF, 2005) to the National Curriculum Framework for Teacher Education (NCFTE, 2009) to bring in quality in teacher education. It is also to bring teacher education in the continuum of NCF. The second initiative was to create a balance in supply and demand as recommended by the Supply and Demand Study (2009-10) of teacher education of all the states and union territory. It was the most challenging task where NCTE banned for opening new teacher education institutions in over supplied states of the country. Apart from these, many other initiatives were taken and executed in order to maintain the house of teacher education in India.

Privatisation of Teacher Education

When the country realised the significance of education for all, there came up the dearth in the number of teachers in the country. As a result there arose a huge requirement of teachers in the country which was not possible to be fulfilled with Government sector only. The private sector intervention thus promoted in the teacher education sector at a large scale. At present, the private sector initiative in teacher education reached almost 90 per cent. Table 1 shows the concurrent status of quantitative growth in teacher education institutions and intake capacity in different regions of the country. Data reflects the institutions and enrollment at Diploma, Degree and Postgraduation level teacher education courses. It further shows the already increased role of private providers in educational provisioning of teacher preparation for more than 90 per cent in India.

Taking a stock at different levels of teacher education, it appears that Diploma level courses are under the government sector in eastern region whereas entire other regions, more than 90 per cent institutions are under the private sectors. B.Ed courses are almost in private sectors with about 90 per cent institutions in all regions of the country, whereas M.Ed level institutions are quite less in number in all the regions of the country, even though merely 10 per cent institutions are under the government sector. Glancing at all India scenario, almost 95 per cent institutions at B.Ed. level are being run by the private sector and less than five per cent are under the government sector. It shows the interest and scenario of government participation in educational provisioning in Indian Teacher Education System.

Table1: Status of Private/Govt. Institution & Intake at different levels of teacher Education in India

Regions	D.El.Ed				B.Ed				M.Ed			
	Govt.		Pvt.		Govt.		Pvt		Govt.		Pvt.	
	Inst.	Intake	Inst.	Intake	Inst	Intake	Inst.	Intake	Inst	Intake	Inst.	Intake
Eastern Region	234	13679	174	8950	56	5533	482	49855	12	420	19	380
Western Region	246	12190	2388	116344	37	3700	1505	149990	27	915	298	10278
Northern Region	160	12240	1256	82771	91	12770	2774	295492	15	705	243	6275
Southern Region	124	7121	2710	154049	42	3828	1861	272981	18	620	277	7243
All India Total	764	45230	6528	362114	226	25831	6622	768318	72	2660	837	24176

Source: MHRD-NCTE(2013)

Source: MHRD-NCTE (2013)

Teacher education in India has been running in its most critical stage due to continuously degrading quality. Immediate need of revamping teacher education (especially secondary level; B.Ed) sector (Sudeep Banerjee Committee Report SBC 2008) and the relevance of the apex teacher education regulatory body, National Council for Teacher Education (NCTE) are among the most alarming demands in the contemporary education policy debates. Apart from these, Sarva Shiksha Abhiyan (SSA 2001), Right to Education (RTE 2009), Rashtriya Madhyamik Shiksha Abhiyan (RMSA, 2009) and the latest Rashtriya Uchchatar Shiksha Abhiyan (RUSA 2013) aimed at achieving 30 per cent in higher education by the year 2020 have indeed given a conspicous reason for an urgent call on revisiting the lost glory of teacher education. The present movement for stabilising the efforts of the professional statutory bodies such as; AICTE, NCTE, etc. by the government due to their poor delivery in maintaining the quality of education led to many politico-legal issues in this sector.

Justice Verma Commission

Skewed supply-demand (2011) and proliferation of commercialisation in teacher education have led the market forces to determine the fate of teacher education which further led to anarchy in this sector. As a result the Supreme Court of India decided to set up a Commission to review the teacher education and NCTE under the chairmanship of Former Chief Justice Shri. J.S. Verma in 2012. Although, recognition of D.Ed. colleges in bulk manner in already over supplied state of Maharashtra was the immediate reason for setting up of the Commission. However, overhauling of the entire teacher education was much needed long ago. The recent upsurge of education privatisation in last decade has also engulfed the secondary teacher education up to the level of almost extinction and as a result, the Justice Verma Commission (JVC) Report 2012 delivered numerous recommendations in order to regain the minimum standards in teacher education. Some of the salient features of Plan of Action (2013) based on JVC recommendations are as discussed here.

Suggested Measures for Improvement of Pre-Service Teacher Education

- Government should increase investment in Eastern and North Eastern states to meet the increasing demand of teacher education;
- Institutionalising the transparent procedure of pre-entry testing of the candidates of pre-service teacher education programmes;

- Teacher education must become a part of higher education with enhancing duration of D.Ed, B.Ed, M.Ed and four year integrated programme;
- Multi and inter-disciplinary approaches to be started in teacher education ;
- Teacher education programmes should be redesigned according to National Curriculum Framework for Teacher Education NCFTE 2009;
- Teacher education institutions should have a dedicated school attached as a pedagogical laboratory for teachers and students;
- Establish a national body for continual reflection and analysis of entire teacher education programme;
- First professional degree/diploma programme should be offered only through face-to-face mode whereas other modes of education may be used for continuous professional development activities in teacher education;
- The institutional capacity should be increased for the preparation of teacher education along with starting two year M.Ed programme;
- A broad-based qualification of teacher educators need to be developed by NCTE;
- Faculty development programmes must be institutionalised through UGC-Academic Staff College;
- Research orientation needs immediate attention in teacher education and establishing Inter University
- Centre in Teacher Education for promoting research culture in this sector.

Suggested Measures for Improvement of In-Service Teacher Education

- An expert group to develop a policy framework for in-service teacher education is required in consultation with national and state level institutions;
- In-service teacher education institutions DIETs, SCERTs, BRCs, CRCs, etc. need to be strengthened for elementary teacher education;
- Continuous professional development programmes for secondary school teachers in arrangement with CTEs, IASEs and University Departments of Education;

Teacher Performance and Audit through a Framework for Assessment of Teacher Performance

Strengthening the Regulatory Functions of the NCTE

- NCTE needs to review the existing Norms and Standards for various teacher education programmes keeping in mind the new curriculum framework guidelines;
- NCTE should formulate appropriate regulation to implement JVC recommendation and also new framework for inspection in order to maintain overall quality;
- NCTE should establish a Teacher Education Assessment and Accreditation Centre (TEAAC);
- NCTE should set up an institutional platform with state govt., Universities, UGC, and other relevant bodies for decision-making on quality and standards in teacher education;
- Transparency in regulations and inspections along with a special vigilance cell in NCTE;
- Tenure of Chairperson and Vice-Chairperson of NCTE should be of five years and age limit should be maximum of 65 years;
- Central government should develop guidelines regarding manner of appointment of members of the council which further will appoint the regional committee members;
- Empowering the council to issue directions to regional committees and also to revise orders of regional committees when required;
- NCTE should appoint a task force to undertake organisational restructuring of NCTE.

Critical Analysis of JVC's Plan of Action

The Plan of Action (2013) based on the recommendations of JVC report uncovered the appropriate pathways for quality maintenance in teacher education. A long awaited reform required in this sector which has been repetitively pronounced by several policies in the recent past and also by SBC Report and now by the JVC Report is still awaited. Some of the major issues in implementing the plan of action of JVC Report are:

- The nexus and conflicts between NCTE and its regional authorities, affiliating body and the management of private institutions and above all the unwillingness of state governments in north-eastern and eastern regions of the country create hindrance in such reformist activities;

- More than 90 per cent of the institutions are private self-financing largely with profit motive. They are unwilling and show inability to offer long duration teacher education courses due to cost effectiveness and also stakeholders' unwillingness to invest almost double amount as of now if two/four year teacher education courses are launched;
- Long duration courses require huge additional infrastructure and capital investment which is again a dead-end for majority of the private self-financing institutions;
- Attracting quality faculty in teacher education institutions appears almost impossible due to lack of quality culture such as ignored teaching and research avenues, low salary structure, job insecurity commercial attitude of private management, etc. in private self financing institutions which further disallow any curriculum level changes and innovations in students input and also for pedagogical changes;
- Dedicated schools attached with teacher education institutions has repetitively been recommended since 1968 Education Policy, but now with suddenly increasing demand due to universalisation of elementary education and also financial infeasibility of creating dedicated attached schools by the private institutions, it appears very difficult to implement such institution-school attachment;
- Professional development and capacity building among faculty members has its own financial deficiency in private institutions and overburdened work-load along with undersupplied manpower in government institutions are the important ones among the implementation challenges in teacher education sector.
- First degree/diploma programme in teacher education should be only of face to face mode as well as of longer duration keeping in mind the large number of untrained school teachers in many of the states, which are undersupplied in terms of teacher education institutions will face further challenges in training the already existing large pool of untrained teachers.
- Presently, a majority of the states are oversupplied in terms of teacher education institutions (NCTE 2009) which will subsequently lessen the demand for in-service teacher education in future, apart from new directions (RTE, 2010) of trained teacher recruitment policy. In case duration gets longer in face

to face teacher education programme then the duration of in-service training programme must become minimum four- year which appears a difficult proposition to be accepted by directorates of distance education of Universities as well as by open Universities (both government institutions) which offer such courses in the country. Since many of the states have a large pool of untrained teachers in the schools, more people are to be trained in coming years due to RTE norms and also to maintain the quality of education.

The above discussed are some of the focal points in terms of implementation of JVC report as directed in plan of action for maintaining quality of teacher education in India.

The second major head Plan of Action of JVC Report discusses about the "Quality of In-service Teacher Education" which largely provides the phenomenal change in the concept of in-service teacher education to an in-service professional development activities through various agencies such as; IASE, CTE, DIET, SCERT, BRC, CRC, etc. Presently, about 22000 in-service teachers receive first teacher education programme in India (NCTE 2012) and accordingly institutional arrangements have been made by various providers of distance mode teacher education in the country. Now, scrapping up suddenly all those courses from directorate of distance education of Universities as well as from open Universities does not appear to be viable and further reemployment or rearrangement of those existing teacher educators needs an entire conceptual shift in teacher education. Along with this, measurement of teachers' performance and auditing them seems a challenging decision since there might be many repercussions for the teachers of socially and economically disadvantaged groups which further need some special strategy of measurement and audit.

Strengthening the regulatory functions of NCTE has been repetitively recommended by SBC (2008) and JVC (2013) apart from suggestions of many renowned policy experts in teacher education in recent years. Formulating new regulations, norms and standards for institutions and changing the curriculum require entire revamping of NCTE and its existing way of work culture. The well known malpractice managed by the visiting team of the NCTE for approval and re-approval, proper regulations of regional committees, apolitical decisions of apex members of NCTE, increasing tenure and age limitation of chairperson and vice-chairperson provided honest leadership given to these bodies, dynamic linkages of NCTE with affiliating Universities, and providing reformist leadership to this apex body are among some of the major trajectories and challenges in order to better the functions of NCTE. Establishment of Teacher Education Assessment and Accreditation Centre (TEAAC) appears better initiative for quality maintenance in teacher education since the role of NAAC in teacher education again has been questioned, but precautions are to be taken in formulating the structure and stakeholders of TEAAC failing which the same old story of malpractices in NCTE and NAAC will be repeated. Formulation of TEAAC and establishing a vigilance cell in NCTE must require a third party intervention in order to have honest function and maintain quality in teacher education institutions. RUSA (2013) has also proposed a similar special body like state level NAAC in order to have quality parameters according to the state's provisions and requirement.

Current Status of JVC

Several debates have been initiated as a follow up of JVC report in 2013-14. Some of these are; Poonam Batra Committee to look after two year D.Ed programme, Prof. Jangira Committee on faculty requirement for B.El.Ed and D.El.Ed, Prof Govinda on Plan of Action of JVC Report, Prof Vinita Kaul on First Degree programme & Professional Development Programme, etc. The above mentioned committees and its deliberations for reform & renovation of teacher education in India could begin largely as a result of JVC report but visible impact is yet to deliver significantly on existing one- year B.Ed programme and its institutions which is the most important concern in teacher education for now. Some of the lobbyists of privatisation from private as well as government sector are extremely not in favour of long duration teacher education programmes which might lead in delaying any stringent action for promoting long duration teacher education courses in order to make it more professional in nature. Long duration teacher education progrmme is a long awaited demand since Kothari Commission report which is yet to be accepted by the authorities and implemented by the Universities. Its already been two years that JVC Report came in public domain and one year of Plan of Action but fruits of these deliberations are yet to be seen.

Concluding Remarks

Recent shift in Indian political regime and conflicting debate among academicians, policy bodies, lobbies of private institutions and bureaucratic set up in entire system have been causing delay in following up of JVC Plan of Action. Dedicated school attachment with the institutions of teacher education, scrapping one year face to face B.Ed and In-service B.Ed as first degree, enhancing M.Ed courses in undersupplied states, revising norms and standards for teacher education courses which are some of the Action Plans for next academic year, needs immediate implementation in order to regain the quality in teacher education. Leadership of any organisation stands for the most crucial agent of reform who furthers change in entire system, so appointment of apex positions in NCTE may bring the expected change in entire functioning of NCTE which shall further lead to maintain the quality of pre-service teacher education, in-service teacher education and will also prevent the lowering dignity of teacher education in India. Curbing the menace of extreme commercialisation in teacher education can be executed by immediately beginning long duration teacher education programmes and banning one-year teacher education course and also creating a harmonious role of university and regional committees of NCTE for approval and affiliation related complexities. Plan of action of JVC (2013) report can be proved as the ultimate instrument in the hands of government and policy-makers to be implemented with immediate effect in order to make a historical change in teacher education in post 1990s.

References

- Siddiqui, M.A. (2012) Quality Teacher Education: A Critique on the Role of NCTE. *University News*. Vol. 50 (29) 06-22, July.
- NCTE (2011) *Demand and Supply Estimates of Intake Capacity of Teacher Education Courses across the States and Union Territories (2009-10 to 2016-17)*. New Delhi: National Council for Teacher Education.
- NCTE (2009) *National Curriculum Framework for Teacher Education*. New Delhi: National Council for Teacher Education.
- Economic and Political Weekly (2007). Educating the Teacher. *EPW*. 25 August 2007.
- NCTE/UGC/MHRD (2007-08). Sudeep Banarjee Committee Report.
- Pritam, B.P. (2009). A Study of Challenges posed by Privatisation to Teacher Education in India. An unpublished M.Phil. Dissertation. New Delhi: NUEPA.
- NCTE (2013). *Plan of Action of Justice Verma Commission Report*. New Delhi: National Council for Teacher Education, http://www.ncte-india.org/Plan%20of%20 Action% 20made% 20by% 20R% 20govinda. pdf

- NCTE (2012). *Justice Verma Commission Report.* New Delhi: National Council for Teacher Education. http:// www.ncte-india.org/ Commission.asp
- MHRD (2010) *Right of the Children to Free and Compulsory Education Act.* New Delhi: Ministry of Human Resource Development.

Note : This paper is already published in University News (November 10-16, 2014).

9

Rashtriya Uchchatar Shiksha Abhiyan: A Trajectory of Indian Higher Education Policy and Implementation Challenges

Bhanu Pratap Pritam

and

Prof. P.F. Rahman

Abstract: *The recent past of Indian politico-economic scenario and its multi-sectoral impact have manifested numerous changes in the country. In education, higher and professional sectors have largely participated and experienced such long lasting changes in terms of increasing GER, budgetary allocations and direct linkage of higher education with economic development of the country. This paper largely deals with the post-independent era policies of education in India leading to Rashtriya Ucchchatar Shiksha Abhiyan (RUSA) 2013. Demographic dividend, empowering slow and steady progress of state higher education sector and universalisation of school education are also some of the immediate reasons to launch such nationwide programme. Finally it also reflects on some of the key issues in planning and implementation of RUSA and status of low performing states which will largely face numerous challenges in order to accomplish the objectives of RUSA within the given timeframe.*

Background Introduction

The President of India, Shri Pranab Mukherjee addressed the Conference of Vice Chancellors of Central Universities (CUs) at Rashtrapati Bhavan 7th February 2014 said :

"India can be a world leader in education, if only we discover the will and leadership to take us to that pinnacle and also Steps are required to improve quality of education in CUs by creating inter-linkages of industry-Academia; Interfacing with Ranking Agencies and use of technology for access, equity and quality in higher education."

The then Prime Minister Dr Manmohan Singh, while addressing the same gathering said, "*The Rashtriya Uchhatar Shiksha Abhiyan which our Government has launched should go a long way in expanding access to Higher Education opportunities.*"

Both the highest authorities in India have expressed the glorious expectation and responsibilities from the leadership and Institutions of higher learning for realizing the ethos of national development through Higher Education.

"Our university system is, in many parts, in a state of disrepair...In almost half the districts in the country, higher education enrollments are abysmally low, almost two-third of our Universities and 90 per cent of our colleges are rated as below average on quality parameters... I am concerned that in many states' university appointments, including that of vice-chancellors, have been politicised and have become subject to caste and communal considerations and there are complaints of favoruitism and corruption."]

- Prime Minister Manmohan Singh in 2007 Prime Minister's address at the 150th Anniversary Function of university of Mumbai.

Continuously degrading quality of higher education has been loudly uttered by the then Prime Minister of India even prior to 11th Five Year Plan and massive institutional growth in private sectors. Expansion, Equity, Excellence and Employability are the roadmap of higher education in contemporary India pronounced in 11th Five Year Plan and accelerated in 12th Five year plan.

Accordingly the fund allocation for education sector including higher education has been enhanced significantly. The country as a vast multi cultural-ethnic society travelled a long journey to come up to the level of excellence which basically began with basic needs of schooling during and after freedom movement leading to independence. Modern Indian education can largely be seen from two different chronological perspectives; first the conventional way of looking policies and development of higher education in pre-and post-independent period; second can be traced with pre-LPG (economic reform 1991) and post-

LPG period which manifested the exponential growth and development of entire education system especially the professional-higher education sector in India. Now, education has started gaining importance in direct linkage with skilled manpower and economic development of the country in the post -LPG era.

Table 1: World Regional GER in Higher Education

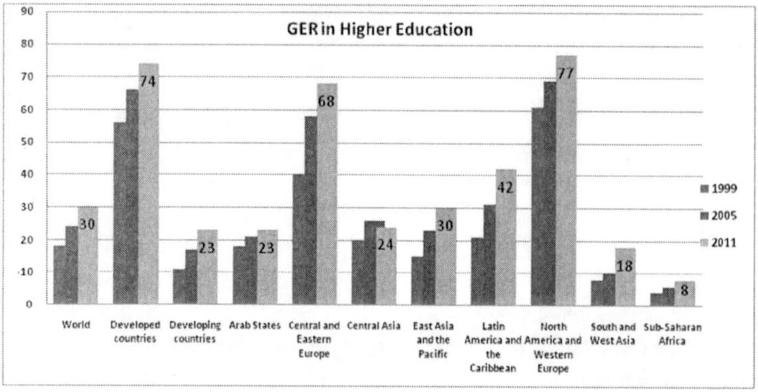

Source: UNESCO Statistics 2013.

Table 1 reflects above the increasing growth in gross enrolment ratio in higher education sector in different regions of the world along with GER in developing and developed countries. There appears a clear distinction between developed and developing countries in terms of growth in GER which reveals that growth of GER in developed countries is about 32 per cent in during 1999 to 2011 whereas more than 100% growth registered in developing countries during the same period. Looking at different regions, Arab countries, Central Asia, North America and Western Europe have manifested comparatively lesser growth (less than 30%)in GER in Higher sector compared to Central and Eastern Europe, East Asia and Pacific, Latin America and Caribbean, South and West Asia and also the Sub-Saharan Africa with more than 80% growth during 1999 to 2011.

Table 2: Developing Countries' GER in Higher Education

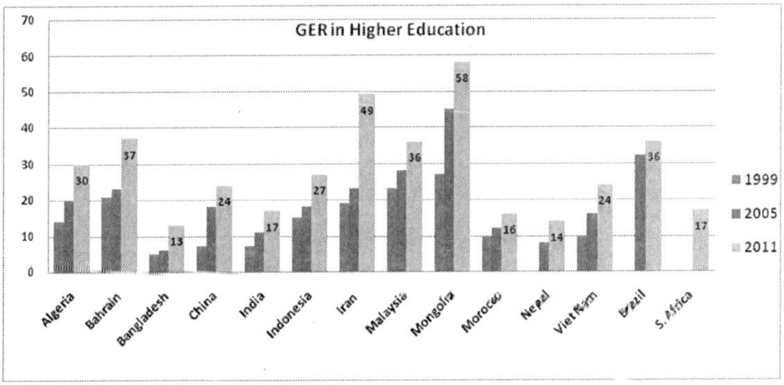

Source: UNESCO Statistics 2013.

Table 2 reflects here the gross enrolment ratio largely in developing countries and their growth pattern in last decade. Important to note here is that countries like Algeria, Bangladesh, China, India, Iran, Mongolia and Vietnam among developing countries have achieved more than 100 Per cent growth in GER of Higher Education in during 1999 to 2011. From both the tables above reflect the potential of the countries as development showed in higher education sector in last decade is remarkable. Apart from this, countries like India which has large population of young people and its sustainable transformation into human resource needs to be properly taken care by different policies of the Indian government and RUSA is one among these.

Demographic Dividend Engineering

According to the estimates of International Labour Organisation, there would be 116 million labour manpower in India in the age group of 20 to 24 by the year 2020. This is also estimated that India would be having 29 years average age of population whereas, now we have more than 60 per cent population in the age group of 15 to 59 years. With above mentioned figures, it is clear that India is passing through the most productive age group population which will not last for very long time. The present time can be visualised as the most appropriate juncture for intervening with such a huge productive manpower to channelize them by producing skilled manpower and employability for the creation of a sustainable long term economic development of the nation. India cannot afford to lose such great opportunity of transforming massive productive population into economic development of the country. Here comes the role of intervention in these productive populations through higher professional education and training.

Higher Education Policies in India

Post-independent era in Indian higher education can be understood as an era of experiments and initiatives which began with University Education Commission (UEC) or Radhakrishnan Commission (1948) which although perceived as remarkable beginning but faced many criticism. Instead of continuing basic education and commissioning universal school education India began with UEC. However, the second landscape in Indian education policies was Secondary Education Commission also known as Mudaliar Commission for improving the status of secondary education in post-independent India. Meanwhile, Constitution of India in 1950 spelled about the achieving universal primary education within 10 years by 1960 which remained an unfulfilled dream for another half century until the early decade of 21st century. Kothari Commission 1964-66 was the first significant policy intervention, in real sense, which caters to entire education system in India under the leadership of Honourable Dr D. S. Kothari. "The destiny of India lies in its classroom" the beginning sentence of Kothari Commission made an effort to relook the entire education right from school to higher professional education sector in India. Almost two decades after Kothari Commission, National Policy on Education 1986 and Programme of Action 1992 came into picture which again revamped entire gamut of education. As a result, operation blackboard, DPEP, CRCs and several state specific plans and projects for primary education providing all minimum facilities for schooling etc. for revamping school education on one hand and, restructuring professional education by modification of AICTE and establishment of NCTE, NAAC for establishment of assessment and accreditation body and initiatives in establishing private institutions, etc. on the other hand were major remarkable initiatives in post 1991 era. The recent resultant factor for RUSA (2013) has its root in, largely, universalisation of elementary education by Sarva Shiksha Abhiyan (2001) and RTE (2009) and also on

Rashtriya Madhyamik Shiksha Abhiyan (2009). The success of universal elementary education transiting to increase GER in secondary education led to launch RUSA in 2013 apart from several other reasons such as global competition, national and international demand for higher education and direct linkage of higher education with economic development of the country in the post-LPG era.

RUSA was launched largely to empower the state higher education sector in 2013 with a goal of achieving 30 per cent of GER in higher education by 2020 with the following objectives.

Objectives of RUSA

- Aid reforms in state higher education system by creating a facilitating institutional structure for planning and monitoring at state level, promoting autonomy in state Universities and improving governance.
- Improve the overall quality of existing state institutions by ensuring that all institutions conform to prescribed norms and standards and adopt accreditation as a mandatory quality assurance framework.
- Expand the institutional base by creating additional capacity in existing institutions and establishing new institutions, to achieve enrolment targets.
- Correct regional imbalances in access to higher education through setting up of higher education institutions in unserved and underserved areas.
- Improve equity in higher education by providing adequate opportunities to socially deprived communities; promote inclusion of women, minorities, SC/ST, OBCs and differently abled persons.
- Ensure adequate availability of quality faculty in all higher educational institutions and ensure capacity building at all levels.
- Create an enabling atmosphere in higher educational institutions to devote themselves to research and innovation.
- Create opportunities for states to undertake reforms in the affiliating system in order to ensure that the reforms and resource requirements of affiliated colleges are adequately met.
- Ensure academic and examination reforms in the higher educational institutions.

Table 3: Enrolment Growth in Higher Education

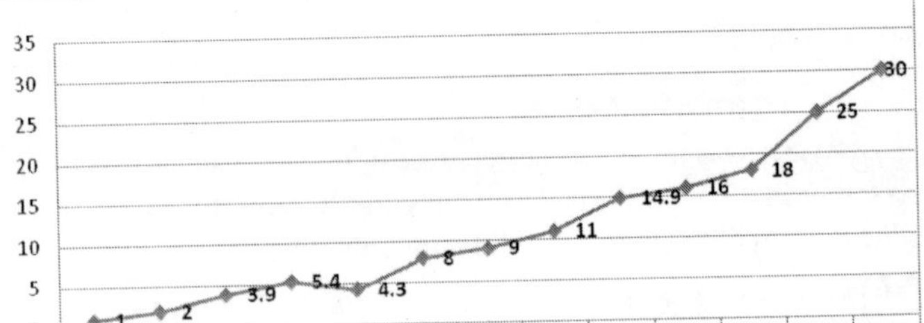

	1950-51	1960-61	1970-71	1980-81	1990-91	2000-01	2002-03	2005-06	2009-10	2011-12	2012-13	2017-18	2020-21
GER % in HE	1	2	3.9	5.4	4.3	8	9	11	14.9	16	18	25	30

Source: RUSA Document 2013.

Post-independent era shows a routine and gradual growth in GER of higher education which began with approximately one per cent in the year 1950-51 and expected to reach 30 per cent by 2020 as per the RUSA objectives. In between there are many policy interventions, programmes, projects and other provisions which resulted in growing GER at national level. The growth of private self-financing institutions in last decade 2000-01 to 2010-11 has enormously contributed in increasing GER especially in professional and technical education sector but quality and excellence of higher education have been repetitively questioned. Currently GER in higher education rose to almost 20 per cent and a target of adding 10 per cent more in coming six year is expected through several provisions provided under the RUSA. A normal growth has been registered till 1990s in terms of GER in higher education but a steep growth pattern can be observed in post-1991 which has been accelerated with the private initiatives in higher education, liberal policies of higher education, increasing demands of professional higher education due to availability of global market in India and many more. Now after 11th Five Year Plan government of India planned to continuously intervene through several initiatives to promote higher education which has also been envisioned in 12th Five Year Plan as well as in RUSA. In the line of National Knowledge Commission (2005) RUSA also proposed to establish 374 model degree colleges, 1000 polytechnics, 800 constituent colleges of central Universities and 30 exclusive Universities for women in the 12th Five Year Plan for enabling India to produce skilled manpower. Such a holistic development plan for increasing institutional infrastructure would certainly lead in achieving the target of 30 per cent GER by the end of 2020.

Table 4: States with low GER and GSDP for HE

	States	GER	% of GSDP on HE	Universities	Colleges
1	**Assam**	13.4	1.02^	15	507
2	**Bihar**	10.5	0.55	22	706
3	**Chhattisgarh**	13.6	0.78	19	681
4	**Jammu & Kashmir**	16.8	1.09^	11	314
5	**Jharkhand**	8.1	0.14*	14	231
6	**Madhya Pradesh**	13.6	0.68	37	2364
7	**Meghalaya**	17.5	0.33*	10	69
8	**Orissa**	16.1	0.56	19	1117
9	**Rajasthan**	18.2	0.41*	59	2753
10	**Tripura**	13.6	1.10^	3	40
11	**Uttar Pradesh**	16.3	0.18*	61	4440
12	**West Bengal**	12.4	0.31*	27	896

Sources: RUSA Document 2013

Here, above Table 4 reflects the states in India which might face much difficulty in implementations of RUSA in coming years leading to achieve the target of 30 per cent GER by the end of year 2020. States lagging behind in terms of GER in higher education sector largely are from eastern and north-eastern India apart from Madhya Pradesh and Rajasthan. Some of the common reasons identified for low GER in such states are low expenditure pattern in term of per cent of GSDP spent on higher education sector, less infrastructure and institutions for higher learning and also the low GER and transition rate in school education. Assam has GER of 13.4 per cent in higher education although 1.02 per cent of GSDP is spent on higher education which is remarkable and near to national average spent on higher education in the country. Similarly Jammu and Kashmir and Tripura are also high expenditure states in terms of per cent of GSDP spent on education but gaining low GER. Such scenario exists due to its increasing cost of higher education provisioning especially being the hilly region and extreme geographical locality.

Further some of the bigger states in terms of demographic structure such as Bihar, West Bengal, Madhya Pradesh, Uttar Pradesh and Rajasthan are also among challenging states where achieving the target of 30 per cent appears much difficult task due to several historical as well as politico-economic reasons. These states are largely called BIMARU reasons due to its underperformed schooling leading to higher education, densely populated area with less economic development, low Human Development Index rate, lower expenditure pattern on education especially on higher education as of GSDP and almost stagnant infrastructure facilities for higher education by the respective state governments. Although privatisations of higher education in some of the states have catered the problem of supply of higher education but focus was largely on professional, technical and IT related sectors linked with market needs and profit generation.

Table 5: Socio-Religious GER Profile

Major categories	% GER	Rural	Urban	Male	Female
Schedule Caste	**12.2**	--	--	13	9
Schedule Tribe	**9.7**	--	--	13.1	**7.5**
OBC	18.7	--	--	--	--
Others	28	--	--	--	--
Hindu	20	14.7	34.9	--	--
Muslim	**11.3**	**6.8**	19.2	--	--
Christian	31.3	24.3	44.2	--	--
Sikh	23.1	18.8	37.3	--	--
Jain	54.6	38.5	56.2	--	--
Buddhism	**17.9**	**11.7**	25.9	--	--
Rural	--	--	--	13.7	**8.3**
Urban	--	--	--	29.6	**13.7**
TOTAL GER	14.0	13.9	32.5	12.7	**17.1**

Source: RUSA-2013, NSSO 66th Round.

The Table 5 here indicates the socio-religious representation in higher education and also those areas where much are needed in order to achieve the objectives of RUSA. Schedule castes which consist of around 18 per cent of country's population have merely 12.2 per cent GER that is much below than the national GER in higher education. Schedule tribes have fairly sufficient GER of 9.7 per cent in higher education which is almost proportionate to their population in the country which again needs further inspection of regional imbalance in development of ST population from North Eastern and Rajasthan region with rest of the country. Whereas, OBCs have comparatively lesser GER of 18.7 in higher education compared to their respective population. Further, among minorities population except Muslim minority, all Christian, Sikh, Jain and Buddhist have better GER (17 per cent+) in higher education as compared with national GER in India. GER in higher education for Muslim population appears in much deteriorated status with merely 11.3 per cent which is much below to the national average as well as other group of minorities.

As far as rural urban profile of GER in higher education is concerned, Christian, Jain and Sikh have more than average national GER even with rural population whereas Muslim minority rural population have merely 6.8 per cent GER in higher education which appears quite alarming compare to any other religious group in the country. However, among the urban segment population, again GER in higher education among Muslim minority is the lowest with merely 19.2 per cent and Buddhist, which largely consists of Schedule caste population, having GER of about 25.9 per cent. Apart from this, all other socio-religious group has comparatively higher GER (more than national average 32.5 per cent) in higher education. Similarly in gender segment, among all socio-religious group, female has much below GER in higher education compare to male.

Concluding Remarks

The potential growth of developing countries in the world and their recent progress in higher education sector needs adequate attention for sustainable development and Indian chapter in developing countries has shown its potential in last two decades in various sectors. Indian higher education system has manifested immense growth in last two decade especially in technical and professional education sector. Such growth resulted in response to continuous policy interventions from post-independent era till the recent time. University Education Commission (1948), Kothari Commission (1964-66) National Education Policy (1986), several initiatives in post 1991 LPG linkages with higher education resulting in establishment of apex bodies NCTE (1993), NAAC (1994), Private Universities and Colleges Establishments Act both by Central and State governments, National Knowledge Commission (2005) along with universalization of school education established great foundations for RUSA. In addition, the age of demographic dividend through which India is passing presently has to be properly managed and channelised in order to make large pool of Indian young population into productive human resources. The present challenges to be faced by higher education with regard to achieving the objectives of RUSA, in many states, largely eastern Indian states and states with low GER and expenditure pattern in higher education sector would face extreme complexities needs to be revisited. Apart from this, performance based funding will further create challenges for poor states which have no potential for financial enhancement in higher education sector. RUSA offers similar funding pattern for all developed states, developing states as well as underdeveloped states which will further enhance the gap between rich and poor states. Rather need based funding and incentive based surplus funding according to the present educational status can better serve the purpose of RUSA in timely achieving the target of 30 per cent GER by the year 2020.

References

- MHRD (2013) Rashtriya Uchchatar Shiksha Abhiyan. Government of India.
- UGC (2012) 12th Five Year Plan: Inclusive and Qualitative Expansion of Higher Education. Delhi: UGC.
- Planning Commission of India (2012) 12th Five Year Plan: Education. Government of India.
- Agarwal.P (2009) Indian Higher Education: Envisioning the Future. New Delhi: Sage Publication.
- Jain. V.P. and Negi.U.R.(2012) Status of Growth and Development of Higher Education in India. New Delhi: Association of Indian Universities.
- UGC (2013), Higher Education at a Glance. New Delhi: University Grants Commission.
- Pillai.L and Manjunath, B.R.(2014). The Indian Universities and Accreditation Question. University News: Vol.52. no. 3
- Tilak, J.B.G. (2013). Higher Education in BRIC Member Countries: Comparative Patterns and Policies. *Economic and Political Weekly*. April 6, 2013 vol xlviii no 14
- Bhushan, S (2013) Rashtriya Uchchatar Shiksha Abhiyan: Implementation Challenges. College Post. Vol.14, No, 4.
- http://www.uis.unesco.org/Pages/default.aspx

Note: This paper is already Published in "College Post" (April-June 2014). **ISSN-2348-084X)**

Economic Perspectives in Higher Education

10

FDI and Public Private Partnership in Higher Education

Dr Saneem Fatima
and
Syed Ahmed Saad

Abstract

India is a fast developing economy of the world and has become a favoured destination for FDI. The economic reforms of early 1990s paved the way for liberalised and more open economy for the private sector as well as foreign investors. The service sector is booming and new investment alternatives are emerging like banking, telecom and education etc. Realising the importance of education in a knowledge economy on one hand and potential market on the other due to the large number of students enrolling for higher education, government has given a liberal hand to private sector which attracted a lot of investment in recent past. In such times the scope of foreign direct investment and public private partnership has gain a lot of momentum. This paper discusses some issues related to foreign direct investment and public private partnership in the field of higher education in India.

Keywords: Higher Education, FDI, PPP, UGC and Planning Commission.

Introduction

Education informs a person and enlightens him about things he does not know and thus initiates him to inquire all sorts of questions about their surroundings like nature, life and people of society. Historically education is being used as an instrument of struggle and liberation by both individual and by the society. Higher education constitutes the topmost stage of formal education and more importantly concerned with processes in the more advanced phases of human learning. Higher education enhances a country's capacity for participation in an increasingly knowledge-based world economy and has the potential to enhance socio-economic development and well being of its citizens.

Education in India comes under concurrent list of Honorable Constitution meaning that its a responsibility of both Centre and State, while the Centre Co-ordinates and determines standards in higher and technical education, school education is the responsibility of the State. The key policy making agencies for higher education are:

1. Ministry of Human Resource Development (Higher Education Department) - lays down the National Policy on Education.

2. Central Advisory Board of Education (CABE) - coordination and cooperation between the Union and the States in the field of education.

3. State Councils for Higher Education – coordination of roles of Government, Universities and apex regulatory agencies in higher education within the State.

An Overview of Higher Education

The Indian education sector has been recognised as a sunrise sector for investment in the recent past and the Government of India has reignited its reforms agenda by opening up certain sensitive sectors to foreign investment like retail and civil aviation, which results in increased economic activity and employment generation.

Public spending on higher education is justified on the grounds that it generates positive externalities since it is a merit good. Equally, there is an argument that public spending on higher education should be discouraged since private benefits far outweigh social benefits. National Institute of Educational Planning and Administration (NIEPA) has recommended that institutions of higher education should make efforts to raise their own resources by raising the fee levels, encouraging private donations and by generating revenues through consultancy and other activities. Various studies shows that with the given levels of India's public spending, GER levels and private sector participation are low, even when compared to developing countries, there appears to be a case for improving the effectiveness of public spending and increase the participation of private players, both domestic and foreign. The Planning Commission in its approach paper to 12th Five Year Plan had suggested that the current "not-for-profit" approach in the education sector should be re-examined in a pragmatic manner so as to ensure quality without losing focus on equity.

India, today, is considered as a talent pool of the world, having qualified and educated human resources in abundance. This has been one of the primary reasons for transformation of India into one of the fastest growing economies in the world since liberalisation in the 1990s. As the economist Clark Kerr observed, "On a global scale, wealth and prosperity have become more dependent on the access to knowledge than the access to natural resources." India's aspirations to establish a knowledge society in the context of increasing globalisation, is based on the assumption that higher and technical education essentially empowers people with the requisite competitive skills and knowledge. It has been realised that it is the quality of education that prepares one for all pursuits of life and in the absence of an acceptable level of quality, higher education becomes a mere formalism devoid of any purpose or substance. As a result, from around the turn of the century, increasing attention has also been paid to quality and excellence in higher education. Post-independence India has witnessed an above average growth in the number of higher educational institutions vis-à-vis its population. While there were just about 20 Universities and 500 Colleges at the time of independence, today these numbers have grown exponentially with 642 Universities.

According to World Bank, Public expenditure on education as per cent of the Gross Domestic Product (GDP) in India has been 3.2, 3.3 and 3.2 in 2009, 2010 and 2011 respectively. Higher education is assuming an upward significance for developing countries like India which is experiencing service-led economic growth. The growth of India's higher educational institutions has indeed been outstandingly rapid. The numbers of Universities have doubled since 1990-91, and enrolment has become more than doubled. But this has been at the expense of quality, increased rigidity in course design, poor absorption of knowledge, and growing lack of access to laboratory facilities, journals and opportunities for field work, etc. India is one of the most attractive destinations for higher education which is characterized by huge market size both in terms of numbers of student and its potential growth rate of 16 per cent for next five years. According to the National Knowledge Commission estimates, the country needs to build 1,500 Universities within a period of five years to endow enough people with the skills to sustain rapid growth. Given this state of higher education in India, could liberalization be the way out? The major concern regarding such liberalisation is that it can lead to commercialisation of higher education which may have an effect on a large section of society adversely. Sunder (2010) concluded that due to budgetary constraints, the government appears to have decided on profit-oriented privatization of higher education as the solution.

Expenditure on Higher Education

Growing youth aspirations and massive expansion of schooling is creating a huge demand for higher education. Higher education is also to build a workforce capable of underpinning a modern, competitive economy. As a consequence, enrollment in higher education would have to be significantly increased in a demand. There must be a strategic shift from mere expansion to improvement in quality higher education. For this, the focus should be not only on larger enrollment, but also on the quality of the expansion.

The latest figures from the government documents shows that there is an urgent need to step up both public and private investment in higher education (including technical), and increase in the efficiency of its utilisation. About 18.0 per cent of all government education spending or about 1.12 per cent of GDP is spent on higher education today. This should be raised to 25.0 per cent and 1.5 per cent respectively. An increase of 0.38 per cent of GDP means an additional allocation of about Rs 25,000 crore to higher education for the Centre and the States taken together. Institutions should be encouraged to raise their own funds through various legitimate means. Reasonable tuition fees in higher education need to be supplemented with appropriate publicly-funded financial aid. State Universities and their affiliated colleges that account for more than 90.0 per cent of the enrollment suffer from severe fund constraints and poor governance leading to poor quality.

Recent Trends in Higher Education

Over the past few decades, the global economy has shifted from being manufacturing-centric to a knowledge-driven one and as countries move up the ladder of development, the contributions of hi-tech manufacturing and high value-added services to the GDP increases. Success in leveraging knowledge and innovation is only possible with a sound infrastructure of higher education. A successful education policy forms the foundation of all fields of national development including political, social, economic, technical, scientific, and environmental. Thus, the higher the quality of university education in a country, the more prosperous and competitive are the people.

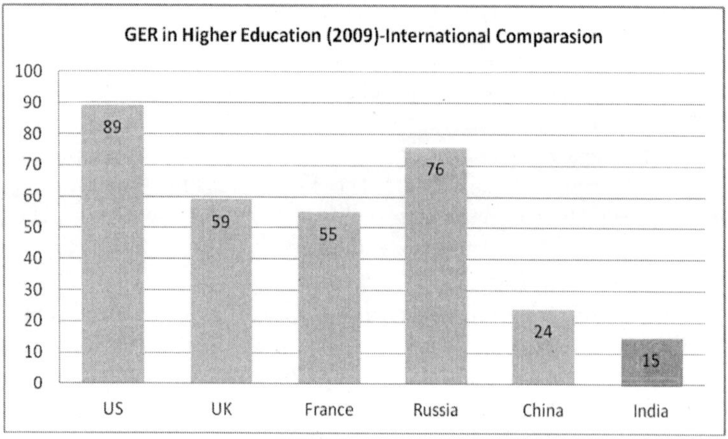

Source: UNESCO Institute of Statistics Database.

The emergence of India as a service-based, knowledge driven economy has put the spot light on human capital. Higher education is essential to build a workforce capable of underpinning a modern, competitive economy.

Role of FDI and PPP in Higher Education

Foreign direct investment provides highly productive advantages both governmental and private companies and organisations of all over the world. Foreign direct investment (FDI) plays a multidimensional role in the overall development of the host economies. It may generate benefits through bringing in non-debt-creating foreign capital resources, technological upgrading, skill enhancement, new employment, spillovers and allocative efficiency effects. Foreign direct investment is profitable both to the country receiving investment (foreign capital and funds) and the investors. Education is gaining lot of importance in India. Education Industry is likely to grow by the size of the public education sector is $40 billion and the private sector amounted to $60 billion in 2011-2012. Foreign Direct Investment up to 100 per cent is allowed in most of the sectors more significantly, there is an expectation that FDI would reach US$ 1000 million this year. India is the second most favoured destination for foreign direct investments as per the survey by UNCTAD after China for transnational corporations during 2010-2012. The education sector has attracted foreign direct investments (FDI) worth Rs 4,596.96 crore (US$ 740.35 million) during April 2000 to September 2013, according to the data released by the Department of Industrial Policy and Promotion (DIPP).

Bahmaid (2007) concluded that FDI as a strategic component of investment is needed by India for its sustained economic development, and presently the market for education have limited competition leading to high prices. But with the government approving 100 per cent FDI in this sector, more and more foreign investments will flow in, with foreign players foraying into this sector. This will bring in more competition in the market, with prices reflecting true costs and quality improvement.

Challenges Ahead

Several reforms in the regulatory framework are currently underway such one is a proper accreditation structure, quick redressal of disputes through educational tribunals and prevention of malpractices and establishment of a national level apex body, that is, National Commission on Higher Education and Research (NCHER) to ensure autonomy of institutions and enhancement of standards and provision for entry of foreign education providers. The lack of long term, reliable and market oriented regulation has proved to be one of the greatest obstacles to infrastructure investment. One of the biggest challenges to governments is achieving a regulatory framework that provides the necessary credibility and accountability for the efficient functioning of the sector, allowing for greater investment inflows. Presently there are following problems:

1. UGC not open to recognizing Foreign Universitiess.
2. Limitations on intake of students (quotas, foreign students, mode of admission etc.).
3. Limited choice of entity – Trust, Society or Section 25 Company.
4. Lack of availability of trained faculty.
5. Course content not in line with the expectations of the industry.
6. High capital expenditure requirements for setting up Higher Education institution with quality infrastructure.

Tough Road for Foreign Universities

AICTE has in place regulations for Foreign Universities/ Institutes which propose to collaborate/ enter into twinning arrangement (where a student does a part of the course in India and part overseas) in Technical Education. The broad features of these regulations are:

1. Franchise is not permitted.

2. Fee/seats prescribed by AICTE.
3. Degree/institution to be recognized in the home country.
4. For degree granting institutions, affiliation / tie-up with Indian University mandatory.

Other than the above stated problems the legislature is also considering some important issue like the Foreign Educational Institutions (Regulation of Entry and Operations) Bill, 2010 having the key features:

1. Own Campus.
2. Franchise route not permitted.
3. Prior Central government approval mandatory.
4. Reservation applicable.
5. Fee and admission policy will be regulated.
6. No profiteering/commercialisation allowed.

But the Foreign Educational Institutions (Regulation of Entry and Operations) Bill 2010 is pending in Parliament as several parties are opposing to some of the provisions which would allow foreign Universities to operate in India. The Parliamentary Standing Committee has made several recommendations to the Bill and they were being considered by the government. Although there are regulatory hurdles it is possible for an overseas education provider to look at opportunities in India, subject to appropriate structuring.

Role of Public Private Partnership

The Government of India has set itself an aggressive target of achieving 30 per cent GER in Higher Education by 2020, which translates into doubling the GER in the next six years. Government resource allocation is inadequate to meet its own targets. As per recent estimates by NUEPA, in order to achieve this target an additional investment of Rs 9.5 lakh crore (USD 190 bn), which includes capital expenditure and operating expenditure. To give a perspective, the total allocation to the entire education sector under the eleventh Five Year Plan (2007-12) was Rs 2.7 lac crore (USD 55 bn) out of which higher education's share was only about 30 per cent. Therefore, given the limited support, which Government can provide to this sector in terms of investment leaving enough scope for private participation and the private sector needs to play a much larger role. The Eleventh Five Year Plan (2007-12) allocation for technical and higher education has been raised by almost nine fold to US $ 18.8 billion from US $ 2.1 billion in the Tenth Plan. However, this is still a fraction of the estimated requirements for achieving the targets.

National Knowledge Commission has recommended that the number of Universities increase up to 1500 by 2015, considered a highly ambitious target, but inadequate to meet demand for quality education and for higher education, an expenditure of US $ 37.13 billion has been projected to achieve the objectives during the 12th Five Year Plan (2012-17). The 12th Five Year Plan focuses on expansion, inclusion and quality to achieve the national goals in education. There is unanimous agreement of the fact that the private sector needs to be involved to complement and supplement the efforts of the Government. As private finance has taken on a greater role in sharing the cost of higher education, it has also increased its role as a conduit for investment in higher education. This has led private finance to gain greater sophistication in this sector, with a handful of countries pioneering innovative financial techniques such as FDI, tax incentives, public-private partnerships, and university-industry collaboration.

Adequate infrastructure is a prerequisite for increased access to global trade and investment flows, increasing competitiveness and thus sustaining regional growth. In fact improved infrastructure reduces transportation costs, excessive inventories and logistical costs, expanding markets and reducing distances between production and consumption centeres. Improved infrastructure also increases the attractiveness of the business environment for Foreign Direct Investment (FDI). The Planning commission also advocated the role of private sector in its approach paper and discussed that the growth of private sector in higher education should be facilitated to achieve the GER target. To counter the present problem of limited support from the government innovative Public-Private Partnerships (PPP) should be explored and developed and the FDI be given a prominent role in the Twelfth Plan.

Private higher education accounts for about four-fifths of enrollment in professional higher education and one-third overall. A clear policy is therefore, required to manage private education and a statutory and transparent framework needs to be established for its operation for driving private growth further in a legitimate and balanced manner. It remains a valuable instrument for infrastructure investment; the framework for such participation must change so as to increase the social and economic benefits. Private investment is not the silver bullet: public sector investment must also increase, and other sources of infrastructure financing must be actively explored. New forms of public-private partnerships (PPPs) have emerged from the experience of the past decades. Currently, PPP in India has been largely concentrated in sectors such as power, telecom, roads and airports. In the field of higher education it constitutes 80 per cent of professional higher education and 33 per cent of overall education. Currently, private PPP can enhance the quality of education, relevance of an education system and funding possibilities to enable the government to improve the educational system.

Key Features of PPPs in Education. Despite their broad scope, it is generally accepted that PPPs share five key characteristics:

[1] In that they are formal in nature,

[2] They involve the development of a long-term relationship between the partners,

[3] They are outcome focused,

[4] They include an element of risk-sharing among the partners, and

[5] They can involve both the voluntary and commercial sectors as private sector partners.

The future of PPP in India looks bright as the country aims for a higher growth trajectory through strong infrastructure investment. With the increasing involvement of PPP modules in development across various sectors, the share of PPP and the private sector in total infrastructure investment is expected to rise to 50 per cent in 12th plan from 30 per cent in the previous one. Education is one of the key sectors witnessing higher role of PPP, and this trend is set to continue over the next decade as well. In order to increase this share, policymakers should look at setting up an independent intuitional structure for PPP handling sector specific regulatory mechanism and higher level of transparency of information for PPP. There are following models:

1. *Basic Infrastructure Model:* The private sector invests in infrastructure; the government manages the operations of the institution, making annualised payments to the private investor.
2. *Outsourcing Model:* The private sector invests in infrastructure, manages operations in lieu of payment from the Government for specified services.
3. *Equity/Hybrid Model:* Here the investment in infrastructure is shared between government and private sector while operation and management is vested with the private sector.

4. *Reverse Outsourcing Model:* As per this model, Government invests in infrastructure and the private sector takes the responsibility of operation and management.

The government policy is keen to open the higher education sector to the private providers, either through public-private participation or foreign direct investment in higher education. If India is to be a global economic powerhouse it is essential to nurture this higher education sector in urban as well as rural areas. Recently, the University Grants Commission (UGC) has recommended four models of Public Private Partnership to the Planning Commission and according to an estimate; the country requires an investment of over US $ 150 billion in the next 10 years.

Challenges PPPs in India: There are following challenges to the establishment of PPPs in the education sector, particularly in developing countries like India the challenges include:

1. There is no independent PPP regulator as of now. In order to attract more domestic and international funding of the infrastructure, a more robust regulatory environment, with an independent regulator is essential.
2. The PPP programme lacks a comprehensive database regarding the project/ studies to be awarded under PPP. An online database, consisting of all project document including feasibility reports, concession agreements and status of various clearances and land acquisition will be helpful to all bidders.
3. The project development activities such as detailed feasibility study, land acquisition, environment/ forest clearances etc., are not given adequate importance by the authorities. The absence of adequate project development by authorities leads to reduced interest by the private sector, mispricing and many times delays at the time of execution.
4. The private sector is dependent upon commercial banks to raise debt for PPP projects. With commercial banks reaching the sectoral exposure limits funding the PPP projects is getting difficult.
5. The partners all have different aims, constituencies and ways of working and it is difficult harnessing their respective demands and requirements for working with each other.

6. Apprehension from both parties for the public sector, education is seen as a non-commercial activity while for the private sector there is concern that policy reversals may reduce the benefits arising from such a partnership arrangement.

Conclusion

Education is a qualitative aspect and not only an important factor for the development of country but for the well being of its people as well. With limited infrastructure and growing demand for higher education, the scope for foreign direct investment and public private partnership is increasing. The exponential increase in numbers of Universities and colleges since independence and especially in last twenty years is quite appreciating. In order to achieve sustenance government increase its spending on higher education and also make policies in such a way that the needs of large population can be served. The role of private sector is praiseworthy and it is expected that the government institutions like UGC, NEUPA and AICTE will work out for the same, keeping the interest of people at priority.

References

- Agarwal P. (2006). "Higher Education in India: The Need for Change". ICRIER Working Paper.
- Bahmaid, SS, (2013). Study on foreign direct investment in education. *International Journal of Advanced Trends in Computer Science and Engineering,* Vol.2 , No.1, p.p. : 519 - 531.
- Kapoor, R. and kelkar, N. (2013). E-Governance: Higher Education in Rural Area. *Proceedings of National Conference on New Horizons in IT* - NCNHIT 2013, ISBN 978-93-82338-79-6.
- Roy, J. and Banerjee, P. (2007). Attracting FDI from the Indian Diaspora: The Way Forward. *Confederation of Indian Industry*
- Scandizzo, S. (2007). Public-Private Partnerships and the Infrastructure Challenge in Latin America.
- Sharma, K. (2007). FDI in Higher Education: Aspirations and Reality.
- Sunder, S. (2010). Higher Education Reforms in India.

Reports

UNESCO Global Education Digest 2010;

MHRD Annual Report 2009-10;

All India Survey on Higher Education 2011-12 Department of Higher Education, Ministry of Human Resource Development, Government of India, New Delhi, 2013.

Internet Links

http://data.worldbank.org/indicator/SE.XPD.TOTL.GD.ZS
http://www.thehindu.com/news/national/article3483922.ece
http://www.ibef.org/industry/education-sector-india.aspx

11

Higher Education of India: Service Revolution and Economic Development

Dr H. Akther Banu[1] S. Mansoor Rahman[2]
Syed Samiuddin Muzamil [3]

Knowledge has always been prime mover of prosperity and power. The acquisition of knowledge has been the thrust area throughout the world....Whether a nation qualifies as knowledge society is judged by how effectively it deals with knowledge creation and knowledge deployment.

-A.P.J. Abdul Kalam

Abstract

The world is experiencing service revolution where "Service and Expertise" are the main business outcomes. The concept of Knowledge Management has become the kingpin and life nerve of organisations. The organisations are responding to the external challenges by modifying their management practices. One of the more prominent features of the organisational landscape in the New Millennium is a focus on a cluster of related ideas such as information, knowledge, and learning. At the centre of this cluster is the notion of Knowledge Management.

Key Words: Knowledge Revolution, Service Revolution, Information Revolution, Knowledge Economy , Market Economy

---

1. Assistant Professor of English, Govt. Degree College Kurnool, (A.P) draktherbanu@gmail.com
2. Associate Professor of Economics, Osmania College (Autonomous) Kurnool, (A.P) drmansoors@gmail.com
3. Associate Professor of Economics, Osmania College (Autonomous) Kurnool, (A.P) drmansoors@gmail.com

Expansion of Service Sector

The growth of higher education in India has been phenomenal. Over the last 50 years, the Government of India has provided full policy support and substantial public funds to create one of the world's largest systems of higher education. These institutions, with the exception of some notable ones, have however, not been able to maintain the high standards of education or keep pace with developments in the fields especially in knowledge and technology.

Starting with 1950- 51, there were only 263,000 students in all disciplines in 750 colleges affiliated to 30 Universities. By 2005, 11 million students in 17,000 Degree colleges affiliated to 230 Universities and non-affiliated university-level institutions. In addition, there are about 10 million students in over 6500 in vocational institutions. The enrolment is growing at the rate of 5.1 per cent per year. However, of the Degree students only five per cent are enrolled into engineering courses, while an overall 20 per cent in sciences.

As of 2010, India has 504 Universities and university – level institutions which include 243 state Universities, 53 state private Universities, 130 deemed Universities, 33 institutions of national importance established under Act of Parliament and five institutions established under various State legislations. In addition, there are 25,951 colleges including around 2,565 women colleges.

In India both public and private institutions operate simultaneously. In 2000-2001, of the 13,072 higher education institutions, 42 per cent were privately owned and run catering to 37 per cent of students enrolled into Higher education, that is, approximately 3.1 million out of total 8.4 million. It is also likely that most of the growth in the rapidly expanding higher education sector took place in private unaided colleges or in self-financing institutions. Since grant-in-aid to private colleges is becoming difficult, many governments/universities have granted recognition/ affiliation to unaided colleges and many Universities have authorised new 'self-financing' courses even in government and aided colleges. It is felt that as of now more than 50 per cent of the higher education in India is imparted through private institutions, mostly unaided.

What is Knowledge?

Today we are living in a knowledge era. This is evident from the common usage of the phrases such as knowledge wealth, knowledge society, knowledge bank, knowledge city, knowledge economy and knowledge based industry. Media are replete with advertisements of centres that claim to offer knowledge and skills that can lead to better professional development. Knowledge has come to be regarded today as a power that is wealthier than self and stronger than might. This scenario brings into close focus the discussion of what is knowledge, what is learning and what is education.

What is Knowledge Revolution?

Human capital is the engine of development. We are undergoing a social and economic revolution which matches the impact of the agricultural and industrial revolutions. Both the agricultural revolution and the industrial revolution had one thing in common: the adoption of new fuels and new knowledge about how to use them. The current revolution is also driven by knowledge. We can call it the Knowledge Revolution. This "Knowledge Revolution" is driven by knowledge and by the technologies for processing and communicating it.

Knowledge Economy – An Overview

While speaking about the need for knowledge society for the development of the country our first Prime Minister Jawaharlal Nehru declared that;

> *If all were well with our educational institutions, all would be well with the nation. Educational institutions are intimately linked with society at large. They are the temples of knowledge.*

Alvin Toffler argues that knowledge is the central resource in the economy of the information society:

> *In a Third Wave economy, the central resource – a single word broadly encompassing data, information, images, symbols, culture, ideology, and values – is actionable knowledge.*

Where as the three waves are

First Wave – Agrarian Revolution

Second Wave – Industrial Revolution

Third Wave – Service Revolution*

According to an eminent Economist Gurnal Myrdal:

> *Education has an independent as well as instrumental value, i.e., the purpose of education must be to rationalize attitudes as well as to impart knowledge and skills. Education for national development should aim at training the young generation the life*

skills, self reliance, personality development, community service social integration and political understanding.

Reasons for the Emergence of Knowledge Management

Today it is important to consider why particular management trends such as KM emerge at a particular time in history. While the notion of knowledge management has been around at least since the 1970s, it is arguably only in the past five years that it has become a widespread management "buzzword." KM's emergence may be seen as arising due to a number of contemporary trends in organisations, technologies, and discourse. The explanation includes both rational and non-rational elements. on access to knowledge or expertise. With the recognition of the importance of knowledge in getting work done comes the concomitant recognition of the need to create processes and structures that enable workers to have access to knowledge resources.

KM may be seen as part of the general trend toward an increase in what is commonly referred to as knowledge work, that is, work such as that done by scientists, consultants, and physicians, which is largely dependent for its success. The rise of knowledge work is the recognition of intellectual capital as a source of organisational success. A concern with intellectual capital is most likely in for-profit organisations concerned with achieving competitive advantage within their industry, although many government agencies and not-for-profit (NFP) organisations also have begun to consider intellectual capital in accounting for their resources. For example, a CEO of an NFP organisation explained the development of a centralised, web-based database system (an example of KM 3) thus: "One of the major reasons for doing this [was that] the knowledge base was appalling. We needed knowledge to make good decisions". Essentially, many organisations have recognised that a resource essential to their success is the collective expertise they have to do their work. This recognition often prompts KM efforts. That is, it prompts managers to attempt to identify, develop, and retain intellectual capital.

- **First Wave** is the society after agrarian revolution and replaced the first hunter-gatherer cultures.
- **Second Wave** is the society during the Industrial Revolution (ca. late 17th century through the mid-20th century). The main components of the Second Wave society are nuclear family, factory-type education system and the corporation. Toffler writes: "The Second Wave Society is industrial and based on

mass production, mass distribution, mass consumption, mass education, mass media, mass recreation, mass entertainment, and weapons of mass destruction. You combine those things with standardization, centralization, concentration, and synchronisation, and you wind up with a style of organisation we call bureaucracy."

- **Third Wave** is the post-industrial society. Toffler would also add that since the late 1950s most countries are moving away from a Second Wave Society into what he would call a Third Wave Society. He coined lots of words to describe it and mentions names invented by him (super-industrial society) and other people (like the Information Age, Space Age, Electronic Era, Global Village, technetronic age, scientific-technological revolution), which to various degrees predicted demassification, diversity, knowledge-based production, and the acceleration of change (one of Toffler's key maxims is "change is non-linear and can go backwards, forwards and sideways").

KM is the fallout from organisational trends of the past decade. Downsizing and Business Process Reengineering (or BPR, which often resulted in downsizing) became enormously popular business strategies in the 1990s, particularly as organisations began to value the ability to become quicker to respond to customer demands and competitors' moves. These strategies led directly and indirectly to organisations' loss of expertise. That is, many knowledge workers were terminated by the organisation as part of downsizing efforts, whereas many others exited from organisational environments that were perceived to be less stable and secure as a result of downsizing. Subsequently, organisational strategists recognised that the mass exodus of expertise made organisations vulnerable. KM became attractive to these strategists as a way to protect the organisation's intellectual capital from the whims of employees. The logic is that, if employees' knowledge could be captured and stored in computer databases, the organisation would be less dependent on its people.

KM has emerged in response to the explosion of information and the subsequent problem of information overload. Recent decades have seen dramatic increases of available information, such that knowledge workers have difficulty keeping up with developments in their fields of expertise. Thus, organisations see the need to find ways to manage information such that knowledge workers have access to useful information and are not overwhelmed by less useful information.

KM is in part a response to problems created by globalised, networked organizations, including the problem of distributed expertise. Large (and even not-so-large) multi-national organisations today find themselves with work forces distributed across the globe. In many cases, workers need to coordinate their efforts with each other, or draw on expertise that may not be easily accessible. For example, international consulting firms such as Accenture or PriceWaterhouse Coopers must provide their consultants with the resources needed to offer comparable services in Jakarta, Berlin, or Hong Kong. Thus, such organisations rely increasingly on KM systems that provide general industry information as well as "best practice" solutions to specific problems. Of course, underlying many of these explanations for the emergence of KM is the fact of advances in ICTs. Developments in ICTs have indirectly contributed to KM's emergence by enabling and encouraging globally networked organisational forms, the explosion of information info and even, to some degree, the trend toward BPR and downsizing. In the latter case, technological solutions were often used to "re-imagine" organisational processes and structures and the replacement of some manual processes with automated ones. In addition to the indirect effects, ICT advancements have contributed more directly to the emergence of KM by enabling methods of capturing, storing, and processing information, and making information immediately available to workers, as well as by suggesting possibilities for collaboration. In other words, the emergence of KM is made possible by advanced ICTs.

Finally, we cannot discuss the reasons for the emergence of KM without considering the "faddishness" of KM. That is, as a bit of historical reflection and the recent research on management fashion suggests, KM is the most recent in a long line of management trends that have emerged with great fanfare as the "next big thing" in management practice.

Knowledge Sharing and Communication Process

Knowledge Management Process is about sharing, collaborating and making the best possible use of a strategic resource. Knowledge sharing is the process where individuals mutually exchange their implicit and explicit knowledge and jointly create new knowledge. Knowledge sharing is also the most important ingredient of innovation. Knowledge sharing process consists of two parts- donating and collecting. Knowledge donating can be defined as "communicating to others what one's personal intellectual capital", whereas knowledge collecting is defined as "consulting colleagues in order to get them share their intellectual capital".

What is Service Revolution ?

The growth experience of India suggests that a Service Revolution—rapid income growth, job creation, gender equality, and poverty reduction led by services—is now possible.

The History of Hyderabad—the capital of the Indian state of Andhra Pradesh—is truly inspiring for latecomers to development. Within two decades, Andhra Pradesh has been catapulted straight from a poor and largely agricultural economy into a major service centre. It has transformed itself from a lagging into a leading region. Fuelled by an increase in service exports of forty-five times between 1998 and 2008, the number of information technology (IT) companies in Hyderabad increased eight times, and employment increased twenty times.

The move from an industrially-based economy to knowledge or information-based one in the 21st Century demands a top-notch knowledge management system to secure a competitive edge and a capacity for learning. The new source of wealth is knowledge, and not labour, land, or financial capital. It is the intangible, intellectual asset that must be managed. The key challenge of the knowledge-based economy is to foster innovation.

> *For several decades the world's best-known forecasters of societal change have predicted the emergence of a new economy in which brainpower, not machine power, is the critical resource. But the future has already turned into the present, and the era of knowledge has arrived.*
>
> —"The Learning Organization," Economist Intelligence Unit

The knowledge economy rests on three pillars:

- The role that knowledge plays in transactions: it is what is being bought and sold; both the raw materials and the finished goods.
- The concurrent rise in importance of knowledge assets, which transform and add value to knowledge products.
- The emergence of ways to manage these materials and assets, or KM.

Information Revolution and Service Revolution

The term **Information Revolution** describes current economic, social and technological trends beyond the Industrial Revolution. Many competing terms have been proposed that focus on different aspects of this societal development. The British polymath crystallographer J. D. Bernal (1939) introduced the term "*scientific and technical revolution*" in his book ***The Social Function of Science*** in order to describe the new role that science and technology are coming to play within society. He asserted that science is becoming a "productive force", using the Marxist Theory of Productive Forces. After some controversy, the term was taken up by authors and institutions of the then-Soviet Block. Their aim was to show that socialism was a safe home for the Scientific and Technical Revolution, referred to by the acronym **STR**. The book *Civilization at the Crossroads*, edited by the Czech philosopher Radovan Richta (1969), became a standard reference for this topic.

Daniel Bell (1980) challenged this theory and advocated *Post Industrial Society*, which would lead to a service economy rather than socialism. Many other authors presented their views, including Zbigniew Brzezinski (1976) with his "Technetronic Society".

The main feature of the information revolution is the growing economic, social and technological role of information. Information-related activities did not come up with the Information Revolution. They existed, in one form or the other, in all human societies, and eventually developed into institutions, such as the Platonic Academy, Aristotle's Peripatetic school in the Lyceum, the Museum and the Library of Alexandria, or the schools of Babylonian astronomy. The Agricultural Revolution and the Industrial Revolution came up when new informational inputs were produced by individual innovators, or by scientific and technical institutions. During the Information Revolution all these activities are experiencing continuous growth, while other information-oriented activities are emerging they are the part of service revolution.

Service Revolution in India

The **Economy of India** is the eleventh largest in the world by nominal GDP and the fourth largest by purchasing power parity (PPP). The country's per capita GDP (PPP) is $3,290 (IMF, 127th) in 2010. Following strong economic reforms from the socialist inspired economy of a post-independence Indian nation, the country began to develop a fast-paced economic growth, as free market principles were initiated in 1990 for international competition and foreign investment. Economists predict that by 2020, India will be among the leading economies of the world. India's top five trade partners are UAE, China, USA, Saudi Arabia and Germany.

India's large service industry accounts for 56.9 per cent of the country's GDP while the industrial and agricultural sector contribute 26 per cent and 17 per cent respectively. It is clear that service sector is steadily expanding since 1950. (Table 1)

Table 1: Share of Service Sector in GDP

Year	*Primary Sector*	*Secondary Sector*	*Service Sector*
1950-51	59.1	13.3	27.6
1970-71	48.1	19.9	32.0
1990-91	34.9	24.5	40.6
2000-01	26.2	24.9	48.9
2010-12	17.4	25.9	56.9

***Source*: Economic Survey of India. 1950 - 2012)**

Agriculture is the predominant occupation in India, accounting for about 51per cent of employment. The service sector makes up a further 27per cent, and industrial sector around 22per cent. (Table 2) The labour force totals half a billion workers. Major agricultural products include rice, wheat, oilseed, cotton, jute, tea, sugarcane, potatoes, cattle, water buffalo, sheep, goats, poultry and fish. Major industries include telecommunications, textiles, chemicals, food processing, steel, transportation equipment, cement, mining, petroleum, machinery, information technology-enabled services and pharmaceuticals. However, Statistics from a 2009-10 government survey, which used a smaller sample

Table 2: Share of Service Sector in Employment

Year	*Primary Sector*	*Secondary Sector*	*Service Sector*
1950-51	72.1	10,7	17.2
1970-71	72.1	11.2	16.7
1990-91	66.8	12.7	20.5
2000-01	56.7	17.5	25.8
2010-12	51.1	22.4	26.6

Source: Economic Survey of India. 1950 - 2012)

size than earlier surveys, suggested that the share of agriculture in employment had dropped to 45.5per cent Previously a closed economy,

India's trade and business sector has grown fast. India currently accounts for 1.5per cent of world trade as of 2007 according to the WTO. According to the World Trade Statistics of the WTO in 2006, India's total merchandise trade (counting exports and imports) was valued at $294 billion in 2006 and India's services trade inclusive of export and import was $143 billion. Thus, India's global economic engagement in 2006 covering both merchandise and services trade was of the order of $437 billion, up by a record 72per cent from a level of $253 billion in 2004. India's total trade in goods and services has reached a share of 43per cent of GDP in 2005–06, up from 16per cent in 1990–91.

India is 13th in services output. The services sector provides employment to 23per cent of the work force and is growing quickly, with a growth rate of 7.5per cent in 1991–2000, up from 4.5% in 1951–80. It has the largest share in the GDP, accounting for 55% in 2007, up from 15per cent in 1950.

Information technology and business process outsourcing are among the fastest growing sectors, having a cumulative growth rate of revenue 33.6% between 1997–98 and 2002–03 and contributing to 25% of the country's total exports in 2007–08.[70] The growth in the IT sector is attributed to

Table 3 Shift of Economic Activity in Andhra Pradesh

Year	*Primary Sector*	*Secondary Sector*	*Service Sector*
1950-70	I	II	III
1970-90	I	II	III
1990-00	III	I	II
After 2000*	III	II	I

Source: Economic Survey of A P.C 1950 - 2010)

(* Age of Super Industrialisation and Service Revolution.)

increased specialisation, and an availability of a large pool of low cost, but highly skilled, educated and fluent English-speaking workers, on the supply side. This is matched on the demand side by an increased demand from foreign consumers interested in India's service exports, or those looking to outsource their operations. The share of the Indian IT industry in the country's GDP increased from 4.8 per cent in 2005–06 to 7 per cent in 2008. In 2009, seven Indian firms were listed among the top 15 technology outsourcing companies in the world. Tourism in India is relatively undeveloped, but growing at double digits. Some hospitals woo medical tourism.

Organised retail supermarkets accounts for 24 per cent of the market as of 2008. Regulations prevent most foreign investment in retailing. Moreover, over thirty regulations such as "signboard licenses" and "anti-hoarding measures" may have to be compiled before a store can open doors. There are taxes for moving goods from state to state, and even within states.

Mining forms an important segment of the Indian economy, with the country producing 79 different minerals (excluding fuel and atomic resources) in 2009–10, including iron ore, manganese, mica, bauxite, chromite, limestone, asbestos, fluorite, gypsum, ochre, phosphorite and silica sand.

Table 4: Human Resource Requirements in Andhra Pradesh for High Growth Industries

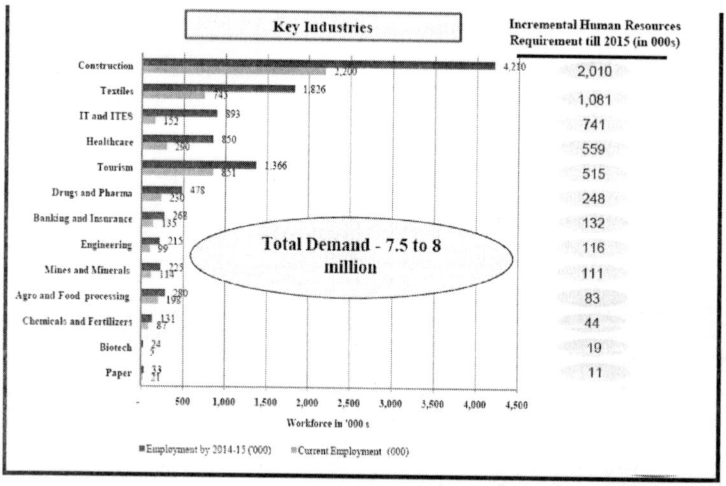

India has the world's third largest road network, covering about 3.3 million kilometers and carrying 65per cent of freight and 80per cent of passenger traffic. Container traffic is growing at 15per cent a year. Internet use is rare; there were only 7.57 million broadband lines in India in November 2009, however it is still growing at slower rate and is expected to boom after the launch of 3G and Wimax services.

India's oil reserves meet 25per cent of the country's domestic oil demand. As of 2009, India's total proven oil reserves stood at 775 million metric tons while gas reserves stood at 1074 billion cubic meters. Oil and natural gas fields are located offshore at Mumbai High, Krishna Godavari Basin and the Cauvery Delta, and onshore mainly in the states of Assam, Gujarat and Rajasthan. India is the fourth largest consumer of oil in the world and imported $82.1 billion worth of oil in the first three quarters of 2010, which had an adverse effect on its current account deficit. The petroleum industry in India mostly consists of public sector companies such as Oil and Natural Gas Corporation (ONGC), Hindustan Petroleum Corporation Limited (HPCL) and Indian Oil Corporation Limited (IOCL). There are some major private Indian companies in the oil sector such as Reliance Industries Limited (RIL) which operates the world's largest oil refining complex.

The Indian money market is classified into the organised sector, comprising private, public and foreign owned commercial banks and cooperative banks, together known as *scheduled banks*, and the unorganised sector, which includes individual or family owned indigenous bankers or money lenders and non-banking financial companies.[84] The unorganised sector and microcredit are still preferred over traditional banks in rural and sub-urban areas, especially for non-productive purposes, like ceremonies and short duration loans.

Today, knowledge has become a major characteristic that differentiates a developed nation from a developing one. Developed nations are the ones that have strengthened their economy by harnessing their scientific knowledge for technological growth and development. A study by Denison of the factors contributing to growth of the US economy from 1929 to 1982 attributes 94per cent of the total to factors relating to knowledge generation and dissemination: 64per cent of this growth is linked to advances in knowledge generation (i.e., research and development) and another 30 per cent to advances in education. Better resource management, which is an application of knowledge, is also identified as a more important factor than capital.

The Indian knowledge scenario is not very heartening in the global perspective, more so, considering our aspiration to reach the status of a developed nation by 2020. Our total investment in R and D is only 1/250th of that of the USA and 1/340th of that of Japan and our share of global scientific output in 1998 was only 1.58 per cent of the world's total. Knowledge generation directly impacts national development when it results in new and improved, patentable industrial processes. Every year more than 500,000 new patent applications are filed globally. Of these China accounts for 96,000 and Korea accounts for 72,000, while India accounts for only 8000.

The roots of this grim scenario can be traced to our educational structures. Our educational system missed knowledge, as its main focus and deviated largely from the natural structures discussed in the first section. Though we have taken impressive strides in expanding our college and University network we have failed to make our educational structures knowledge oriented, knowledge centric and knowledge intensive. According to a recent survey by INSA (2004) it was found that only 3.6 per cent of talented students opt for science after school and only 157 out of every million people in India opt to become scientists as compared to 2,666 in Britain, 4095 in the US and 5095 in Japan.

However, we should draw inspiration from the fact that knowledge is not new to India. Our glorious cultural heritage brings home to us that Indian civilisation had flourished as a knowledge society in the ancient times. Mahatma Gandhi who fought the mighty British Empire through his weapons of Truth and Nonviolence was modest in mentioning that he did not tell the world anything new. He said, "The principles of truth and nonviolence are as old as these hillocks". Just as Gandhi demonstrated the powers of these ancient tenets of Indian philosophy to the world through his convictions in their fundamental strength a knowledge revolution aimed at development also demands such a deep faith in our glorious legacy. In a sense our march towards vision 2020 has also to be a march towards our own rediscovery.

Another important factor in favour of India is that she will be enjoying a unique demographic advantage of having the largest young population in the coming decades. We can capitalize on this advantage by reforming our education structures in order to bring majority of this youth under their fold so as to trigger a knowledge revolution. The Prime Minister Dr Manmohan Singh, in his speech at the launch of National Knowledge Commission, observed in this context, "it might be our opportunity to leapfrog in the race for social and economic development."

Growth in the service economy also facilitates growth in the rest of the economy. Services such as energy, telecommunications and transportation are important to all sectors of the economy; financial services facilitate transactions and investment; health and education services that contribute to a fit, well-trained workforce; and legal and accountancy services allow an institutional framework required to run a successful market economy.

Summing Up

The Yashpal Committee and also the National Knowledge Commission have dealt with various issues affecting the higher education system in the country and both have suggested definite framework for improvement by way of institutional as well as policy reforms.

- The knowledge revolution is changing society.
- Knowledge is an intangible privately produced public good, and is today the key determinant of economic and social progress.
- In a knowledge-based society markets behave differently and require more egalitarian patterns of distribution of resources in order to achieve efficiency.
- The primacy of human capital can lead to changes in the distribution of income and wealth, in corporate structure and financial markets, and in the environmental impact of economic activity.
- The knowledge society is more innovative, the cross-fertilization of different ideas and ways of thinking may prove valuable.
- Knowledge-intensive development is the key to economic progress. It replaces resource-intensive growth.
- The knowledge society is innovative and diverse, but deeply conservative in the use of the earth's resources. Humans and human capital are at the center of economic progress, replacing capital and material property.

Biswas Kanti rightly pointed out: *Higher Education is the process by which people not only acquire knowledge and information skill, but also values and ability to live and interact within and with social groups, as well as participate in cultural life and productive activities which may not always be economic. Though not a fundamental right in India, higher education is considered essential for any nation's cultural, social and economic development.*

References

- Bhagwati, Jagdish, (1984). Splintering and Disembodiment of Services and Developing Nations, *World Economy.*
- Garry Jacobs and N. Asokan,(2003). 'Towards a knowledge society', final draft for the Vision 2020 Committee, January 1.
- Jeanne S. Steffes, (2004). " Creating Powerful Environments Beyond the Class Room", *Change*, May/June.
- Hansda, Sanjay Kumar, (2002). "Services Sector in the Indian Economy: A Status Report" RBI Staff Studies, Department of Economic Analysis and Policy, RBI.
- Karan Singh, 'Education for the global society', the UNESCO (1996), Learning : the Treasures Within, Paris.
- Robert M.. Moorf, (2004). " The Rising Tide" *Change*, May/June.
- Salgado, Ranil (2003). India's Global Integration and The Role of the IT Sector, *India:Selected Issues*, IMF.
- Virmani, Arvind, (2002). Bhartiya Rate of Growth: The role of services, Planning Commission, New Delhi.

12

Higher Education and its Labour Market Aspects: A Review of Selected Issues and Evidences from India

Dr Fayaz Ahmad Bhat

Abstract

The main objective of this review is to highlight the major research questions and methodological paradigms which had showed linkage between levels of higher education and its labour market aspects. The related literature was critically evaluated in terms of theoretical bases and empirical findings.

Key Words: Higher Education, Labour Market Experiences, Trainings, Growth Trends.

Introduction

Education does not alone create jobs; it can, however, cut unemployment by enhancing the match-ability of labour force skills with employer needs. When the task is attaining and maintaining full employment, education is not an adequate substitute for effective government fiscal and monetary policies. It also is not the substitute for consumer and business demand. However, it is also valuable complement. The economists are giving more and more attention to understanding social institutions, which strongly influence the pattern of economic growth. Labour institutions (viz-wage systems, trade union, labour market segmentation etc) influence the nature of production processes and pattern of personal income distribution in any economy.

Schooling, training and other similar qualifications, which are usually termed as social institutions, can well be recognised as labour institutions. These institutions affect the demand and supply of labour, level and processes of economic growth and income distribution. These also effect particularly to the level of market premium for human capital variables, such as educational achievements and the labour market experiences of individual workers especially in urban labour markets. The labour markets have changed over the years in nature and composition. Boyer *et al.* (2001) opines that this particular set of labour institutions can form and support a particular growth path. Labour institutions vary in strength across different parts of production system. To Roger (1994) labour force is the critical determinant of labour market segmentation and other forms of inequality. Certain sets of labour institutions may promote "social and economic exclusion". The "exclusion discourse" therefore focuses much more on the way social and labour institutions interact with each other to create particular gaps in society which are excluded from each other as regards their relative social economic and political power.

India faces a paradox of mounting skills shortages co-existing with rising graduate's unemployment and underemployment. This makes it necessary to understand dynamics of linkage between higher education and labour market, especially in the context of globalisation. Globalisation is integrating the labour market of skilled people. There is rising wave of internationalisation of higher education market marked by increased flow of students programme providers across national borders. There are many issues, which call for an in-depth economic analysis. The various analyses like RoR, human capital earning function, manpower planning approach etc had been chosen. These will bridge the gap of lack of coordination between educational investment decision-making and economic planning in general and employment planning in particular. Several interesting findings emerge from review of literature; the general stylized facts have observed from various countries that higher the education, higher is the level of earnings and returns decrease with the decrease in level of education. This accepted fact is true for all types of education in India are yet to be proved. The estimates at all India level are either dated or based on small geographical regions. Most of the researchers have not provided firm empirical evidences in support of notion that how women's returns to education are higher than men at all levels of education, denying the fact that women are economically inefficient than men. All the subject specific studies on returns have shown higher returns to one over another without takings costs, particularly opportunity costs to two different levels of education separately. The comparative studies on higher education development are very less in number in India. The comparative studies are of great importance in the field of returns to education and knowing the extent of inequalities in higher educational sector. The newly emerging area of study is substitutability between levels of higher education and work experiences in labour market. There are many questions which need empirical evidences like:

1. Does education only produce mobility of labour force from Non-formal to formal, Rural to urban sectors of employment? Does it contribute positively?
2. Does education has any role in employment in the non-formal and informal sector of economy and how?
3. What is the relationship between the structure of educational provision and responsiveness of labour supply to change in pattern of demands for labour?
4. How to understand the link between education and training on the one hand and economic, social inequality on the other? How to relate the structure and inequality in the distribution of amounts invested in human capital?

Therefore to overcome such problems the RoR Analysis to higher education is best option and broadly speaking it helps us to understand higher education sector of India. India is one among the countries with largest higher educational systems in the world.The Government of India initiated a planned economic development since independence and various important policy initiatives were taken in the educational sector. The landmark reports of 1948-49 (Radhakrishnan Commission) and the Education Commission Report 1964-66 (Kothari Commission) laid foundations for the remarkable initiatives taken in the Policy and Action Plan (1986). The Action Plan of 1992 included schemes and programmes which were directed towards expansion of intake capacity in general and that of disadvantageous groups such as poor, schedule caste, schedule tribe, minorities, girls, the physically challenged persons and those of educationally backwards regions.

The following table shows the history, growth, trends in student's enrollments, Universities, colleges, teaching staff and total expenditure spend as percentage of GDP.

Table 1.1: Higher Education Growth in India 1950-2012: Basic Statistics

Year	Total Enrollments in 000's	Girls Enrollments in 000's	No. of universities	No. of Colleges	Teaching Staff	Education Expenditure as percentage of Public Expenditure	Education Expenditure as percentage of GDP
1950-51	397	43	30	695	23549	7.92	0.64
1960-61	1050	170	55	1542	59673	11.99	1.48
1970-71	1954	431	103	3604	128876	10.16	2.11
1980-81	2752	749	133	4722	193341	10.67	2.98
1990-91	4925	1437	190	7346	263126	13.37	3.84
2000-01	8399	3306	256	12806	411628	14.42	4.28
2010-11	16975	7049	564	33023	816966	13.63	3.77*
2011-12	NA	NA	634	NA	NA	NA	NA

Source: Annual Reports of Ministry of Human Resource Development.

The above table depicts manifold increase in every sphere of higher education. But after 2000 onwards the growth shows manifold exponential path even though education expenditure as percentage of GDP decreases. In the year 2011-12 nearly 70 Universities were set up, out of these 25per cent were private Universities, so making room for private sector participation in higher education. In normal terms the public expenditure per student in elementary, secondary and higher education stands at INR 2162, 6852 and 12518 respectively in 2003-04. The figures show that the increase is not that marked, if we consider the growth in enrollment. In fact the nominal public expenditure per student in higher education has gone up by nearly 40% during 1993-94 to 2003-04. In real terms however the public expenditure per student in higher education has declined from INR 8961 in 1993-94 to INR 7117 in 2003-04[1].

Direct estimates of private spending on higher education in India are not available. Based on estimates by compiling data on the share of tuition fee income in annual budgets of the higher education institutions, it is seen that the contribution of households to the revenue stream of higher education institutions in India is around 50 per cent. This is surprising considering that 43 per cent of the number of institutions and 30 per cent of enrolment is in private unaided institutions; many public institutions have self-financing courses and most public institutions have high tuition fees. As per NSS (2003), there has been sharp hike in private spending on education over the last decade or so. The per capita private expenditure on education almost quadrupled from 1.2per cent in 1983 to 4.4per cent in 2003. In urban areas, the growth was a strapping 200per

1 Draft Report of working Group on Higher Education 11th Five Year Plan.

cent from 2.1per cent in 1983 to 6.3per cent in 2003. The rural sector showed a high growth of 262per cent from a mere 0.8per cent in 1983 to 2.9per cent in 2003. In absolute terms, households spent nearly INR 335 billion on education in 2003. It is estimated that almost half of it goes into higher education. There are, however, wide interstate variations. Private spending is higher in richer states, where government spending also tends to be high. Interestingly, private spending as a proportion of the total spending on education tends to be higher even in poor states. The reason is possibly due to the fact that government spending on education in poor states is so low that households need to spend more to fill in this gap. It would be fair to expect that a significant amount of this flows to the higher education sector.

International comparison shows us that amount of funds allotted to higher education determines both the size and quality of higher education system in a country. There are several ways to measure the overall level of financial commitment to higher education, each with its strengths and weaknesses. While comparing the public expenditure on higher education described as percentage of gross domestic product (GDP), it is seen that there are few differences between the developed and the developing countries. Both the developed Scandinavian countries and poor African countries spend a high percentage of their GDP on higher education. Whereas the public expenditure of 0.37 per cent of GDP on higher education is comparable to that of Korea (0.34per cent), China (0.50per cent), and Japan (0.54per cent), it is much lower than the U.S (1.41per cent), Germany (1.13per cent), and UK (1.07per cent). The differences in the level of GDP and also different participation rates in higher education mask the relative efforts of different countries towards higher education. Another measure is to compare the public expenditure per student across countries. It is noted that whereas developed countries spend close to US$10,000 per student per year, developing countries spend less than US$1000 per student. India spends merely US $400 per student. Even with currency adjustment, it works out to be much lower than the developed countries or even China (at US$2728 per student). Here again, at the very top of the list of countries with the highest per student spending is an odd mix of developed and less-developed countries. High fixed costs in Universities result in very high cost per student in very small higher education systems. Globally, responsibility of bearing the cost of higher education (HE) has shifted from the government (or taxpayer) to the parents and students. The limitations of public finance make charging of tuition fees inevitable.

Education loans have not been particularly popular way of financing higher education in India. A National Loan Scholarship Scheme started by the Central Government in 1963 was discontinued in 1991 because of its dismal performance, very low rate of recovery, unrealistic rate of scholarship and thin spread. In pursuance to a Supreme Court direction in 1995, the Reserve Bank of India circulated a loan scheme to all public sector banks in 1995. It started to pick up, however the education loan portfolio of banks in India remained small amount till late nineties. It was from the year 2001/02, when the Government of India announced a new comprehensive educational loan scheme to be implemented by the public sector banks in India that the education loan portfolio grew in India. As of 30th June 2005, Public Sector Banks had a total outstanding exposure of INR71 billion against 488,000 education loan accounts. With less than 100,000 students (out of 3.5 million students graduating each year) availing education loans, financing of higher education through student loans is still insignificant. Only two-three per cent students avail of student loans. In comparison, 85 % students in UK and Sweden, 50% in USA and Canada and 77 % in Australia had availed of student's loans in recent years. (Usher 2005) majority of students who availed of loans were pursuing professional degree programmes with 46.17% studying engineering, 22.64 % pursuing MBA and 12.71% doing medical programmes. Around 12.1per cent of the students also took loans to pursue higher studies abroad. Only about 19% of the students who took loans were females.

Therefore, many studies were carried out to look at private financing to higher education mechanism. But these studies were carried out in accordance to higher education enrollment and expansion of higher education institutions.

Students Enrollment in India by Stages in Higher Education as on 2010-11 is shown below:

Table 1.2: Students Enrollment in India by levels of Higher Education 2010-11

S. No.	*Stages*	*Total Enrolments*	*Percentage Share*
1.	Graduate	14616473	86
2.	Post Graduate	2049124	12
3.	Research	137668	1
4.	Diploma/ Certificate	171618	1

Source: Reports MHRD and UGC.

Despite these achievements human resource in India is untapped, only six-seven per cent of Indian youth in the age group of 17-23 has access to higher education, of whom again only 12per cent receives an opportunity to join post graduate classes and only 1 per centcan pursue M.Phil. or Ph.D. programmes[1]. This scenario of participation in higher education is not only in stark contrast to situation in developed countries where the ratio of access to higher education varies from 50per cent and above. While making comparison of India with UK, USA and Canada, situation seems quite surprising. The participation rate in higher education is 50per cent, 81per cent and 100per cent in case of UK, USA and Canada respectively. India even compares unfavourably with developing countries such as Indonesia, Brazil, Mexico and Thailand where the proportion of youth entering in higher education is 11per cent, 12per cent, 13per cent, and 19per cent respectively. In quantitative terms India has been also far behind to china's educational progress. For example, in 2004 enrollment of China's students increased by 21% compared to Indian figure of 5.3per cent. The percentage adult illiteracy in China and India as per 2001 census is 15 and 39 respectively. The birth places of human capital are Universities, colleges, knowledge centre's and vocational training institutes. India is having shortage of all of them e.g. China has 900 Universities while India has 600. USA and Japan has 3650 and 4000 Universities respectively. It is estimated that nearly 110000 to 120000 students leave India every year for studying aboard, at any given time these students cost the country in terms foreign exchange outflow of nearly $ 10 billion per year. We need INR 46000 crores per year to build 40 IIM's or 20 IIT's. India has a third largest scientific and technical manpower in world but comparing with population it is very less e.g. India has only 158 scientists and engineers per million populations where Japan has 5183, USA has 4103 and China has 459. The human capital needs policy framework so that India can come ahead in every field. The faculty-wise distribution of enrolled students in higher educational institutions is shown below:

Table 1.3: Faculty-Wise Students Enrollment in Higher Education in India 2010-11

S. No	*Faculty*	*Total no.*	*Percentage Share*
1.	Agriculture	93166	0.55
2.	Arts	6177730	36.39
3.	Commerce and Management	2904752	17.11

(continied....)

4.	Education	569951	3.36
5.	Engineering and Technology	2862439	16.86
6.	Law	327146	1.93
7.	Medicine	652533	3.85
8.	Science	3127042	18.42
9.	Veterinary	27423	0.16

Source: UGC and MHRD Reports.

The domain of present study was engineering, technology, commerce and management. These collectively share 35 per cent of total higher educational system, so study is of immense importance to look into their costs and benefits. While comparing, female in engineering and technology is 801000 compared to 2062000 men and in commerce and management is 1137000 females to 1768000 men. So over all female enrolment is much lesser than males. Out of total engineering and technology only nine per cent pursue more than masters i.e., research, while in case of commerce and management is seven per cent. The growth of private stake holders in higher education is very high especially in technical and professional education.The following table depicts the growth trend of Technical and Professional Higher Education Institutions in India.

Table No. 1.4:Technical and Professional Higher Education Institutions in India (1999-2006)

S.No	*Education Type*	*No. of Institutions*	*No. of Institutions 1999-2000*	*Percentage Increase 2005-06*	*Public Share 2003-04*	*Private Share 2003-04*
1.	Engineering	669	1478	121	12	88
2.	MBA	682	1052	55	36	62
3.	MCA	780	976	25	38	25

Source: Professional Council and their websites

The above table shows rapid increase in growth of technical / professional (T/P) institutes. This can be because of high returns associated with these professional degrees. The question needs to be answered in broader perspectives, which includes distributional pattern of degree awarding institutes. The below table shows distribution of degree awarding institutes.

Table No.1.5: Distribution of Degree Awarding Universities / Institutions: December, 2011

S. no	Institute Type	Total no.	Percentage Share
1.	Central Universities	43	7
2.	State Universities	297	47
3.	Deemed Universities	129	20
4.	Private Universities	100	16
5.	Institutes of National Importance and Other University Level Institutions	65	10

Source: University Grants Commission, New Delhi.

The education being in concurrent list, state's share in total higher education system is higher. The central bears the responsibility of only 17per cent, including central Universities as well as institutes of national importance.

Till 1980, the growth of higher education was largely confined to arts, science and commerce. The government not only supported higher education by setting up Universities and colleges, but also took over the responsibility of running the institutions set up through private sector. The concerns arising out of growth pattern is that the expansion of higher education system in India has been chaotic and unplanned. The drive to make higher education socially inclusive has led to a sudden and dramatic increase in numbers of institutions without a proportionate increase in material and intellectual resources.

Higher education needs to be viewed as social investment for the promotion of economic growth, cultural development, social cohesion, equity and justice. An analysis of enrolment in higher education across nations suggests that there is a positive correlation between gross enrolment ratio (GER) in higher education and per capita GDP of nations. There is near unanimity about the fact that the economic role of higher education is not its primary role. Yet, employability of graduates is a significant factor in determining the success of higher education effort in country. In light of the above, it is not surprising that the unemployment rate of graduates at 17.2per cent is significantly higher. than the overall rate of unemployment in the country. Nearly 40per cent of the graduates are not productively employed. Of the total unemployed population of 44.5 million, unemployed graduates are 4.8 million (Census of India, 2001). This number is now estimated at 5.3 million. Ghose (2004) pointed out the fact that the young people with some education would not want to engage in low productivity, low-income work in the informal sector. They want non-manual work, preferably in the organised sector. The fact that they have some education, indirectly means that their families have some capacity to support them. Visaria (1998) noted that many of the unemployed have rather poor qualifications in terms of their performance at the examinations and have little aptitude or the capacity for the type of work they aspire for. Many of the unemployed are also perceived as unemployable by the industry.

So today, we face the harsh reality of growing unemployment among graduates that co-exist with skill shortages in many areas. The emergence of a global economy due to increased trade, investment and mobility of people and more recently work across borders has forced nations, states to adapt their systems of higher education to the changed global realities. In recent decades parts of production processes are being increasingly subcontracted, even to unorganised sectors. In the Indian context more than 90per cent of labour force is working in unorganised sector[2]. This has resulted in the growth of temporary help industries or 'call-inns'. The part time employment increased and employment contracts have become in-formalized. Integration of rural and urban labour markets, the accesses pattern of various jobs has changed and the role of intermediaries in the process has become very important. Potential workers came into the labour market with the variety of background characteristics, the most important of which is amount of education. While there is less number of workers, who immediately perform in the production process, they do affect the costs of training, which is acquired formally or informally on the job. Potential workers are then ranked in the labour queue according to the expected training costs. Based on such a queue jobs distributed with employers offering high productivity jobs to those at the head and working down.

The higher education system and labour market institutions mismatch is increasing day by day, creating wide gap between academia and industry. There is lack of formal policy framework with regard to education system and manpower planning. The Ministry of Human Resource Development

(MHRD) Government of India took some steps in this regard but much more needed to be done. The present study of technical and professional higher education system and their labour market aspects is an effort towards the end.

The Indian economy has been growing fast in recent years. This has been driven by the growing knowledge sector bringing to focus the need for human capital formation through its large and expanding higher education system. Due to market imperfections, pricing plays a limited role in clearing of demand and supply in higher education. For fear of market failure arising primarily from information asymmetry and concern for equity, tuition fees and admission policies are often subject to government intervention. The expansion in professional and technical higher education has been largely due to the private initiatives. The fundamental changes taking place in the Indian economy and the rising tide of entrepreneurship reflect India's strength in the knowledge sector. The growth of higher education in the post-1980 period in India through private enterprise has been demand-driven. This has been largely in vocational/technical streams and in employment oriented courses. Huge capacities have been created mainly through private initiatives without much public investment. Entrepreneurship in higher education and training has given a dynamism and vibrancy to this sector.

Due to technological changes, a global occupational structure is emerging. Both skilled worker and non-skilled workers are moving across borders. India has a huge pool of skilled workers with the knowledge of English and good analytical skills. As a result the country has the potential to corner a big slice of the available work in the knowledge sector. Despite some resistance, economic forces and demographic shift will make this inevitable. With increasing affluence and the growing middle class, a larger section of people can afford to pay for higher education. There is already a greater reliance on tuition fees by higher education institutions rather than on government grants. A further shift in this direction is possible. In fact, this appears to be only practical option to address the financial crisis that is being faced by higher education in India. Increased contribution of households for higher education is resulting in the demand for greater accountability of the higher education institutions to the students and parents. Students and parents now give demand value for money. Despite loopholes and weaknesses in the recognition system for degrees in India, India's recent visibility in information technology/ information technology enabled services (ITeS) have created a distinct brand of Indian higher education. Graduates from the Indian higher education institutions, particularly from some of the prestigious institutions, are sought after globally. The Indian brand of higher education can be creatively used to the country's advantage. Though there are structural defects in the accreditation system in India, the process and practice used for voluntary accreditation follow international norms. The process makes use of instruments that are comparable to the best in the world. The practice of external peer review is similar to the practice followed by most accreditation systems in other countries. A large section of academic community in India now has hands-on experience with accreditation processes. The dynamism in the knowledge sector in India is changing the job market for the academic profession. With opportunities for career growth and consultancy available in academic profession, bright people would get attracted to this profession.

New technologies can be used in many creative ways to improve governance both at the institution and the system level. Technology now enables greater collaboration for working in groups across institutions. Teaching-learning processes can be improved using technology. New technologies would enable data collection and compilation to become easy to get correct facts and figures for informed decision-making and policy support. As a strategy, the country needs to build on these strengths and harness new opportunities that are now available.

Duraisamy and Duraisamy (1996) examined substitutability between education and experience in Indian labour market using large scale data namely, the Degree Holders and Technical Personnel Survey (DHTPS) 1981. Their results were based upon Mincerian Semi-Logarithmic Earnings Function. To them there was positive interaction between education and earnings. There was negative interaction between education and experiences implying that these two forms of Human capital are readily substitutable in labour market. To them substitutability was higher among females than males and at higher levels of education than at lower levels of education. They also tested their estimates on Cobb-Douglas and Cross Elasticity of Substitution production functions and suggested that elasticity of substitution between the education and experiences is not significantly different from unity.

Mincer (1974) found a significant negative interaction effect between higher education and labour market aspects for the US economy. Anderson (1980) for El-Salvador; Knight and Sabot (1981) for Tanzania also reported negative interaction coefficients)[3].

---

3. National Statistical Office (2012), "Report of the Committee on Unorganized Sector Statistics". www.mospi.gov.in. Accessed on November 2012.

In the Indian context Tilak (1979) found negative coefficient of statistically insignificant interaction effect, where Datta (1985)[4] reported a significant negative coefficient of interaction term. Both these results were sensitive to functional form of the earning function. The coefficient turned out to be positive in both the studies in linear form of earning function but it was statistically significant at five per cent level. However, Psacharopoulos (1977) found no significant effect for Morocco.

To Duraisamy (1993, 1995), there are two main ways of examining the data for interaction between education and experiences. One has to introduce an interaction term in the earning function. The second approach is to examine the coefficient on experiences in regression equation stratified by length of employment experience. The former method has the advantage of providing significance tests of interactions, but runs the risk of colinearity between a product term and its component predators.

Knight and Sabot (1981) took sample of 777 African employees (working on regular monthly basis) in a manufacturing sector of Dar-el-salam Tanzania in 1971. They stratified it by firm size. The sampling of employees within firms was random stratified by the department. Neither HCT nor screening theory in simplest form predicts the positive interaction results. If HC based on formal education depreciates over time, simplest HCT predicts that the influence of education on earnings declines as employment expenditure increases. To explain the increasing returns to education with expenditure, a HC theorist have argued that the possession of education itself facilities skill acquisition on the job, i.e., prior education is an input into production function of skill formation.

It is also in the spirit of the screening hypothesis that the partial effect of education on earnings should fall with length of employment expenditure. If screening by education explains the higher starting wages earned by the educated, the influence of education on earnings declines as employment experience lengthens; as employers get to know their Workers they can obtain more direct evidence on productivity and need no longer rely on educational qualifications. This tendency may not be strong because it is difficult for an employer to discover the productivity of one individual in a complex production, nevertheless the interaction effect can be expected to be negative. The number of school leavers

4. Cited in Duraisamy and M Duraisamy (1996).
5. *ibid.*

increased faster than demand for labour. This caused the relationship between the attainments of workers with their occupations to change. There occurred a process of filtering down. In a perfect competition labour market, any increase in the relative supply of workers would result into a general reduction in the premium paid to the educated. Both reductions of workers in lesser jobs could produce a compression of the occupational wage structure.The authors took five occupation variables (supervisory, clerical, skilled manual, semi-skilled manual and unskilled manual). In addition to personal economic characteristics, which he/she brings to a job, the occupation of a worker makes a difference to his earnings. The economic value is not only of employment experience but also experience depends upon the occupation on which they are applied. There is also a tendency for average years of education and the employment experiences to increase with skill level. In HCT the job the person does is irrelevant to his earnings. It is the economic characteristics which he brings to bear on the job that determines his productivity. The HC theorists has argued that the significant occupational dummy coefficients are acting as proxies for HC, not otherwise measured. The explanation, however, begs the question of why occupation and unmeasured HC happen to be correlated. In a large sample of whites, the authors found that years of schooling explain only seven per cent of the variation in 1959 annual earnings. But when the model includes work experiences, the explained variation rose to more than 30per cent.

Leigh (1976) attempted to extend Mincer's empirical analysis into two directions. First longitudinal panel data were exploited to provide an improved specification of the post-school investment variable. Mincerian analysis was also extended to examine the work experience of black-men and extended it to racial differences. The accumulated job experience contributed to explaining black white differentials in earnings. Leigh's sample included only middle aged men so that variation in age and years of work experience is limited relative to the variation for the male population.

Brunello,Comiand Lucifora (2000)[6] used cohort panel data from 11 European countries to study whether experience earnings profiles differ by educational attainment. They found evidence that employee with tertiary education have steeper experience earning profiles than employee

---

6 www.etla.fi/PURE PuRE Briefing Paper Public Funding and Private Returns to Education (2000) "A Cross Country Policy-Oriented Perspectives on the Private Benefits of Education".

with upper secondary or lower education. Hence education provides not only an initial labour market advantage that increases with time in labour market. They also find differences in growth of earnings by education are higher in countries which have experienced faster labour productivity growth.

Psacharopoulos and Layard (1979) were the first to show that experiences earnings profiles are steeper for individuals with higher education attainment. They interpreted their results in the light of human capital model as evidence that education and trainings are compliments and trainings increases productivity (or wages) and individuals with higher education are more likely to receive additional oral training over their working life. Knight and Sabot (1987) and Altonji and Pierret (1996) arrived at the same conclusions.

The bias of technological change towards the human capital means that the wages of educated workers increase faster with labour market experience in all sectors or in all the countries with more productivity growth. By employing educated persons in lower job hierarchy or by rising the qualifications required for each job, the productivity of an economy is enhanced (Lewis 1972).

Most of the analyses of the growth processes have generally assigned a casual role to the labour force and indeed few have identified possible source of growth. However, a central notion of any theory of growth must evidently be productivity. The role of skilled manpower to growth and development of a nation's economy is no longer controversial. The capacity of a country to advance economically depends on the availability and utilisation of manpower resources (Denison 1964). Skill is produced factor of production, in the sense that it is different from ordinary labour, which may be called natural factor of production. Analogous to the concept of capital, skill has been described as HC (Walsh 1935; Bowman 1966). The supply of skilled labour presupposes an activity of skill formation through investment in education and training[7].

---

7. Investments being an act of undertaking risk, expectations about internalization of benefits successfully and completely play an important role in determining an enterprise of the investor. The societal investor in this regard is a more advantageous position than the private investor in two respects; first the expected risk of the state being more objective than the private investor's subjective risk, the degree of uncertainty is lower for societal investor. Second, if the time horizon consideration for society, which is longer than the *(contd.)*

To Menon (2003) RoR is not a perfect measure of the profitability of educational investment understanding. No doubt its limitations may vary from case to case, that will enable policy-makers to retain RoR analysis as a basis for decision-making in HC. The criticism of RoR analyses had also highlighted that when the sample is split by the gender, typically the returns to female education are higher than males. It should be remembered that such calculations are based on the observed wages of the women who are working in the labour market several other women have chosen to work at home, tacitly placing a higher value to their household's activities time than market wages. In addition the truncation of women's earning samples leads to classic econometric biases documented by Heckman (1979). In recent works correction for selectivity bias doesn't appear to change significantly the returns on investment in women's education. However, the fact remains that RoR for women don't take into account household production. With regard to the earning which reflects productivity, it was assumed that returns in the private/ competitive sector of the economy are higher than those who work in public sector. Dabos and Psacharopoulos (1991) analysed the earning of Brazilian male in 1980 and found sizable returns to education across labour markets segments especially among rural workers and self-employed. This finding was upheld even after correcting for dependent variable selectivity bias regarding (i.e. who enters into a particular economic sector). The best and most cited finding in this area refer to agriculture production. Jamison and Lau (1982) found that other things being equal, four years of education for the farmer translated to a nearly 10 per cent increase in physical agricultural productivity.

---

of any private investor. In other words society's rates of time preferences are largely weaker than of any individual or private firm. Because of these two reasons the societal investor is capable of undertaking greater risk of uncertainty.Private individual decisions are usually based on the experience of the past. If in the past, attempts at investing in particular branches of skill formation have for one reason come to grief, private enterprise is likely to take a dim view of future investment prospectus. In this regard he would however always be in a better position than the private entrepreneur. This is because former expectations would have as their basics the economy wide data available with the state which the private investor can neither have nor can handle. Secondly the societal investor is capable of undertaking greater uncertainty precisely because the time horizon over which it can and does optimize social welfare functions is longer than the time horizon over which the private investor has to maximise his utility of earnings function. The private calculation of the firm or an individual is usually based on current or short run calculations of rector's costs and prices.

Conclusion

The key focus of review was on the theme of linkages between higher education and its labour market aspects

1. More skilled worked have higher annual earnings both because they are paid more per hour and because they work more during the year. The question is ignored by researchers especially in Indian context.
2. When work experience is measured in time units, the total work experience could be segmented into a sequence of jobs constituting the work history of the individual. If the data is available whether in chronological or in panel form, is ultimately the way in which the analysis of labour mobility should be incorporated into the HC framework. Which is not highlighted in most of studies documented above.
3. The research on school to working transition has tended to concentrate on job searches and the probability of getting a job. Limited work has been carried out on issues of school to working transitions.
4. The returns on education studies move in and around the themes of occupation earning relationship without relating it to different types/levels of education and training, migration and job search and movement out of the labour market. The studies also failed on empirical grounds to show returns to education in relation to new household formation, i.e., housing changes, marriage arrangements, minimum wages legislation and unemployment benefits.
5. There is substantial overlap of educational levels i.e., over-qualification of workers or under-utilising of employers education skills. The effectiveness of youth training and employment schemes have not been comparatively evaluated in different states of India.
6. There is a lack of relationship between rapid global economic and technological change, economic/occupational change, wider social change and changes in provision of educational training and labour market systems.
7. The way technical and educational change are related to companies and industrial strategies for the adaptation of technical and market changes has not been the central point of research.

8. Literature in India showed that there is lack of coordination between the education sector and labour market. No information networking system has been developed yet, as a result there is perhaps no proper manpower planning.

The above highlighted research questions and issues have been dealt by economists since 1950's. The questions have been tested on different contexts world over. There has been methodological advancement in RoR and Earning Functions, but still it is the methodology which becomes a hurdle in estimating returns to education.

References

- Abraham, K. and H. Farber (1987). "Job Duration, Seniority and Earnings" *American Economic Review* 77: 278-297.
- Alagh, Yoginder K. (2008). "Education and Skills in 11th Plan" *The Indian Journal of Labour Economics* **51** (1): 25-30.
- Altonji, Joseph G. and Charles R. Pierret, (1996). "Employer Learning and the Signalling Value of Education" IPR Working Papers 96-11, Institute for Policy Research at North-Western University.
- Altonji, Joseph G. and Nicolas Williams (2005). "Do Wages Rise with Job Seniority? A Reassessment" *Industrial and Labour Relations Review* **58** (3): 370-397.
- Aslam, Monazza (2009). "Education Gender Gaps in Pakistan: Is the Labour Market to Blame" *Economic Development and Cultural Change* **57** (4): 747-784.
- Autor, D., Lawrence Katz and Alan B. Krueger (1999). "Computing Inequality: Have Computers Changed the Labour Market?" *Quarterly Journal of Economics* **113**: 1169-1214.
- Autor, David H., Lawrence F. Katz and Melissa S. Kearney (2006). "The Polarization of the U.S. Labour Market" *American Economic Review Papers and Proceedings*, **96** (2): 189 - 194.
- Azam, J. P. (1994). "Labour Market Integration in Bangladesh" in Hafez Ghanem et al. (eds.) *Labour Market in Bangladesh* World Bank/ International Labour Organization.
- Blaug, M. (1973). *The Education and Employment Problem in Developing Countries*. Geneva International Labour Organization.
- Blaug, M. (1987). "Educated Unemployment in Asia: A Contrast Between India and Philippines" in Shiro Armstrong and Bruce Chapman (eds.) *The Economics of Education and Education of an Economist*. (Edward Elgar Aldershot) pp.100-128.

- Blaug, M., P. R. G. Layard, and M. Woodhall (1969). *The Causes of Graduate Unemployment in India.* London Allen Lane the Penguin Press.
- Blundell, Richard, Lorraine Dearden, Costas Meghir and Barbara Sianesi (1999). "Human Capital Investment: The Returns from Education and Training to the Individual, the Firm and the Economy" *Fiscal Studies* (Institute for Fiscal Studies) **20** (1): 1-23.
- Bose, P. K., B. C. Sanyal and S.P.Mukherjee (1983). *Graduate Employment and Higher Education in West Bengal.* Wiley Eastern Ltd. UNESCO New Delhi; International Institute of Educational Planning (IIEP) Paris.
- Boyer, George and Robert Smith. (2001) ."The Neoclassical Tradition in Labour Economics" *Industrial and Labour Relations Review* **54** (2): 199-223.
- Cain, G. G., R. B. Freeman and W. L. Hansen (1973). *Labour Market Analysis of Engineers and Technical Workers.* Baltimore John Hopkins Press.
- Carnoy, M. (1987). "Higher Education and Graduate Employment in India: Summary of Three Case Studies" Research Report No. 64. Paris International Institute of Educational Planning.
- Carnoy, M. (2006). "Higher Education and Economic Development: India, China and 21th Century" Paper presented at the *Pan Asia Conference: Focus on Economic Challenges,* Stanford Centre for International Development May 31- June 3.
- Combs, Philips. H. (1968). *The World Educational Crisis- A System Analysis.* Allahabad A M Wheeler and Co. Ltd.
- Dearden, L., Richard Blundell, Costas Meghir and Barbara Sianesi (1999b). *Human Capital Investment: The Returns from Education and Training to Individuals' Firms in the Economy.* London: CEE LSE. http://cee.lse.ac.uk/research/default.asp. Accessed on March 2008.
- DiNardo, John E., Nicole Fortin and Thomas Lemieux (1996). "Labour Market Institutions and the Distribution of Wages, 1973-1992: A Semi-Parametric Approach" *Econometrica* **64**: 1001-1044.
- Duraisamy, P. and M. Duraisamy (1996). "Substitutability between Education and Experience in Labour Market Experience" *Journal of Educational Planning and Administration* **10 (3)**: 271-279.
- Duraisamy, P. and M. Duraisamy (1997). "Male-Female Earnings Differentials in the Scientific and Technical Labour Market in India" *Research in Labour Economics* 16: 209-234.
- Ghosh, Ajit K. (2004). "The Employment Challenge in India" *Economic and Political Weekly,* November 27, XXXIX (48).

- Ginitis, Herbert and Tsuneo Ishikawa (1987). "Wages, Work Discipline and Unemployment" *Journal of Japanese and International Economics* (1): 195-228.
- Hinchliffe, K. (1987a). "Education and Labour Market" in G. Psacharopoulos (eds.) *Economics of Education, Research and Studies*. Washington D.C. Pergamon Press.
- Leigh, Duane E. (1976). "Job Experiences and Earnings among Middle Aged Men" *Industrial Relation* 5 (2): 130-146.
- Mincer, J. (1974a), *Schooling Experience and Earnings*. Columbia University Press, New York.
- Mincer, J. and Haimofek (1982). "Interrupted Work Careers: Depreciation and Restoration of Human Capital" *Journal of Human Resources* 17 (1): 3-24.
- Monhanty, Sanjay (1990) *Unemployment in Educated Labour Market*. M-Phil Dissertation (JawaharLal Nehru University, Zakir Hussain Centre of Education Studies).
- Panchmukhi, P. R. (1987). "Graduates and Job Markets: a Quantitative Study of Two Universities of India" Occasional Paper No. 74 International Institute of Educational Planning Paris.
- Polaski, Sandra (2004). "Job Anxiety is Real– and it's Global" Carnegie Endowment Policy Brief No. 30. http://carnegieendowment.org/publications. accessed on February 2010.
- Prakash, Brain and N. V. Varghese (1985)."Education and Employment Linkages" *Manpower Journal*20: 90-109.
- Pryor, F. and D. Schaffer (1999) *Who's not Working and Why: Employment, Cognitive Skills, Wages and changing US labour Market*. London Cambridge University Press.
- Psacharopoulos, G. (1968) *An Economic Analysis of Labour Skill, Requirement in Greece, (1954-1965)*. Ph.D. Dissertation (University of Chicago, Department of Economics).
- Psacharopoulos, G. (1981). "Education, Employment and Inequality in LDC's" *World Development* 9 (1):37-54.
- Psacharopoulos, G. (1986b). "Links between Education and Labour Market: A Broader Perspective" *European Journal of Education* **21** (4): 409-415.
- Psacharopoulos, G. and F. Steir (1988). "Education and Labour Market in Venezuela (1975-1984)" *Economics of Education Review* 7 (3): 321-332.
- Sanyal B. C. (1987). *Higher Education and Employment: An International Comparative Analysis*. UNESCO: Sussex Falmer Press.

- Thakur, C. P. (1979). "Skill Generation and Labour Market in a Developing Economy" *Economic Development and Cultural Change* **27** (2): 343-356.
- Thonstad, Tore (1968). *Education and Manpower- Models and Empirical Applications, Theoretical Economics and Statistical Studies on Higher Education*, London School of Economics and Political Science Edinburgh London. Report No. 5.
- Tilak, J. B. J. (1979). "Schooling, Experience and Earnings" *Margin* **11** (4): 82-88.
- Tolles, N. Arnold et al. (1964). "The Structure of Economists' Employment and Salaries" *American Economic Review,* Supplement to December 1965.
- Velaso, Salas Manual (2007). "Graduates in the Labour Markets: Formal and Informal Post School Training Investments" *Higher Education: An International Journal of Higher Education and Educational Planning* **52** (2): 227-245.
- Visaria, A. (1998). Unemployment among Youth in India, Level, Nature and policy Implications. International Labour Organisation, Employment and Training Papers, 36, Institute of Economic Growth (IEG). New Delhi.
- World Bank (2006a). "Skill Development in India: The Vocational Education and Training System" Human Development Unit South Asia Region, The World Bank. Washington D.C. www.ibrd.org. Accessed on June 2009.
- World Bank (2006b). *India's Employment Challenge: Creating Jobs, Helping Workers*. Oxford University Press. Washington D.C.www.ibrd.org. Accessed on June 2009.

Excellence in Higher Education

13

Assuring Quality and Excellence in Higher Educational Institutions of India: Critical Role of NAAC— —A Case Study of MANUU

Dr Shazli Hasan Khan
and
Abdul Rasheed Shaik

Abstract

In the present era of knowledge driven economy, every country in the world is striving hard to improve the quality of their human resources. Now a days all the "products are branded" and not all of them are "popular". Only those products which are known for "quality" and "standards" are among popular brands, to name a few "Colgate", "Godrej", "Sony" etc. There is benchmark for maintenance of quality for these products i.e., ISO, which certifies the "Standard and quality" of the product. Similarly, on these lines, if the case of Educational Institutions of higher learning is compared. There are a number of Educational Institutions of higher learning at Regional, State and National level. Only those Educational Institutions of higher learning are known for their "Academic performance" and "Sustainable products" in the form of students, which are popular and well known Educational Institutions of higher learning viz., NITs and IITs, for both the key factors of quality assessment—"Academic performance" and "Excellent output". Although in the past sixty odd years, the Indian higher education system has grown rapidly on a massive scale, but inspite of all these expansion and development, the quality of higher education remained the main criteria for all stakeholders in the education system. There are external pressures from funding agencies, accreditating professional bodies etc. In the backdrop of such a dismal scenario of Indian higher education, quality has taken a back seat. Mushroom and unchecked growth of Universities and colleges has become the main cause for the lack of quality in higher educational institutions. There has to be a benchmark to these policy decisions as regards to opening of new educational institutions. The Quality Assurance is a key factor which is to be seriously applied to the system of higher education. Accreditation and assessment are continuous process to be implemented properly in all the higher learning institutions to draw the line of standard through NAAC. Establishment of an Internal Quality Assurance Cell (IQAC) is mandatory task that should be undertaken by all the institutions on an urgent basis. The focus of the present research paper is to highlight the need to maintain and assure quality in Higher Educational Institutes of India. The authors have investigated the role of "principal accreditating agency"- the NAAC and establishment of "Internal Quality Assurance Cell" in assuring sustained quality in institutes of higher learning-with reference to a case study of Maulana Azad National Urdu University (MANUU). In a nutshell, it can be said that sustaining and nurturing a quality and a continuous quality culture holds the key to growth and development of an institution and a Nation as a whole.

Keywords: Higher Education, Quality, Accreditation, Internal Quality Assurance Cell, Audit, *Quality Management, Quality Monitoring, MANUU.*

Introduction

Quality Higher Education is a powerful tool to build modern, value-based, knowledge-based, culture-based and peaceful society that lead the country towards becoming superpower in the world. It could be seen that higher education at present is developing fast with emerging new trends and subjects. Quality Higher education contributes to the growth of society in particular and nation as a whole by providing specialised knowledge and skilled manpower. Development of any nation in general and of an institution in particular depends on the quality of higher education. But it is often observed that everywhere quality is treated as a casualty. Quality should be the main criteria of academicians, administrators and the government at large. Most of the quality-related problems are embedded in the system that can be improved only when it is viewed as a prevention mindset than that of an inspection mindset. The house, the school, the college, the community, the institution and the organisation are the places where the parameters and importance of quality, sustenance and enhancement of quality emanates, infact, these are deep-rooted and are driven factors for success and survival.

Indian Higher Education system is the third largest in the world after US and China. At the time of independence there were 20 Universities, 500 colleges with 0.1 million enrolled students community. As of now, India has 43 Central Universities, 289 state Universities, 130 deemed Universities, 94 private Universities, 05 institutions established and functioning under the State Act, and 50 institutions of National importance. Others institutions include 33,000 colleges as Government Degree Colleges and Private Degree colleges, including 1800 exclusive women's colleges, functioning under these Universities and institutions as reported by the UGC in its Annual Report 2012. Distance learning and open education is a key factor of the Indian Higher Education, and is viewed after by the Distance Education Council (DEC). Indira Gandhi National Open University (IGNOU) is the largest Indian National University in the world with highest enrolment of students, approximately 4.5 million students across the globe. In-spite of all these developments, and growth, quality remained the main concern for all stakeholders in higher education system i.e. students, parents, institution management, faculty members, policy-makers and society as a whole, however Indian higher education is far away from the modern educational standards. India doesn't stand in the recently released (year 2011) world Universities rankings. Not a single university of India is able to figure out in worlds' top 100 Universities. The three rankings—Times Higher Education World University Rankings, Academic rankings of world Universities compiled by Shanghai Jiao Tong University and QS World University—are just out and none of our prestigious institutions of learning like the IITs and the IIMs make it to the top200. In the QS rankings, IIT Bombay finds itself at the 225th position far beyond of 187th position in 2010, IIT Delhi is on 218th position and IIT Chennai is on 281st position.

Today the world economy is in volatile condition and is experiencing a remarkable change. New era trends and modern developments in science and technology, internationalisation of education and the ever changing competitive environment are revolutionising the educational sector. In the present scenario, quality higher education is a paradigm shift remarkably noticed in higher education sector from '*National education*' to '*Global education'*, from '*one time education for a few'* to '*lifelong education for all*', from '*teacher-centric education*' to '*learner centric education*', infact learner-assisted. These changes demands fresh challenges to the established education system. India, like any other knowledge economy, depends on the development of Higher Education, which drives the competitiveness and employment generation (John Morton, 2007)[8].

The higher educational system in India is still today in a state of inertia—resistant to change. Though large, our educational system is neither relevant nor effective. India's educational policies and ethos needs major reforms in the context of changes that are sweeping across the country. Indian society is undergoing transformation that warrants rejuvenation in the way we teach and how we teach. Unplanned institutional proliferation and unabated expansion of students' enrolment should be effectively and vehemently discouraged. It is, however, more important and pertinent to safeguard against mistakes than to unnecessarily expand. Funds alone cannot help to improve the quality of our higher education. It is high time that we assess the quality and accredit the higher educational institutions in India, the impact of which shall be fulfilment of objectives and targets in India's National Policy on Education and Programme of Action.

Objectives of the Study

The main objectives of the present study are as follows:

1. To focus on the need for assuring quality in Higher Educational Institutes (HEIs) of India.
2. To explore the initiatives taken by India in promoting quality in its higher educational institutes.
3. To highlight upon the current challenges and issues in assuring quality among the HEIs of India.
4. To investigate the role of accreditation agency-NAAC and Internal Quality Assurance Cell in promoting quality among HEIs of India.
5. To discuss upon the benchmarks and frontline strategies that have been adopted and evolved for assuring and sustaining quality in Higher Educational Institutes of India.
6. To elaborate upon the role of accreditation agency-NAAC-vis-à-vis Internal Quality Assurance Cell in sustaining and assuring quality in MANUU (A case study undertaken).

Methodology of the Study

The study was conducted with an objective of knowing the role of NAAC and Internal Quality Assurance Cell in the accreditation of MANUU, Hyderabad. The authors conducted their studies on the basis of Secondary sources of data. The authors used some important Secondary sources of data like past research studies, NAAC documents, various Commission reports, books, Journals, magazines, Annual reports of MANUU and retrieved some information and data from websites of various organizations like MANUU, UGC, NAAC, MHRD etc. Thus, the authors exhausted all resources available and carried out extensive studies for the present research paper.

Assuring Quality and Excellence in Indian Higher Education

The concept of quality is drawn from industry. In the recent past, education and industry functioned independent of each other and displayed a very contrasting ethos and values. Quality is an elusive attribute of values, which cannot be easily measured or quantified. Webster's dictionary describes it among the other things as, '*degree of excellence*' and '*superiority in kind*'. Quality is the ability of a product or service to deliver its function. Quality does not apply only to the product or service itself; it also applies to the people, processes and organizational environment associated with it. For instance the quality of an institution is judged by the quality of faculty, staff and courses offered and also by the efficiency and accuracy of processing paper work. Quality means performance, reliability, durability, service ability, tangible factors, consistency, responsiveness to students' needs/friendliness, timeliness and conducive atmosphere. Juran (1989)[5] defined quality as '*fitness for purpose*'. According to him, "*A product or service can meet its specifications and yet not be fit for its purpose. The specification may be faulty and thus specification should be what the customer wants*". Broadly interpreted, quality mean quality of work, quality of service, quality of information, quality of process, quality of division, quality of system, quality of company, quality of objectives and quality of outcome. The British Standard Institution (BSI) [1] defines quality as "*the totality of features and characteristics of a product or service that bear on its ability to satisfy stated or implied needs*". Quality is an attribute which can be seen or observed when no one is watching you. Thus, in the field of higher education, while addressing the quality, the focus of all the stakeholders shall be the facilities provided, of academic environment, teachers and the teaching/learning process. The result shall be measured through the score or grades achieved, and of prospective employers on the nature of the output. A quality higher education depends on institutions' '*objectives and the outcome of the education*'. Defining a quality education depends on the stake of results of the institution that provides the education, whether you are a professor, student, administrator, or a company that hires students and graduates. In addition, a definition of quality education must recognise that any education is a part of system (Stoner et al., 2008)[17]. Quality of higher education completely depends on the quality of infrastructure, faculty and the quality of students' support system. In simple words, "*quality is purity of knowledge acquired by faculty*" and standards set up by the higher education institution to transform the present state of knowledge acquired by faculty and standards set up by the higher education institution and to transform the present state of knowledge of the students' community, so that they can face the forthcoming challenges efficiently and comprehensively. Quality in higher education sector consists of quality assurance, quality control and quality improvements to overcome the change.

During the past fifty years there has been a sharp increase in the awareness amongst, all connected with quality higher education—regarding the need for maintaining quality in university-level institutions and the desirability for adopting formalised quality assurance procedures. The Indian Higher Education is in a constant state of flux and change due to the increasing needs of expanding higher education, impact of modern technology on the delivery of education, increasing market volatility, increasing private participation and the impact of globalization.

The subject of assessment and accreditation was new till 1994, to Indian higher education system. The Indian system of Higher Education has (Prasad, 2004)[14] always responded well to the challenges of the time. When the system came under severe criticism that it has allowed mushrooming of HEIs, the Ministry of Human Resource Development and the UGC took initiatives to restore the standards of higher education. Consequently, the National Policy on Education (NPE, 1986) that laid special emphasis on upholding the quality of higher education in India noted certain policy initiatives. India has presently two national level accreditation bodies for assessment and accreditation of HEIs. As a follow-up action to the NPE 1986 policy statement and in pursuance of the function specified in the AICTE Act 1988, the AICTE has constituted the National Board of Accreditation (NBA), which has a clientele in professional; disciplines like engineering, management and pharmacy. On the recommendations of the Programme of Action (1992)[4] document that provided the guidelines for the implementation of the National Policy on Education (1986)[3], in 1994, the UGC established NAAC, as an autonomous body to assess and accredit institutions of higher education and its units thereof, with its headquarters at Bangalore (Prasad, 2004)[14]. The mandate of NAAC is in making quality assurance an integral part of the functioning of the HEIs. The vision of NAAC is to make quality the element of higher education in India through combination of self and external quality evaluation, promotion and sustenance initiatives. The mission statements of the NAAC aim at translating the NAAC's vision into action plans and define specific tasks of NAAC engagement and endeavour as given below:

- To arrange for periodic assessment and accreditation of higher education or units thereof, or specific academic programmes or projects;
- To stimulate the academic environment for promotion of quality in teaching-learning and research in higher education institutions;
- To encourage self-evaluation, accountability, autonomy and innovations in higher education;
- To undertake quality-related research studies, consultancy and training programmes, and
- To collaborate with other stakeholders of higher education for quality evaluation, promotion and sustenance.

NAAC primarily focuses on assessment of the quality of higher education institutions in the country. The NAAC methodology for Assessment and accreditation is very much similar to that followed by Quality Assurance (QA) agencies across the world and consists of self-assessment by the institution and external peer assessment by NAAC. Till March 2008, NAAC has accredited 3,796 Colleges and 156 Universities in the country on the basis of several parameters like qualifications of faculty, library and sport facilities, infrastructure etc (Ranganath, 2008). Under the methodology introduced by NAAC in 2007, the higher education institutions were assessed and accredited by a two-step approach. In the first step, the institutions is required to seek 'Intuitional Eligibility for Quality Assessment (IEQA)' and in the second step, assessment and accreditation of the institute is done under the grades, 'A', 'B', 'C' for accredited institutions and 'D' for those which are not accredited. NAAC has identified seven criteria so as to measure excellence and quality. These are in fact the main processes for developing the capabilities of an institution. These seven criteria are: Curricular aspects; Teaching, learning and evaluation; Research, consultancy and extension; Infrastructure and learning resources; Student support and progression; Governance and leadership; and Innovative practices. NAAC has been continuously fine-tuning its assessments and accreditation methodologies in tune with regional, National and global changes in higher education scenario. Many new initiatives such as Annual National Meet of State Commissioners/ Directors of Higher Education have been undertaken by NAAC. Best practices series like Internal Quality Assurance Cell (IQAC), Library and Information Services, Community Engagement, Evaluation of Students, Students feedback and participation, Curriculum Development have been bought out. The revised NAAC methodology, (*The Hindu*, 2013)[18], for grading educational institutions draws attention of colleges to hitherto neglected areas such as energy efficiency, water conservation and harvesting, gender neutrality and institutional social responsibility. NAAC developed assessment and accreditation instruments through nationwide seminars, conferences, workshops, discussions, meetings etc. and involved senior academics of high competency from all over the country. The success of NAAC (Ranganath, 2013)[15] is often measured by the number of higher education institutions it has accredited. However, it is to be understood that this is not to measure NAAC's performance. NAAC has established successful collaborations with many accrediting bodies of other countries. NAAC is an active member of International Network for Quality Assurance Agencies in Higher Education (INQAHEE) and Asia-Pacific Quality Network (APQN). NAAC has an active MoU with AUQA-Australia, COL-Ca nada, HEEACT-Taiwan, IEEE-USA, HEQC-South Africa, NQA-Nepal and other countries.

The NAAC has completed till 6th January, 2000, the assessment of around 100 institutions and the institutional grades have been announced for 85 institutions, which include six Universities and 79 colleges from only 11 States in India. Latest statistics as on 16th June, 2013 (Raganath, 2013)[15] is that, so far 179 Universities and 5,115 colleges have been assessed by NAAC, out of 620 Universities and 35,000 colleges in the country (Ranganath, 2013)[15]. Of these, only 35 per cent of Universities and 10 percent of colleges are graded 'A'. The current scenario is dismal. In other words, more than 400 Universities and 30,000 colleges have still not come forward to get assessed at the hands of NAAC. NAAC advocates every accredited institution to establish an Internal Quality Assurance Cell (IQAC) as a quality sustenance measure. With an intension to monitor and improve the institution's quality in all the seven criteria given by NAAC, establishment of IQAC is imperative. IQAC would become part of an institution's system and work towards realising the goals of quality sustenance enhancement. More than 3000 accredited institutions have established IQAC and they are engaged in developing strategies to internalize the quality culture. NAAC should insist on Minimum Institutional Requirements (MIRs) for Re-accreditation, Functional IQAC, Website, compliance on previous report and yearly submission of Annual Quality Assurance Report to it. NAAC has brought out State-wise analysis of the accredited institutions. About 10 States reports have been published and had interaction with Higher Education Secretaries, Vice-Chancellors, Director Higher Education and Principals of the Accredited Colleges. The grading system followed from 2002 to 2007 is given in Table 1

Table 1: Grading System from 2002-2007

Grading System

S.No.	*Grade*	*Institutional Score (Upper limit exclusive)*
1.	A++	95-100
2.	A+	90-95
3.	A	85-90
4.	B++	80-85
5.	B+	75-80
6.	B	70-75
7.	C++	65-70
8.	C+	60-65
9.	C	55-60

If the overall score is more than 55per cent, the institution gets the "Accredited status" and any score less than that would lead to, "Not Accredited" status. The accredited institutions were graded on a nine-point scale with the above scale values. More than 3500 institutions were assesses during this period. The grade-wise analysis is given in Table 2.

Table 2: Grading Analysis (2002-2007)

Grading System- Nine point scale(upper limit exclusive)

S.No.	*Grade*	*Universities*	*Colleges*	*Total*
1.	A++ (95-100)	02	—	02
2.	A+ (90-95)	04	51	55
3.	A (85-90)	19	256	275
4.	B++ (80-85)	31	619	650
5.	B+ (75-80)	23	857	880
6.	B (70-75)	10	851	861
7.	C++ (65-70)	03	419	422
8.	C+ (60-65)	01	248	249
9.	C (55-60)	—	110	110
10.	**Total**	93	3411	3504

Source: *NAAC Annual Report (2009-10)*

Based on NAAC's recommendations, 28 states have state-level quality assurance cells (SQACs) and several institutions have Internal Quality Assurance Cells (IQACs). *With robust growth and expansion of higher education, NAAC is an initiative towards quality higher education.* NAAC clearly specify its functioning highlighting quality assurance mechanism in Higher Education Institutions with the combination of self and external quality evaluation, promotion and sustenance, activities and initiatives. From external quality assurance, the emphasis now has shifted to internal quality assurance. It has to be institutionalised. The IQAC being promoted by NAAC has the task of building on the self study process. The IQAC is to make the internal quality checks and robust functioning in upgrading of the specific areas viz., curriculum design and development, teaching, learning and evaluation process; research and consultancy; infrastructure development which are essential to get a prominent response from NAAC. As per NAAC guidelines, establishment of IQAC in every higher education institution who is planning to get NAAC grading is an imperative task to continuously monitor the quality of higher education. Quality assurance is the core responsibility of everyone in an educational institution, though the think-tank of the institution sets the policies and priorities. Hence, assuring quality should be an incessant and enduring process in delivering the best services in any higher education institution. It should not be mull over as a one time activity for accreditation along. Here, IQAC has to take up the responsibility to maintain consistency in delivery of quality higher education services to the students' community by frequent monitoring of all the quality dimensions in higher education viz., various tangibles, competence of academic staff in the institution, relevance of content and delivery, and reliability in every aspect.

NAAC is continuously revising and reviewing its methodology in order to keep itself abreast in higher education. After assessing and accrediting more than 3500 institutions of higher education, it has decided to fine tune its manuals, to focus on the quality parameters and indicators. The purpose of this exercise of change is to implement an appropriate strategy for improvement in line with its vision and mission. The new methodology was introduced from April 1st, 2007. The criterion, key aspects as well as core-indicators as guidelines were introduced to make the methodology more rigorous and robust. The grading pattern has now changed to three letter grades: A, B, C, with Cumulative Grade Percentage Average (CGPA) for accredited institutions and 'D' for not accredited. The table 3 shows the present grading pattern.

Table 3: Present Grading Pattern

S.No.	*Range of institutional CGPA*	*Letter Grade*	*Performance Descriptor*
1.	3.01-4.00	A	Very Good (Accredited)
2.	2.01-3.00	B	Good (Accredited)
3.	1.51-2.00	C	Satisfactory (Accredited)
4.	below 1.50	D	Unsatisfactory (Not accredited)

Source: *NAAC'S Manuals for Self Study (2010); Bangalore.*

Under the new grading system, a Cumulative Grade Point Average (CGPA) is arrived at, which reflects the quality status of the institution. NAAC initiated formalised steps to constantly empower higher education institutions. For instance, NAAC provides grants of Rs 75,000 for each IQAC to conduct seminars and workshops. Over all since its inception, NAAC as an apex body for Quality Assurance of institutions of higher learning has accredited 257 Universities and 6472 colleges as on 8th July, 2013 (Ranganath, 2013)[15].

Emerging Challenges and Issues in Assuring Quality in Indian Higher Education System

There are many quality issues that need to be addressed here. The quality of education being delivered in institutions of higher learning in India needs substantial improvement. In this regard, UGC has been giving financial help to the central and state governments. From the given below discussion, we can see that although higher education in India has made a significant progress, but because of certain reasons, it cannot be said to be encouraging and satisfactory.

The various problems and their solutions for quality education at the level of higher education are as following:

1. Lack of Qualified Faculty

In the present context of Indian higher education, there is a significant dearth of qualified faculty, as a result of which the quality of education has deteriorated. Recently, in the newspaper, it was reported that more than fifty per cent of the posts at the level of Assistant Professors are vacant in Indian Institutes of Technology (IITs). Out of 11,723 sanctioned teaching posts in the 43 odd central Universities in India, about 20 percent, i.e. 2,334 teaching posts are vacant (Annual Report, UGC, 2009) and another 32,723 odd vacant teaching posts are available in the proposed forthcoming 23 more central Universities in India, under the XII Plan of University Grants Commission (Annual Report, UGC, 2010-2011)[19]. Table 4 shows the number of candidates with UGC-NET qualification and PhD degree in respective years.

Table 4: Candidates with UGC-NET Qualification and PhD degree

S.No.	Year	UGC-NET	Qualified PhD Degree holders
1.	2004	7,242	15,328
2.	2005	13,833	17,853
3.	2006	12,187	17,898
4.	2010	23,187	24,684

Source: *UGC-Annual Report-2010-2011.*

In view of these exorbitant figures (Table 4), the Parliamentary Standing Committee cited that, "*Considering the large number of UGC-NET qualified and Doctoral candidates, it is surprising that suitable candidates were not available for teaching jobs. If it is so, it indicates serious malaise of sub-standard quality of higher education where we have the numbers but not the quality*". It must also be noted here, that about 30per cent of PhD holder candidates, who have earned their doctorate degrees from central Universities, are working either in private sector or are engaged in their self-entrepreneurial jobs, but they are not employed in the public service sector (*Economic & Political Weekly*, 2010)[2]. Thus, there are almost fifty per cent of the doctorate graduates who are employable, yet they are working either in private sector or are underemployed in the public sector. So, there is lot of exploitation of qualified teacher who are working in the private B.Ed and M.Ed degree colleges on one hand and on the other hand, many of these institutions are neither recognised by NCTE (National Council for Teacher Education) nor they are accredited by the NAAC and they are just working like moving stalls without any roof or permanent place.

2. Inadequate Funding

It must be realized that the colleges require financial as well as non-financial resources to run it. These resources should be either through UGC/any other Govt. funded schemes or through support from Non-Governmental Organisations like *Pratham* or *Educomp*. UGC should also provide adequate funds to the concerned colleges which are recognised for better quality of higher education. So, lack of financial resources should not be a hindrance for any educational institution of higher learning.

3. Obsolete Curricula

The present day curricula have not kept pace with the changing times. The higher education has undergone a paradigm shift from regional level to National to Global level, from the teacher centred to student-centred. Therefore, the present curriculum should be revised and updated in the background of National Curriculum Framework Teacher Education (NCFTE) [11] 2010, National Curriculum Framework (NCF) [10] 2005 and National Knowledge Commission (NKC) [12] 2006.

4. Poor and Sub-standard Research and Quality Development work

Research is an indispensable part of quality higher education, the others being teaching, training and extension. A reputed Institution of higher learning is known by its output of research papers published by their faculty, as the major and essential function of quality higher education. Problem of shortage of adequate funds, lack of infrastructural facilities, lack of interest among faculty members and research students (MPhil and PhD scholars) and the Assistant Professors or Associate Professors, lack the quality content and conceptual clarity nor do they have any quality knowledge of Research methodology. Such type of problems should be solved by the government, faculty, researchers and administrative and academic authorities.

5. Obsolete Examination System

The problem of examination system in India is as serious as the problem of curriculum and the methods of teaching. The aim of our education has become only to pass the examination and get degrees. The Government should ensure that quality higher education is being imparted in institutions of higher learning. In private institutions the annual examination is just a routine paper work being done primarily, so that the students just get degrees and the situation is even worse in private colleges of engineering and management and other technical institutes. In this regard, regulatory authorities — NAAC, AICTE, UPTU and NCTE may come forward and guide these private institutions, to stop churning out half-baked students, fake and unrecognised degrees.

6. Lack of Academic Staff Colleges

UGC- Academic Staff Colleges are playing a key role in developing and improving the quality of teachers in the field of higher education. But the existing Academic Staff Colleges are not adequate enough to cover all the staff in the Universities and colleges. More quality Academic Staff Colleges should be established and motivational modulus including research-oriented training programmes should be included in the Orientation/Refresher programmes of the said colleges.

7. Poor Administration

Administration is the major organ for sustenance of any system for achieving quality. There are many slippages in schedule so much so that the conduct of examinations and display of results are delayed by 6-12 months. One of the weakest links between policy, planning and practice is the lack of proper data and research base for the purpose of policy-making, implementation and execution. This is close to reality but the crucial aspects are often overlooked which one learns through critical analysis of the system.

8. Gap between Theory and Practical Aspects

The students should be subjected to hands-on-experience of the theories learned within the four walls of the institution and should be made to acquire sound knowledge of the applied aspect of the theories learned, which would bridge the gap between theory learned in the classrooms and its practical aspects.

9. Lack of Accountability

Every individual of an institution either teacher or administrator should have the sense of responsibility and be accountable. When it comes to the question of accountability on the part of administration, then it is generally seen that some of the recruited teaching staff even after two to three years of their service, they are not given even the basic infrastructure for which they are entitled.

So it could be noticed that the present state of affairs is a very pathetic and dismal. There is rampant corruption and the government is not paying any heed to the woes and problems of the teaching fraternity, which are always being exploited on one pretext or the other. There is also no importance given to faculty development programmes by the Academic Staff Colleges.

Benchmarks for Quality Assurance in Higher Education

A large number of calibrated initiatives have been covered in Eleventh and Twelfth Five Year Plans so as to promote and nurture quality across institutions of higher learning. They are as follows:

1. Regulatory Reforms

The Eleventh Five Year Plan laid a good deal of emphasis on the reforms agenda in higher education. Guided by the recommendations of the National Knowledge Commission (2006)[12], and later as suggested by the Yashpal Committee, it prescribed a series of measures for reforming the higher education system and for reviewing the regulatory mechanism for higher education at the National as well as state level. The following legislative proposals have been developed in this context (UGC, 2011)[19].

(a) The Educational Tribunals Bill, 2010;

(b) The Foreign Educational Institutions (Regulation Entry and Operations) Bill, 2010;

(c) The National Accreditation Regulatory Authority for Higher Institutions Bill, 2010 (NARAHEI);

(d) The Prohibition of Unfair Practices in Technical Educational Institutions, Medical Educational Institutions Bill, 2010;

(e) Higher Education and Research Bill, 2010.

Moreover, all the regulatory bodies like All India Council for Technical Education (AICTE), UGC, Distance Education Council (DEC), National Council for Teacher Education (NCTE) should be replaced by an apex regulatory body—*National Commission on Higher Education and Research (NCHER).*

2. Curricular Reforms

Besides reforms in the regulatory system and structures, the Eleventh Five Year Plan also highlighted the need for quality reforms in the process of admission, curricula and assessment. Accordingly, it was emphasised that admission in higher education should be based on a single common entrance examination with due regard to past academic track records of the applicants. The examination reforms provided for introduction of Semester System, Continuous and Comprehensive Internal Assessment, Choice Based Credit System and mobility of students through effective mechanism of credit transfer across institutions of higher education. It was mandated that the present curricula should be revised at least once every three years and the syllabi be made in tune with job market dynamics. HEIs were also expected to evolve appropriate pedagogical processes for effective transaction of institutional materials.

3. Accreditation Mandatory

The Eleventh Five year Plan made process of accreditation mandatory for all institutions of higher education. It envisaged the setting up of multiple accrediting agencies and institutional accreditation. The National Accreditation Regulatory Authority for Higher Educational Institutions Bill, 2010 was introduced in the Parliament with a view to achieving reforms in accreditation. The Bill is under active consideration of the Parliament.

4. Promoting Quality Faculty andContinuous Faculty Development Programmes

The 12th Five Year Plan envisaged effective implementation of the brain gain policy. Substantial initiatives were taken to attract and retain quality faculty coupled with mobility. Facilitation of faculty movement from one institution to another for a period of six months to two years was undertaken during the exchange programmes. Increasing the strength of Academic Staff Colleges (ASC) from present 66 to 100 for faculty development programmes.

5. Student Mobility

It is an integral component of quality enhancement which involves opening admission to students of other states and countries.

6. Evaluation of Teachers by Students and Peer Assessment

It is recommended that peer assessment, teachers' and students' assessment and self-appraisal need to be implemented with serious thought by all the institutions.

7. Establishment of Navratna Universities

These Navratana Universities are having the following features:

(a) The number of programmes and departments offered in the university;

(b) The rate of expansion during the last five years;

(c) Number of students seeking admission;

(d) Plurality and demographic diversity of faculty and students;

(e) Number of SAP departments, CAS schemes, National facilities;

(f) Number of research projects undertaken;

(g) Number of quality of research papers published with Impact Factor of more than three in National and International journals.

8. Effective and Proficient use of ICTs and ICT related technologies

(a) **National Mission on Education through Information and Communication Technology (NMEICT)**

NMEICT was launched with the aim of making educational institutions equipped with latest digital technologies and Information technology-related tools. Several communication technology related tools and equipments such as establishment of Smart classrooms, video conference classrooms, Wi-Fi connectivity in hostels, Internet faculties etc.

9. Promotion of Autonomous Colleges

The UGC has to review and renew its efforts so as to achieve a target of 50 additional autonomous colleges during its 12th Five Year Plan.

10. Strengthening and expanding E-resource facilities and initiatives

A National Educational Resource Portal (NERP) needs to be created and the data of all educational institutions of the country should be made available on the portal. Moreover all state Universities as well as centrally-funded institutions should avail the e-resources funded by the UGC through INFLIBNET.

11. Availability of Research Facilities

(i) Maximising the utilisation of research facilities of National Institutes and Laboratories

The 12th Five Year Plan encouraged collaboration between National Research Laboratory and selected Universities through fellowship/ scholarship supported programmes.

(ii) Strengthening Research facilitates for science teachers in State Universities and colleges

Research opportunities will be provided to the science teachers in order to upgrade their knowledge.

(iii) Research fellowship

Awarding fellowship will now be extended to colleges and Universities covered under the SAP/CPE and UPE programmes.

(iv) Curbing Menace of Plagiarism

In order to stop plagiarism, mandatory installation of essential software, *turnitin* in all libraries by UGC funding and introduction of compulsory check of all theses before they are evaluated would bring in enormous scientific ethics and will effectively curb plagiarism. In a recent report, it was found that 59 out of 61 projects submitted at Jamia Millia Islamia University were found to be plagiarised. As per the regulatory check-up authorities, found that as many as 11 research submissions had 75-100 per cent copied content, only two were found to be 100 per cent original. From lifting an entire chapter from another research paper to copying articles from journals, the problems were similar in many dissertation works submitted by research scholars and faculty members. The NAAC and other regulatory bodies should put a stringent check on the menace of plagiarism.

12. Establishment of Internal Quality Assurance Cell

To achieve the goal of aiming quality assurance as an ongoing focus and priority integral to the functioning of Indian institutions of higher education, a number of post-accreditation activities have been developed. NAAC, for the last six-seven years has been promoting the establishment of IQACs at all higher education institutions as a post-accreditation quality measure. The IQAC may channelise and systematise the efforts and measures of an institution towards academic excellence. It should not be yet another hierarchical structure or record keeping exercise in the institution; it would be a facilitative and participative organ of the institution. The IQAC is meant for planning, guiding and monitoring quality assurance and quality enhancement activities of higher education institutions. The IQAC should become a driving force for ushering in quality by working out intervention strategies to remove deficiencies and enhance quality. Active participation of the IQAC in the quality enhancement of the institution would enable the institutions to keep them in high position. The UGC has recognised this initiative and it has taken a policy decision to direct all HEIs to establish IQACs for which it has decided to provide financial assistance. Every HEI should have an Internal Quality Assurance System, with appropriate structure and processes, and with enough flexibility to meet the diverse needs of the stakeholders. Kamble (2009) emphasised that IQAC is the major device to be used in the improvement of the institutional functioning in the post-accreditation period. Every year IQAC has to prepare plan of action at the beginning of the academic year and devise programmes for successful implementation. IQAC helps the institution in preparing it's quality academic, administrative, cultural, co-curriculum activities and training programmes for the teacher, supporting staff and the students. IQAC guides in resource mobilisation and development of infrastructural requirements, and invaluable cooperation and encouragement from all the stakeholders, required to achieve the objectives of IQAC, so as to build the institution as a "*Centre of Excellence*".

Success of an institution in enhancing the quality of higher education solely depends upon how effectively IQAC plan, implement and execute its plan of academic and administrative activities, how effectively interact with and seek the cooperation from all stakeholders engaged with higher education. Every institution should submit its Annual Quality Assurance Report (AQAR) to NAAC every year. AQAR has to be placed before the syndicate in case of Universities as well as aided and private colleges in management; and before the Directorate of Higher Education, in case of the Govt. Colleges, for further strengthening institutions. The NAAC need to prepare a statistical format in the Self-Appraisal report so that when the institution submits its report, it would be able to analyse and present it to the peer team members. The institutional part which is submitted to NAAC may be uploaded in their institutional website.

A Case Study of Maulana Azad National Urdu University (MANUU), Hyderabad

Maulana Azad National Urdu University (MANUU) is a Central University, established by an act of Parliament in 1998. The University received an 'A' grade from NAAC in March, 2009. The University offers both Campus and Distance Modes of Education so as to cater to the higher education aspirations and needs of the Urdu knowing and the Urdu speaking community.

"The objectives of the University are to promote and develop Urdu language; and to impart education and training in vocational and technical subjects through the medium of Urdu; to provide wider access to people desirous of pursuing programmes of higher education and training in Urdu medium through teaching on the campus as well as at a distance and to provide focus on women education". With this objective, the vision of Urdu University is to provide access to quality higher education through Urdu as the medium of instruction. There is a need "*to strike a balance between access and equity so as to ensure national stability leading to an all-round growth*" is the vision of this university.

The mission, hence, is to empower the socially, economically and linguistically disadvantaged and marginalised sections of society so that they can be streamlined into the mainstream of education system and thereby contribute to the socio-economic development of the nation. The propagation of Urdu language, literature and culture is the proclaimed mission of this university. The twin concerns that serve the activities and programs of MANUU are: higher education and social activism. Quality higher education has always been associated with a certain elitism projected as intellectualism and as a tool of empowerment. To put it succinctly, the university moves ahead of the conventional role accorded to institutions of higher learning by taking charge of an area of social life which was hitherto considered to be out of bounds for an educational institution. It can be claimed with utmost candour that in the decade-long stint as a centre of quality higher education through the Distance Learning mode and as well as through Regular learning mode, MANUU has amply proved that it is a front-runner, in the way it has stepped out in an extension of its given role and in paving the way for constructive nation building.

Assuring Quality in MANUU through Establishment of Internal Quality Assurance Cell

The special features of the academic programmes in MANUU that need to be highlighted are:

- Beyond-the-curriculum-Training in Communication Skills in English.
- Across the curriculum ICT and ICT related tools skills and proficiency.
- Enhanced global relevance with introduction of courses in International Human Resource Management, e-marketing etc;
- Course in Human Rights and Disabled Studies.

The UGC-Academic Staff college is the hub of feedback and on Campus academic activities, which offers opportunity of self-development to teachers, and also arranges for a continual assessment of teachers who are participants in the programs as also of the resource persons. The pattern has been taken up at a more comprehensive level, and one round of evaluating the programmes, courses and teachers by the students has been completed in 2008. Apart from introducing the leaner to the latest courses, and innovative programmes, MANUU also exposes the students to the use of the state-of-art technology through units like the IMC, Computer Centre and INFLIBNET etc. Research and Research Development are among the major concern of the administration as well as the academia of the University. The Regular mode Campus departments are forging ahead in the Research development programmes with Departments one after the other launching the M.Phil and PhD programmes. By promoting research, the university is serving those who are interested in advanced studies and careers in higher education. All the departments are paying very close attention to the issues of quality in research. The University has set up a Committee of Research Programmes in order to bring in necessary reforms in the research environment in the different schools of MANUU. The guidelines for admission and evaluation of Research Projects are put up to detailed scrutiny in order to assure quality and uniformity of access and opportunity. The constant focus on theses issues is a sign of quality assurance and efficiency.

The society and the other stakeholders like the parents, prospective employers' and sister institutions have all played a great role in validating the MANUU enterprise by simply laying trust in it. The university approached the issue of development in the most positive and proactive manner. The suggestions for improvement are considered with seriousness and, where feasible, they are adopted. Examination reforms are set in motion after assessment of existing practices. By initiating good governance systems, the institution establishes its own credibility. The recent trend of immediate repair and reform in the organisation of examinations has set the benchmark of trust and validates the good practices of MANUU. The university maintains its quality-based perspective by taking bold stands at critical and crucial times.

The University in order to maintain its quality has established an Internal Quality Assurance Cell (IQAC).

The IQAC of the University projected the following parameters towards quality enhancement for one of the academic years:

- To encourage Faculty in research activities so as to make campus research vibrant, i.e., presentation of papers at National and International level by the faculty members.
- To focus on Distance Education Programmes vis-à-vis development of Regional Centres;
- To organise National and International Seminars/Conferences by the University Departments and Centres;
- To develop ICT enabled Library vis-à-vis web-enabled user friendly Library;
- To encourage Faculty members in conduct of Research projects;
- To encourage students through learner-welfare and learner-progression relied schemes accessed by MANUU with the support of UGC and MHRD;
- To encourage students in Community Service;
- To focus on "*Development of Urdu*", a step towards achieving the mandate of the University.

Some new academic programmes have been initiated during the year 2012-2013. Some of the new Programmes that have been introduced through Regular Mode are :

(i) U.G. Programmes: B.Tech (Proposed)

(ii) P.G. Programmes: M.A. (Political Science); P.G. Diploma in Graphics and Animation

(iii) Research Programmes: M.Phil—Management: PhD—Social Exclusion and Inclusive Policy and PhD. — Management

Several inter-disciplinary programmes have also been started through regular or distance mode by the university.

Many new innovations have been done in Curricular Design and transaction aspect by the University. Various new examination reforms have been implemented by the university. Reforms in assessment, printing of Degree certificates, Remuneration Policy, Student Grievances, Technology introduction, Changes in Question Paper Patterns, Criteria for paper checkers and several other initiatives have been undertaken by the examination branch of the university. Initiatives have been taken for Faculty Development Programmes by the UGC-Academic Staff College of the University by conducting Refresher Courses, Orientation courses, Professional Development programmes, Extension Lectures, organization of Symposia/seminar/workshop for staff members. The Faculty of various Departments of the university have presented a large number of papers at several National and International level seminars and conferences. The faculty of various departments have also published a huge number of research papers in several reputed National, International Journals. Therefore, the seminars, conferences, workshops and the lectures that the university conducted during the 2012-2013 are a testimony to its commitment to research and inculcating of research culture amongst the students. These seminars, conferences and workshops are a proof enough to highlight the drive and dedication of the university, and its unceasing effort to upgrade its faculty and acquaint its students with the latest trends of study, and requirements of research. The seminars and conferences initiate students into university's culture of cooperative curiosity for the furtherance of research. The University has been awarded around 12 Major/ Minor Research Projects, out of the 16 proposals submitted to the UGC, in the month of March, 2009 (14th Annual Report, MANUU, 2012)[7]. The university established a special cell for UGC Schemes in the month of July, 2008. The function of the cell is to collect data, monitor UGC Programmes and to correspond with UGC. The UGC granted hundred per cent financial assistance to the allocated research projects. A total of 91 M.Phil and 45 PhDs (2013-14) have been enrolled in M.Phil and PhD Programmes of the university. Similarly 102 students have been enrolled in various Certificates and Diploma courses of the university. The number of students enrolled at U.G. programmes is 145 at B.Ed and 49 in B.Tech (Computer Science), while there are 756 students enrolled in the 17 P.G. Programmes of the university, including both first year and second year students (2013-14) (www.manuu.ac.in). Uptill now, in the Distance Mode of education, the University has admitted about one lakh fifty three thousand and fifty one (153051) students. Out of forty four thousand three hundred and eighty seven (44387) students have passed out.

At satellite campus, Lucknow, the total number of students enrolled are 99 (including first year and second year), out of intake capacity of 80 students, during the year 2013-14, while students enrolled at the Three CTEs (Srinagar, Bhopal, Darbhanga) are 314, out of intake capacity 320 students (2013-14). The total strength of the teaching faculty is presently 306, and of non-teaching staff is 366 (14th Annual Report, MANUU, 2012)[7]. The University library boasts of 39429 books and has subscribed 159 print and electronic International and National Journals.

Various honours and awards have been given to the faculty members of various department of the university. All the records in the university pertaining to students, teaching staff and other non-teaching staff have been completely computerized. There has been constant increase in Infrastructural facilities in the university, ever since its establishment. There has been continuous technological up-gradation in the university's technological development and advancement. Latest ICT gadgets and Audio-visual teaching aids are being used in classroom teaching. Continuous telecast of lessons in Urdu is being done on Door Darshan Urdu channel. Setting up of Computer Labs, equipped Central library with latest books/journals, availability of *Wifi* in the campus; well equipped auditorium at DDE/CPDUMT/library with 500/200/150 seats capacity respectively; seminar halls in School of Languages and Indology, School of Education, a Lecture Hall Complex; a conference hall in Administrative building; and meeting rooms in Guest House are indicators that MANUU is totally committed to providing functional and constructive infrastructure to the academics, researchers and students. As a result of beautiful and huge infrastructure, the third Hyderabad Literary Festival was organized in MANUU campus, from 18th to 20th January, 2013. All the students and the teaching staff has been given separate Internet connection and has free access to Internet, which is 24 hours available. Sports activities are going on in the Campus every year and latest sports equipments have been provided to all the student community. Independence and Republic Days are celebrated every year with great enthusiasm and patriotic fervour in the university. On these days debates, seminars, symposia and other cultural activities are performed.

The university has well established Guidance and Counselling Cell. The Departments of MBA, MCJ and MSW and Polytechnic have Guidance and Counselling Cells separately. The Departments conducted field trip; educational tours; industrial tour; and conducts special lectures as part of the curriculum. The University feels very proud, that almost all its students of MBA, MSW and Polytechnic are successfully placed in various organisations and companies all around the country. Many students of Polytechnic have been placed in several world class companies like Kazafooni (Dubai based Company), EASSO Lift Company, Refrigeration and Conditioning Trade Company in Libya and in APCPDCL company, Hyderabad. Many MBA students have been successfully placed in Private banks and in Reliance group of Companies. The university is fully committed to its goal and objective of advancement of Urdu language and culture, dissemination of Urdu literature, broadening of educational access to women, and offering professionalised training to Urdu teachers. These are the goals which the university's IQAC has endeavoured to address effectively, through its established six centres. As per the IQAC initiative, more and more students are being drawn through out India through publication of University News outside headquarters and through conduct of Entrance tests for various Professional Programmes offered through distance as well as regular mode. Thus, taking into account all the University's achievement and developments in the past ten years, NAAC, has given very rightly given 'A' grade status to MANUU on 7th March, 2009. What more needs to be done is that the university should also provide hands-on training to its entire teaching staff in latest Information and Communication Technologies (ICTs) and ICT related modern gadgets. Installation of latest gadgets and equipments like Interactive White Boards (IWBs) should be done, so as to facilitate the process of teaching and learning efficiently.

Now the next inspection of NAAC is due this year, 2014. Looking at the rapid growth and expansion of the University in terms of it infrastructure, students' enrolment and above all, imparting of highest quality of education, I hope, the university, definitely this year, would get "A^{+}" or "A^{++}" status from NAAC.

Conclusion

The concept and scope of quality cannot be concluded. However, this article is being concluded as follows:- The conclusion of the article is based on the phenomenon of the "*Quality*", "*Sustenance of quality*", "*Continuous assessment of quality*" and "*Maintenance of quality Standards*" for the survival in the present day volatile market conditions. As is well known fact that, "*Educational Institutions of Higher Learning*" are "*ever enduring organisations*" of any Nation, the quality should be the remarkable benchmark for all the Educational Institutions of Higher Learning. These factors are, "*Academic performance*", "*provision of new technological equipments*", and availability of "*ICT enabled vis-à-vis Web-enabled*" facilities for all the stakeholders of the educational institutions. Administrators of Educational Institutions should play a "*facilitator role*". These are some of the key factors of Quality Assurance. However, "*the quality has many and never ending dimensions that are still to be explored*".

India cannot progress until its higher education system is qualitatively strong enough, because this poor quality higher education is resulting in low employability, low performance of the specialised individuals, lack of innovative and creative ideas etc. There is an urgent need to enlarge the adaptive capacity and quality of the higher education system, so that it is more responsive to the changing world of work and meets the diversified needs of the economy—both domestic and global. Enhanced quality of higher education also helps in setting the goals and in formulating National planning through practical application of knowledge for solving the everyday problems of life. The process of '*Quality' and 'Excellence*' in higher education cannot be achieved overnight. Organized and systematic efforts are needed. These systematic efforts include adopting best practices to improve quality in higher education, internal-institutional audit, access and equity, economics of higher education, promotion of professional ethics and value education, proper evaluation and assessment system, quality assurance in higher education, assessment and accreditation, sustaining quality in higher education institutions, changing the core-aspects of the students' learning-experience, fair and objective recruitment of qualified faculty in National Universities, role of UGC-Academic Staff Colleges in professional development of teachers, organizing seminars, conferences, workshops, symposia, taking up of major and minor research projects of UGC and ICSSR by the competent faculty etc are needed to achieve the ultimate objective of quality and quality sustenance in institutes of higher education. All the parameters of a strong quality culture should be strictly enforced in Higher Educational Institutes, so as to ensure innovative and quality learning and teaching. All the regulatory bodies should work in tandem in assuring quality in higher education. An Internal Quality

Assurance Cell (IQAC) has to be established in every HEI of India, so that they can play a pivotal role in maintaining the quality of education service in India. All the accrediting and assessment agencies like UGC, AICTE, NAAC etc. should come under one roof, so that they are able to impose certain kind of restrictions on every HEI on quality aspects of the service delivery which would place them under certain pressure on different quality dimensions.

An effective quality control of the academic performance to maintain the standard of the higher education, examination and research in all institutions should continuously be undertaken. Incentives and awards both for the institution and individual teacher be instituted for good and excellent job they do. Decisive and effective measures have to be taken to curb the inferior quality education. MANUU, Hyderabad has been taken as case study—with regard to assessment and accreditation of HEIs in India. On March 7th, 2009, NAAC has rightly accredited MANUU an 'A' grade status. The university has well established IQAC that assures in maintaining quality in the institution on all its dimensions. Now, with sixteen years of establishment of the university, the university has made rapid strides both in qualitative expansion and in achieving excellence in all its academic and administrative endeavours. The university in a very short span of time is among the top five Universities of the Asia (Outlook, Dec 2010)[13]. MANUU's Distance Mode education programme has the second highest student enrolment (1.70 lakhs) in India, after IGNOU (MANUU Annual Report, 2012)[7]. The next assessment and accreditation of the university is now due this year and I have not an iota of doubt that the university would get A+ or A++ grade from NAAC. Looking at the rapid pace of expansion, growth and development in terms of academic performance, better infrastructure facilities, ICT enabled classrooms and SMART camp us are few to name and the day is not very far when the university would definitely find its place among the top most Universities of India and would be the topmost university in Asia also.

It would be absolutely right here to state the statement of the International Conference held at Bangkok in year 2000. ***The core statement of the Bangkok Conference is as follows***:

"Quality Assurance in higher education has become a global issue. Universities throughout the world focus special attention on implementing quality assurance system in order to be classified as world-class quality education. The quality of higher education is judged mainly by the strength of ethical and pedagogical principles it embodies. —

(The Ba`ngkok Conference Brochure: 2).

References

- British Standards Institution (1990). *Quality Systems*, part 1-3, 1987; Part 4, BSI, London.
- Panda, K.C. (2010). "Is Accreditation an Answer to Quality Assurance?" *Economic and Political Weekly*, Sept, 2010, Vol. 54, No.34.
- Govt. of India (1986). *National Policy on Education*, New Delhi.
- Govt. of India (1992). *National Policy on Education* (Revised), 1992, New Delhi.
- Juran, J (1984). Leadership for Quality: An Executive Handbook. New York: *Free Press*.
- Manuals for Self Study (2010), *NAAC's Publication*. Bangalore; retrieved from http://www.naac.gov.in/publications.asp, accessed on 28th Jan, 2014.
- Maulana Azad National Urdu Univeirsty-14th Annual Report (2011-2012), MANUU, Hyderabad.
- Morton, John (2007). "Engineering Skills: the Threat from China andIndia?" paper presented at the *Meeting of European Engineers Forum*, Hanover, England, April, 2007.
- NAAC Annual Reports 2006-07 to 2009-10, Retrieved from:- http://www.naac.gov.in/sites/naac.gov.in/files/naac%20Anual%20 Report. PDF
- National Curriculum Framework (2005), New Delhi, NCERT.
- National Curriculum Framework for Teacher Education (NCFTE), 2010, New Delhi, NCTE.
- National Knowledge Commission. 2007, 2008. *Report to the Nation*, 2006, MHRD, GOI.
- Outlook (2010). "*Top Universities in Asia*", Vol. 18, 2010.
- Prasad, V.S. (2004). *Value Framework for Assessment of Higher Education Institutions, Bangalore*: *NAAC*.
- Prasad, V.S. "Best Practices in Higher Education for quality Management" *University News*, 43 (46), 2005.
- Ranganath, Dr. HA., (2013). "*A Call for Stringent Accreditation*": Text of the Interview taken by a Correspondent Shri Bharat Joshi-for and New-item appeared on 17th June, 2013, in the *New Indian Express*, Bangalore Edition. Retrieved from: file:///I:/A%20 Call% 20for% 20stringent % 20accreditation% 20% 20The%20New%20Indian%20 express.htm.

- Stoner, A.F. James, R.E. Freeman and D.R.Gilbert, 2008. *Management*. 6th Edition, Education, New Delhi, pp: 236.
- The Hindu (2013). New NAAC Guidelines Draw Attention of Colleges to Hitherto Neglected Areas, *News item Bangalore*, April 17th. 2013, Retrieved from: http://www.thehindu.com/news/national/Karnataka/new-naac-guiidelines-draw-attention-of colleges-to-hitherto-neglected-areas/article4624025.ece.
- UGC (2011). Booklet "Inclusive and Qualitative Expansion of Higher Education": *Compilation* based on the Deliberation of the Working Group for Higher Education in the 12th Five Year *Plan (2012-17), UGC Publication*, Novemeber, 2011, Chapter1, pp. 1-10 and Chapter 4. 66-73.

14

Professional Ethics: The Crisis in Higher Education

Dr Tanu Shukla

Abstract

The literature about professional is deficient that attempts to intensify thoughts pertinent to an ethical code, which needs to cultivate professionalism among teachers. The quality of the services of the teaching profession influences the nation and its citizens, teachers shall exert every effort to maintain and raise professional standards, to promote a climate that encourages the exercise of professional judgment, and to achieve conditions that attract persons worthy of trust to careers in education. The teacher stands for as a righteous and a virtuous stature for moral influence and abides accountability to make sense of transformation of the society. Teachers are vested by the public with trust and responsibility, together with an expectation that they will help prepare students for life in society in the broadest sense and so, ethics outlines the profession and considered to be an integral part of the teaching profession. The paper, in this light, shall discuss the crisis of professional ethics and the importance of various aspects of work ethics in higher education. It also highlights that teachers need to be sensitized for ethical contemplation involved in the teaching profession for effective and quality educational organisations in the contemporary context.

Key Words: Professional ethics, globalisation, code of conduct, educational institutions.

Introduction

Education is considered as a powerful agency, which is instrumental in bringing about the desired changes in the socio-cultural life of the nation. Education is not knowledge alone, but also the capacity to utilis e it. The quality of education depends upon the ability it imparts to make proper use of learning. Importance of education has been recognised for centuries by all societies in the world, but it has got special attention in the modern age. Education can rarely free itself from social and cultural norms and has to relate it to the ferments within the society. It has to deal with, transmit the cultural heritage and the tradition as a prime mover of change. The status of the teacher reflects the socio-cultural ethos of a society and code of ethics enables to set out the ideals and responsibilities of the profession as what and how teachers are supposed to perform. The human being is moving rapidly towards its formation of one world family and the people of one part of the world cannot remain indifferent to what is happening elsewhere. Earlier, we had more or less static society and a static outlook. Our goal was to make our children good citizens who would be physically and mentally fit to move in the world and serve our society and country as well. It is not that these needs have been out of place now. Nonetheless, new responsibilities have been vested and the world situation has changed to such an enormous extent that we are now required to revise the whole perspective. All these require a complete and total change in the outlook of a man, a transformation of character and a sincere, real respect for the values of universal brotherhood and unity of man irrespective of caste, colour, race, religion, region and class. Students must be taught to be a universal man who can cross the walls of social or national egocentric existence and look upon humanity as tied by the bonds of unity, justice and brotherhood. The current generation is not being educated in that manner, although we have been encountered several times about the goals of education, such as; individual, social, national and international development. Now, one has to proceed differently, thinking above than just self-development, but time is demanding for global thinking, global competition and global goals as well.

The quality of education depends upon the ability it imparts to make proper use of learning. The most essential domain for the quality of higher education institutions is the set of beliefs and moral standards about the rules of right conduct or practice that becomes professional ethics when carrying out professional practice of teachers in educational settings. It becomes incredibly important to discuss about 'ethics' prior to have an argument about professional ethics. Generally, 'Ethics' has been defined as the science of morals or moral principles. The term 'ethics', derived from the Greek word, ethos (character), refer to the philosophical science that deals with the rightness and wrongness of human actions. Ethics convey the rules of right conduct or practice, especially the ethical standards of a profession. The ethics provides people in the organization with a standard of what is right in a particular context, but sometimes people lack the skills and knowledge required to make effective and high quality ethical decisions. These beliefs help to shape the character of the people in that society, teaching them what is good or bad.

The ethics of a professional group refer to the essential values,principles and kinds of behaviour that are thought appropriate to the profession. When we discuss about ethics in teaching profession, it implies the meaning of the task of a teacher inside and outside the classroom and also a kind of value judgment which is realised by the teacher towards the teaching profession. Professional ethics of teachers can be understood by the normative moral values directed by the governing authority and self judgment of the individual in order to perform his/her duty and responsibility in the profession with full accountability.

Prominence of Professional Ethics in Teaching as a Profession

A code of ethics is nothing but a kind of mission statement for human beings to live by; similarly ethics for teachers is nothing but a kind of mission statement for learners and teaching learning activities to be performed by the teachers. The organisation seeks to establish congruence between the social values associated with or implied by their activities and the norms of their acceptable behavior in the larger social system of which they are a part (Allen, 2003). It flows out of the overriding necessity to ensure that any given task is undertaken and completed in conformity with the principles of accountability, equity, propriety, prudence, decency, morality, honesty, integrity and transparency. Teaching does make moral demands on the teacher, specifically evident in teachers' relationships with a number of stakeholders (Sockett, 1993).

Ethics is ultimately a matter of conscience for the individual and professional ethics concerns one's conduct of behaviour and practice when carrying out professional work (Scriven, 2006).

Ethics implies knowledge of these basic principles and responsibility to make the appropriate choice when necessary. Ethics has several attributes, and are also considered synonymous with the expression of norms, and values, something to do with a sense of right or wrong (Enderle, 2007).

The Professional Code of Conduct provides the text for teachers that allowed them to respond to questions and problems, and to redefine relations with different stakeholders in education. Professional Code of Ethics makes common and collective claims in so far as they construct a set of uniform guidelines for teachers that articulate what it means to be a teacher in the current context. Although many professional organisations have adopted formal and well-established codes of ethics, the academic profession has not, is being emphasised by Felicio and Pieniad (1999). Durkhiem (1956) recognised the importance of Education for the preparation of individuals who will assume responsibility for society and emphasized on inculcating a certain number of physical, intellectual and moral states is similar to the current focus on the lack of ethical training in higher education. Ahmed Commission Report (1985) has suggested some recommendations such as; pursuit of excellence and relevance for curricula, enforcement of minimum standards, autonomy and linkages with community, resources and management of education, living and working conditions of teachers, work culture and environment all which substantiate in building up the professional ethics and values in education set up. In the era of globalisation, part of the reform movement has focused on quality education for all students, and most reform is framed in terms of better outcomes for students (A. Hargreaves and Evans, 1997).

Wallerstein (1991) suggests that cultural practices and the shared premises of the cultural attributes of these practices are often shared subconsciously between classes and thus elude discussion. The UGC (1988) adopted the code of professional ethics for university and college teachers on the recommendations of the Task Force it had constituted for the purpose. The code has been placed under seven sections, namely, teachers and their responsibilities; teachers and their students; teachers and colleagues; teachers and authorities; teachers and non teaching staff; teachers and guardians; teachers and society. *The National Policy on Education* (1986) stated that professional organizations of teachers shall develop a code of professional ethics and shall also see to its observance. The central thesis about the ethical claims of teaching concerning the causal relationship between the moral claims of teachers and the influences on their students. For Socket (1996), the concept of professional virtue underpins the development of the profession. If taken further, the virtue extends into teachers' dealings the important function of transmitting the knowledge which provides access to practice of many professions.

Crisis of Professional Ethics in Higher Education

The notion of how societies change and development are not new in the present discourse, but it is started from ancient time and still going on right up to the modern period. There have always been ideas and theories about how societies change and develop. Teachers in such concerns become the central agent for change. There is a lack of accountability of teachers in higher education and teachers is not acquainted with the existence of a Code of Conduct in higher education. Professional Code of Ethics makes common and collective claims in so far as they construct a set of uniform guidelines for teachers that articulate what it means to be a teacher in the current context. In making these claims, attention is given both to external demands, for example, the demands of different stakeholders, and to internal demands, such as the need for ongoing conversations about what it means to be a teacher. The ethical guidelines aim to unpack the notion of ethical behaviour and move towards greater precision in making visible professional obligations.

The Code of Ethics forms the beginnings of defining teachers' identity, according to teachers. Shils (1983) states that the academic profession has done very little to disseminate a set of guiding principles which should govern the role in the internal conduct of Universities and its participation in the public sphere. The teacher symbolises as a principled figure, assigned as with moral authority, able to make sense of change, and in doing so, can help students to make sense of change. The code addresses teachers' social agency and political commitment. It answers the challenge for teachers' unions to move forward and outward into global and local communities in search of the common good that addresses social and educational needs for all. University's autonomy and academic freedom are very important concerns in all the activities and rests on a certain legal traditions and requires the emergence of a modern society, moreover there is no profession which is exempt from fundamental ethical obligations. Scott (2002) argues that the important organisational values are five basically as honest communication, respect for property, respect for religion, and respect for justice which allow parallel constructs at individual and organisational level.

Academic profession has not received adequate attention and has been captured in negative terms, but the professional responsibility includes a distinctive positive dimension, so there is a special reason to value a profession as the profession contributes to human excellence and is solely committed to enlarge the power and influence of reasoned discourse (Baumgarten, 1982). By reaching out to global organisations that have used teacher ethics as a way to unite the profession at the global level, teaching fraternity can align themselves to powerful coalitions that give greater capacity for teachers to empower their own profession and be a force in determining what it means to be a teacher in the new century. According to Abbott (1983), the five basic properties of professional ethics include universal distribution, enforceable visibility, and allowance for individuality, collegial obligations, as well as alignment with recognized status, also states that both intra-and extra-professional status needs to be taken into account when forging professional ethics. These properties present the basis for a collective agreement about teachers' ethical obligations. Rather than promoting ethical teaching as a personal obligation and preference, ethical deliberations, taking into account the types of properties suggested by Abbott, become part of the negotiations in defining the profession. The code of ethics stresses the public duties and moral commitment of teachers as public employees entrusted by society.

Higher education has witnessed massive change for restructuring and reforming institutions with the passage of time in the last few decades. In the era of change, higher education has been facing value paucity due to increasing influences of global and commercial orientation in this sector. Such changes in new world order also influence the culture and traditions which largely depends on capability, skill and talent as much as it depends on practice of such knowledge. Higher Education is often conceived in terms of broadening its knowledge to extended stakeholders i.e. the society, keeping in mind the harmonious nature, values and morality between institution and society. So, ethical considerations and values are presumed to be imperative for the effective and efficient internal coordination of the university. It is crucial to identify the problems and address the fundamental reality to begin to discern between substantial and insubstantial aspects required to promote the moral principles in academia.

Conclusion

General observation and text also suggest that teachers are failing in their services, not because they are deficient in command of subject matter, but for the reason that they lack adequate understanding of their students and are so unskillful in their efforts within the complex processes of interpersonal relationships. The most essential domain for the quality of educational institutions is the set of beliefs and moral standards about the rules of right conduct or practice that becomes professional ethics when carrying out professional practice of teachers in educational settings. This trust requires teachers to adhere to a moral code of conduct where true professionalism is guided by high ethical standards. As evident professional ethics deal not only with conduct but also with motives and character. Ethics constitute a higher standard of moral and values which are quite individual in nature than just rules, regulations and laws.

The literature about professional is deficient that attempts to intensify thoughts pertinent to an ethical code, which needs to cultivate professionalism among teachers. The quality of the services of the teaching profession influences the nation and its citizens, teachers shall exert every effort to maintain and raise professional standards, to promote a climate that encourages the exercise of professional judgment, and to achieve conditions that attract persons worthy of trust to careers in education. Quality enhancement in higher education is a deliberate process of change that leads to improvement and teachers are the only agents who can bring about the significant changes in the quality upgradation of educational institutions. Consequently, it can be said that professional values, ethics and quality are inseparable since these are embedded into every aspect of teaching. Hence, it can be concluded that teachers need to come to a sensitive wakefulness of ethical contemplation involved in teaching profession for effective and quality educational organisations.

References

- Allen, D.K. (2003). Organizational Climate and strategic change in higher education: organizational insecurity higher education, Vol. 46, No.3.
- Abbot, A. (1983). Professional Ethics. American Journal of Sociology, Vol. 88, No.5.
- Baumgarten E. (1982). Ethics in the Academic Profession: A Socratic View, *Journal of Higher Education* , Vol. 53, No.5.
- Durkheim, E. (1956). Education And Sociology, Translated With An Introduction By Sherwood D. Fox. Glencoeil: The Free Press.
- Felicio, D.M. and J. Pieniad (1999). Ethics in Higher Education: Red Flags and Grey Areas, Vol 9, No.1.
- Hargreaves, D. H. (2000). The production, mediation and use of professional knowledge among teachers and doctors: A comparative analysis. Paris: OECD.
- National Commission of Teachers In Higher Education(1986), Ahmed Commission Report, New Delhi: University Grants Commission.
- Report of the Task Force on Code of Professional Ethics for University Teachers, (1989). New Delhi: University Grants Commission.

- Scriven, M., (2006). Professonal Ethics. *The Journal of Higher Education*, Ethics and the Academic Profession, Vol 5, No.9.
- Soltis, J. F. (1986). Teaching Professional Ethics. *Journal Of Teacher Education*, Vol. 37, No.3.
- Sockett, H. (1996). The Moral Base for Teacher Professionalism. New York: Teachers College Press.
- Shills, E. (1983), The Academic Ethic, Minerva, Vol.97, No.104.
- Scott, E.D., (2002). Organizational Moral Values. *Business Ethics Quarterly.* Vol.12 (1).
- Wallerstein, I. (1991). The Heritage of Sociology: The Promise of Social Science. *Current Sociology*, Vol. 47, No. 1.

15

Cognizance of Media Literacy in Higher Education

"Enabling Youth for Knowledge Economy"

Dr Gajendra Singh Chauhan

Introduction

There is rising unanimity for better transparency in the process for determining the promising education system in the country. In this respect, the role of higher education system is very critical in the current scenario. It is all about enabling youth's critical and imaginative capabilities when it comes to the media. Democratic values and civil obligations are two of the leading aspects of it where information dissemination emerges out to be important as information is the currency of the new age. It is possible only through awareness about media and with rapid globalization, the distances have decreased significantly. As the mediums of information dissipation increase, so does the amount of information. The superhighway is jammed with news from around the globe. In such an inter-connected world, an earthquake in Japan affects a Tsunami in the Indian Ocean. A major Cancer research in Moscow affects millions in Delhi. The sources of information are varied according to nature, availability and impact. With information, people associate freedom; the freedom of having an opinion which requires information as a precursor. The concept of informing people of the incidents and news from far away took its birth as a consequence of human curiosity and care. With the discovery of radio waves by Marconi and other contemporaries, the watershed moment had arrived. Today's media is all pervasive as it has touched everyone's life. It has not only changed the pace of dispatch but more critically the content for the consumers. A piece of information has become a product and it is offered 24x7 worldwide. The Breaking News format is the most exploited news presentation technique by news channels which are on the air the whole day. The format boasts of speed, exclusivity and news of immediate relevance. The reality of it is something quite different. More recently, news of questionable relevance, news without official confirmation and news without in-depth analysis, are presented as fresh and exclusive "Breaking News". Media is both mirror and torch of the society. Bagchi and Rath rightly observes that news media, whether it is newspaper or news magazine or news bulletins or news channels, works like a mirror. But a mirror should work like a plain mirror which should reflect the exact picture of the society. But many a time media works like a concave or convex mirror which reflects the enlarged or reversed or imaginary picture of the society.[1] To bring back media education into the mainstream of the education system, there is a need for proper application of media literacy in education.

Massive Media Industry

India has more than 70,000 newspapers and over 690 satellite channels (more than 80 are news channels) and is the biggest newspaper market in the world where over 100 million copies sold every day. India Media is gigantic and ubiquitous. There's no sphere that is not influenced by the growing power of media. The Indian media and entertainment (M&E) industry is one of the fastest growing industries in the world. Its various segments—film, television, advertising, prints media and music among others—have witnessed tremendous growth in the last one decade. Media is not only a source of entertainment but also a source of information. Keeping in view the importance of media in society and students' continuous engagement with media, it is important that the students start understanding media rather than just being passive viewers or readers. Students knowingly or unknowingly learn a lot from the continuous flow of media messages in their life. Sometimes the learning that takes place is good whereas sometimes they also learn things which can affect their life adversely. Hence a media discourse is necessary at schools. [2] The Ofcom report on Media Literacy in Global Village strongly asserts that it is this convergence between media and education, between entertainment and learning, that is driving major change in the sources and the content of what we learn and how we learn in today's world. Media literacy is not needed in the future, it is needed now, urgently, to assure that our citizens are equipped to make the decisions and contributions a global economy and global culture demand of them.[3]

Media Education Scenario

We are living in a media driven world where our youths are completely hooked on media. Televisions, laptops, smartphones, tablets, social media, video games... the list goes on. Mostly this dependence is talked with concern. 'Should our students be spending so much time ...?' or 'How does this media exposure affect their lives?' These are some of issues that must be taken into account for media literacy programme for youngsters in India. Unfortunately, there is no organised approach to impart media education to the students in schools and colleges. Lately many institutes of higher learning started catering various programmes in media education without realising the socio-culture fabric of the society. Mostly these institute train the students to master the various formats of media and hardly expose them to the potential power of media literacy as a means to counter manipulation by powerful interests. Moreover, it is optional to pursue these programmes depending upon students' aptitude and interests, not available compulsorily to everyone as a basic course.

UNESCO and Media Literacy

UNESCO has a long standing experience in enhancing media literacy, founding the Grünwald Declaration of 1982 which recognizes the need for political and educational systems to promote citizens' critical understanding of the phenomena of communication. Access to quality media and information content and participation in media and communication networks are necessary to realise Article 19 of the Universal Declaration of Human Rights. This underpins all other rights. Recognizing the close link between media literacy and information literacy, UNESCO has redirected its strategy to treat Media and Information Literacy (MIL) as a composite concept.[4] Media literacy has become an international education campaign for effective global citizenship, democratic values and youth empowerment. In US, it is widespread at all levels of education upto K-12 classroom, the education administration feels that even the adults need the opportunity to gain the skills they now find missing in their educational background. The American Diploma Project (2004) called for rigorous national standards to better reflect the challenges faced by high school graduates. This is good news for advocates of media education. National standards in all countries would ensure that every child has access to this valuable instruction. Furthermore, it would lead to a consistent, measurable definition of media literacy and to a set of competencies to guide curriculum development.[5] Media has connected the world in an unprecedented speed and it is a commitment to the idea of universal implementation of media literacy would give an opportunity and understanding to our youths to charter the international boundaries and get engaged meaningfully with the other world. Thomas and Jolls feel that the field has matured to a greater understanding of its potential, not just as a new kind of literacy but also as the engine for transforming the very nature of learning in a global multimedia environment.[6] It is quite sensible to see the media literacy in the right perspective as it is in inquiry-based, process-oriented pedagogy, offers not a new subject to teach but rather a new way to teach and even more important, a new way to learn.[7] The worldwide research data indicate that media literacy is an integral part of education either school or higher education. Here is a scope for Indian education to fill the gap by offering its support and sensitivity to make media literacy an integrated component at every level in school education.

India and Media Literacy

Media education in India is still in a nascent stage and some initiatives by the school education are yet to see its long term impact. As the media industry grows steadily over the years and allures the young audiences to its fold, the need for media literacy has never been felt so essential than now. The new media has redefined the entire concept of communication - the way we look each other, the manner in which we interact, and the pace in which it is offered. New technologies of communication have reorganised existing relationships: between the state and citizens, local and global powers, producers and consumers, and that between experts, administrators and beneficiaries.[8] It's altogether a new ballgame that needs training, skills and more importantly technical expertise to handle it. We can witness an exponential growth in all the segments of media but the scenario of media education is largely bleak and dull. Aram and Paul in their study state that it finds no mention in school and college programmes in general. Media education is normally imparted in the form of workshops, seminars, or as one subject in the school/college curriculum. The older day media educators are not able to comprehend the present day media technologies. The developments in the media have gone beyond their grasp. But there are no serious attempts on the part of the media centres to deal with the situation. Most of the media education teachers are self-taught. Many of them are from a social action background. They want to criticise the media from the political and moral point of view rather than providing tools to analyse and understand them. Most of them have neither studied about the media nor have any working experience in the media. More so, media education enjoys a low priority in educational institutions and communication centres.[9] Exchange of information is shaping the world around us by the minute. Media with its vast network has become most influential business in the current society. The excessive penetration of media creates a new enthusiasm, cultural entity but also a distorted reality. City folk and village people alike swallow what is being offered in the news channels and newspapers. The consequences of such media practices are identified by the critics and researchers and they voiced their concern to countercheck it with wide media literacy programme in India.[10] A new beginning was made at national level where Central Institute for Education and Training, NCERT, New Delhi began an initiative to make media literacy as part of school curricula. Their target audience is the secondary and senior secondary students. The institute started Media clubs in schools.[11] The major drawback of the curriculum is that it does not cover the critical thinking, lacks wide spread reach and too general in structure. Kumar identifies another problem in media education itself. It should be taught as a cross-curricular theme, as a subject 'media education' would overvalue the media and separate it from its social context. This over-evaluation would then again lead to a theory of manipulation.[12] The present media scene is very chaotic and confused and it's pertinent to evaluate the media literacy programs offered in schools and empower the students with right set of skills to differentiate between news and nonsense. What Bagchi and Rath notice that the socio-economic status of the mass media is completely neglected. The role of media in the society and comparative analysis of media and society are not well represented in the curriculum.[13] A systematic course plan, sharing of live media stories in the classroom and trained media teachers would enthuse the news directions in media literacy for the students and nation as well.

Understanding the Multicultural India

India has always been culturally diverse and linguistically vibrant. Media literacy prepares the young people in schools and colleges, their parents and teachers to explore our enriching cultural diversity and assimilate the spirit of tolerance, freedom and equality for all. India is a nation of young people and this generation is hi-tech but yet to be nurtured as media savvy responsible citizens. They enjoy articulating through digital gadgets but they fail sometimes to read and understand the nature and structure of media technology. They are growing in an era where they face many issues of changing values and traditional upbringings leading to a state of restlessness and non-entity. Media literacy comes handy to educate youths how to respect the differences and promote communal harmony and enrich our blessed cultural diversity. This media literacy programme enables the students to bring these issues into the classroom in a fair and free environment and encourages them to resolve these conflicts among themselves.

Understanding the Consumerist Culture

The marketers love to pamper us with their striking messages and stunning visuals. Buy Now ! Zero Interest ! Lose 10 kgs in a week ! They constantly tell our children why to buy and as young consumers they don't have the understanding how to receive, buy and act upon. Media and market work in tandem and they have the power and money to showcase their brands in a very irresistible way so that these connect easily to impressionable minds. Robyn Silverman writes that we need to talk about the silent and hidden advertising messages that we receive about people, their bodies, genders, ethnicities or colours. We needn't make our youngsters to be passive recipients. We want them to be in charge of the way they understand media.[14] There is strong need to develop this understanding among the young people so that become more media literate in a world that delivers their messages in surround sound.

Understanding Social Media

Media literacy programme focuses on helping young people become more cautious of the power of media in their lives. Young students are termed as 'digital natives' as they are strongly connected to web- based and mobile communications technologies. However, most of them are available on social media but are ignorant of its potential implications. They are ubiquitously socialising through mobiles and laptops as they update facebook post, tweet something or upload farewell or convocation video, they completely immerse themselves in media without paying much attention how to conduct themselves or consume content without harming anyone. The worst aspect of poor media literacy is often noticed in the daily news stories where issues relating to cyber bulling leading to teen suicides, threatening messages, covert sexual advancements, racial conduct and stalking are reported.

Way Forward

We consider the media as a strong pillar of our democracy and nation, the media literacy can act as gatekeeper for our information crazy youths. But empowering Media literacy is not the priority of our education. While Media promotes consumerism, on the other hand the media literacy leads to effective decision-making and right understanding of the media content. Jackie J Scott feels that teaching media literacy is a compelling way to move students from passive consumers of images to active citizens who can think critically about how they want to shape their own lives. Studies show that students who have access to media literacy skills that foster critical thinking begin to see themselves as agents of change.[15] It is deemed as the ability to understand the media content of everyday affairs in a critical way. NCERT realised the significance of media literacy and initiated the Media Clubs in schools on experimental basis. It suggests that media messages if consumed wisely can broaden their horizon and help them to understand world in a better way but if these messages are not consumed wisely and judiciously it can create havoc. [16] It is high time that our education system should strive for media literacy especially for youths so that they can read between the lines and grasp the meaning better as active media users. Media literacy enables them to make clear distinction between an informed argument and an unsubstantiated opinion. It offers greater sense of freedom and empowerment to our students by accessing, analysing, evaluating and creating media content. Media literacy programme is an important tool in addressing alcohol, tobacco and other drug use; obesity and eating disorders; bullying and violence; gender identity and sexuality; racism and other forms of discrimination and oppression; and life skills.[17]

Conclusion

Higher education has the distinct role in bringing change in the society and the awareness could be generated through the programs offered at higher education level as it can mobilise the masses of the contemporary generation. Media literacy drive is the reality of contemporary society, specifically the challenge is to pursue it in higher education. Henceforth, we necessarily have to think its relevance in the spectrum of higher education. It is an opportunity to prepare our young generation for the knowledge economy and hence we cannot afford our youngsters to be media illiterate. The issue is if we cannot perceive the media messages in the right sense, then how can we plan to change its negative influence on our lives? Media literacy should be an educational priority where we may teach our students the role of media in shaping and understanding the way

people think about the world and their existence in it. We believe that by empowering and equipping young people with right knowledge and skills to make informed media choices and decisions will have great benefits - both in their own lives, and also for that of their families and communities.

References

- Gopa Bagchi and Pradosh Kumar Rath. Media education in the era of globalization: A study of India. http://www.mediamimansa.com/11th%20issue/11eng_68-71.pdf
- Media Clubs in Schools. http://ciet.nic.in/MediaClub/about_media_clubs.html
- Barbara J. Walkosz, Tessa Jolls and Mary Ann Sund. 'Global/Local: Media Literacy for the Global Village' International Media Literacy Research Forum, Ofcom, London,14-16 May 2008.
- UNESCO http://www.unesco.org/new/en/communication-and-information/media-development/media-literacy/
- American Diploma Project (2004). Ready or not: Creating a high school diploma that counts. Retrieved from http://www.achieve.org.
- Thoman, E. and Jolls, T. (2004). Media Literacy: A National Priority for a Changing World, American Behavioral Scientist, pp. 18-29: Sage Publications.
- Barbara J. Walkosz, Tessa Jolls and Mary Ann Sund. 'Global/Local: Media Literacy for the Global Village' International Media Literacy Research Forum, Ofcom, London,14-16 May 2008.
- Roadmap for media education in India: Emerging challenges and prospects. A mapping study by Centre for Culture, Media and Governance, Jamia Millia Islamia.
- Arul Aram, Suresh Paul. "Challenges Facing Media Education in India." Media Education in India. Springer 2009.
- Indian Media Literacy: A Critical Analysis of Television Experiences from itv to iptv. The Freire Project.
- Gopa Bagchi and Pradosh Kumar Rath. Media education in the era of globalization: A study of India. http://www.mediamimansa.com/11th%20issue/11eng_68-71.pdf
- Media Clubs in Schools. http://ciet.nic.in/MediaClub/about_media_clubs.html
- Keval Kumar. 'Media Education, Communications and Public Policy' Bombay: Himalaya Publishing House.
- Robyn Silverman. "3 Ways to Teach Your Kids to Be Media Literate". http://www.huffingtonpost.com/knowmore-tv/3-ways-to-teach-your-kids-to-be-media-literate_b_6019070.html

- Jackie Jenkins Scott. "Media Literacy in Digital Age". http://www.huffingtonpost.com/jackie-jenkinsscott/media-literacy_b_1941421.html
- Media Clubs in Schools. http://ciet.nic.in/MediaClub/about_media_clubs.html
- Indian Media Literacy: A Critical Analysis of Television Experiences from itv to iptv. The Freire Project.

Social Concerns in Higher Education

16

Structural Barriers at Work Place: Gender in Higher Education

Dr Tanu Shukla

Abstract

The professional seclusion based on gender has become conspicuous as a problem with the mainstream trend of progress towards gender equity of women's capabilities. It portrays marginalisation, discrimination and inequality experienced by women, especially belonging to minority sections. It vanquishes the goal of women's social and economic status over the past few years in developing world. The overriding discourses claimed that women's priority must be families which affect their professional lives. There is a strong interaction amongst various factors which leads to differences in academic output of women, thus, the present study would focus on different aspects related to social and psychological barriers faced by women in the developing world. The study is empirical in nature and employs a qualitative method to identify the factors accountable for the aforesaid issue. It focuses on marginalization, hereafter researcher would contribute in the area of inclusive education.

KEYWORDS: Gender, Education, Discrimination, Marginalisation

1. Gender Discrimination and Higher Education

In the contemporary age, higher education in India has seen a huge escalation, especially in the establishment of higher education institutions and student enrolment ratio challenging various repressed factors at different levels of higher education. The state introduced various programs to endorse higher education for marginalized sections of the society. It is an acknowledged fact that higher education is crucial for economic and social growth of any country. It is also needed that access to higher education should be open to every native of the state, including all the marginalised sections of the society for the overall human development. The issue of attaining gender equality in India is mainly considered a socio-cultural problem, frequently gets identified as solely an economic problem, related to merely quantitative restrictions. It is also a qualitative dimension which influences the different facets of working patterns in any sector. The recognised parameters of human development demands equal access and opportunity to all, including marginalised sections. Gender discrimination is one such massive issue which can be considered an agreed hurdle for the development of the country. The biological aspects of maleness or femaleness cannot be understood as distinct from the social processes and practices that give meaning to these characteristics. It is thus impossible to neatly separate the realm of sex from that of gender when trying to explain any aspect of social life.

The distinct socialisation process can be regarded by noting the interactions in childhood where children imitate behaviours they see which would suggest that those interfaces with their same-sex parent or other role model that they tend to emulate. Peers are more important bases of gender socialisation and role of parents and influence exerted by them in socialisation process is of little influence with regards to gender. Schools are also impactful sources of gender socialization as interaction with teachers reveals their expectations towards male and female students and relations with peers of both sexes encourage individuals to learn gender-related skills and self-concepts (Anderson, 2000). Thus gender differences learned through diverse socialisation which begin at home and such differential treatment even though it might be unconsciously done forms the basis for an understanding of gender identity for children. With little or no knowledge of biological differences in males and females, they have these different constructs of gender in society to be indicative of the existence of two categorically distinct groups.

Gender disparity in education is an age old phenomenon. Traditionally, girls have been at a disadvantage in most parts of the globe and they continue to be so even today (Jha and Kelleher, 2006). Many studies reveal that modern educated women are neither happy nor contended. A modern view education as an instrument for women's equality and development. According to Jha and Kelleher, there are two aspects in women's education, individual and social. Generally, females who start working in organisations do often face gender stereotype problems. Like men, women also desire for professional growth, work passionately for their goals, but cannot avoid few unwanted circumstances like marriage and motherhood.

There are few other factors like glass ceiling effects that halt their progress. One of the objectives, here, is to explore the various factors related to discrimination at work place. There appears to be an insistent practice of inquiring women's career assurance founded on the belief that women's commitment to their family threatens their work promise. The customary view that women will always put family before career and the inferred belief that this is not true for men is not only a discriminating issue in the recruitment process, but also it distresses women negatively at other stages in their career progression.

2. Methodology

The study attempts to understand the nature of the dual burden faced by women and the factors answerable in women's professional development. The study also tries to understand the aspects responsible for glass ceiling effects. The study was dealt in a qualitative approach, a lot of information was gathered on specific aspects of the women's life; systematic analysis was done based on narratives obtained through interviews. The study used interviews as a tool for data collection. Female faculties were used as sample from one of the Universities of Andhra Pradesh through purposive sampling technique. Qualitative method was given the priority as it helped to explore the social psychological barriers when one face the discrimination at work place, that too at various levels. Questions were asked from varied domain, ranging from personal to professional concerns which influence the performance at job place.

3 Results and Discussion

After the analysis of the narratives, researcher figured out that dissimilar types of roles assigned to boys and girls at home, and different kind of rearing are blamable for the discerning. There is a strong interaction amongst various factors which leads to differences in academic output of women, thus, the present study would focus on different aspects related to social and psychological barriers faced by women in the developing world. The mindset of the society with the stereotypical assumptions of the society, the unjustified belief associated with the marriage of the girl child demands the radical transformation, so that the achievement of inclusive education is achieved leading to change in the psyche of individuals. Specific variances in biases may lessen stereotype-based judgments and behaviour, and prejudice towards women are unique. When stereotype based expectations are low, the comparison of an individual to the stereotype of the group to which one belongs often results in counter-stereotypical appraisals of the individuals, i.e. women are at times judged more favourably than similar men. An unexpected case is found out that a woman has exceeded low stereotype-based performance expectation, such as gender-based evaluation has a hidden meaning which can be responsible for undesirable experience for women at work place. When women sometimes receive preference than others and they perform better than the male colleagues, they are marginalised as high-performing females. Inspiration and constant encouragement are imperative for better performance at work place for women. If the notion of prevention is better than cure, is considered then preventing gender typing will be more effective than providing encouragement later to make up for the stereotypes that have been rooted into the brains of the fairer sex. Perhaps it will also help to clear the ambiguity and whether women are inherently disinterested in higher education or whether they are conforming consciously or unconsciously to what the society expects from them. It is the agreed notion that gender differences in these parameters decrease as societies lessen their gender norms. This noticeably suggests that socialisation does have something to do with gender differences in interest and self-efficacy. It would also, therefore, be relevant to check how impactful encouragement in alleviating these differences is.

Gender roles form a system of social practices that creates and maintains gender distinctions which lead to unequal relations based on these gender distinctions (Wharton, 2002). While nature makes us biologically male or female, society makes us socially feminine or masculine. It is gender and society which determines the appearances, attitudes, behavioral roles, responsibility rights, access and control over resources etc. Stereotype content is derived from perceptions of the extent that members of a particular group are perceived as threatening and in competition with the in-group, according to Fiske (2002). The crossing of competence and warmth results in four cases of prejudice. Groups are perceived as warm and competent, warm, but incompetent, not warm, but competent and neither warm nor competent, in this typology woman fall into the two ambivalent groups. Within the ambivalent sexism framework (Glick and Fiske, 2002), benevolent sexism treats women as warm but incompetent. Alternatively, women who are viewed as not warm, but respected, subject to hostile sexism. These women are respected for their high status and in turn perceived as competent, but disliked for lack of human qualities. In other words, different kinds of prejudice turn against these different types of women: hostility is directed toward nontraditional women and paternalistic benevolence toward traditional women (Glick, Diebold, Bailey-Werner, and Zhu, 1997).

The results of the interviews reveal that females have a greater emotional feelings than males, which help them to handle relationships efficiently in work domain i.e. getting and giving emotional support to the partner at the same time social beliefs and societal norms restricts males to express their problems resulting in stress which results into decline in academic/professional performance. Women bear a relatively complicated cognitive framework, they tend to consider multiple points-of-view while making their decisions which results in their in-depth thinking. This result can also be explained by this fact.

Women are more emotionally attached to family and nation which weighs more for them than taking up a job abroad. Cognitive framework and preferences have a remarkable effect on decision-making. Boserup (1970) argued that women were marginalised in the modernisation process and practices of growth, development, and development policy threatened to actually make women worse off. Researchers noticed varied differences in decision‘- making patterns among female faculty members. The main reasons were found as improbability, anxiety, social burden, time constraints, beliefs, motivation etc. Chanana (2004) focuses on the access and participation of women students in higher education in India in the pre-and-post economic liberalisation phase, women gained access to higher education gradually during the first four decades after independence, it could be possible as higher education was fully state funded and highly subsidised. Socio-cultural and economic factors acted as barriers to their ability to access higher education. The pressures for change emanating from globalisation came when the higher education system was unable to meet the rising social demand for professional education. It is argued that the researchers join as faculty members when they are in their early thirties, a time when women are either married or have to be married soon. They need a break to raise a family and after the break cannot compete with men in research and professional experience. Again, more women than men are holding junior faculty positions, (Bal, 2004).

Major issue driving this trend could be the societal norms, men are supposed to support the family in the Indian milieu. The fact indirectly impacts the judgmental capacity of an individual and drives him to choose an option where he can earn more irrespective of his interest. It can be categorised as a belief bias which has a chief role in individual choices. Evans, Barston, & Pollard, (1983) gave a theory on cognitive biases which included belief bias that males and females also differed on the parameters on which they would choose their jobs.

4. Conclusion

A gender neutral image will be beneficial for both the sexes in work domain, as it will improve the overall performance without restricting individuals on the basis of their gender identity. Analysis performed on the responses supported the existence of a perceivable organisational barrier which hinder the rise of women professionals to senior administration and top level positions. Different standards of performance evaluation for men and women employees, lack of opportunities for mid-career function shifts, lack of mentorship programmes and beneficial training sessions for women are the major factors responsible for this unseen barrier.

Reviewing the administration policies, discovering employees' perceptions about organisational culture and employees' career expectations, identifying the best practices of development of women can be instrumental in eliminating the unseen barrier which prevents women from rising to top positions. Implementing retention strategies for women, initiating leadership training programmes for women, monitoring recruitment strategies for female employees and improving the departmental ambience to promote the integration of female faculty would also prove to be effective in ensuring a significant representation of women professionals in top-level positions in the long run.

References

- Bal, V. (2004). Women scientists in India: Nowhere near the glass ceiling. *Economic and Political Weekly,* 7 August, pp. 3647-53.
- Boserup, E. (1970). *Woman's Role in Economic Development.* Women's Committee of the Washington DC Chapter of the Society for International Development, Women in Development (Wid).
- Chanana, K. (2004). *Gender and Disciplinary Choices: Women in Higher Education in India.* UNESCO Colloquium on Research and Higher Education Policy 'Knowledge, Access and Governance: Strategies for Change', 1-3 December, 2004, Paris.
- Chanana, K. (2007). Globalization, higher education and gender: Changing subject choices of Indian women students, *Economic and Political Weekly*, February 17 2007, 42(7), pp. 590–598.
- Evans, J.ST. , Barston, J.L., and Pollard, P. (1983). On the conflict between logic and belief in syllogistic reasoning. *Memory & Cognition,* 11(3), pp. 295-306.

- Glick, P. and Fiske, S. T. (1996*)*. The Ambivalent Sexism Inventory: Differentiating hostile and benevolent sexism, *Journal of Personality and Social Psychology*, 70, pp 491–512.
- Glick, P., Diebold, J., Bailey-Werner, B., and Zhu, L. (1997). The two faces of Adam: Ambivalent sexism and polarized attitudes towards women, *Personality and Social Psychology Bulletin*, 23, pp. 1323–1334.
- Jha, J. and Kelleher, F. 2006. *Boys' Underachievement in education: an exploration in selected commonwealth countries*. London, Canada, Commonwealth Secretariat of Learning .

17

Inclusive Growth and Public Expenditure in Higher Education- Issues and Suggestions

Dr Arifa S Makandar

Abstract

Since the last decade of 20th century we saw huge economic fluctuations in the form of reforms. The focus of the government in recent years is towards building Inclusive India. Inclusive growth basically means "broad-based growth and pro-poor growth". The objectives of an inclusive growth agenda is to reduce poverty, improve quality of life, and ensure to the extent possible, that all segments of society benefit from the economic growth of the country. Education especially higher education is an important tool to attain the objectives of Inclusive Growth.

The present research paper highlights the current structure of higher education in india. The states approach towards the higher education is to be change. The paper highlights the views of experts on the problems of higher education in India and suggest policy measure to improve the same.

Introduction

India has emerged as one of the world's fastest growing economy in post reforms period. The Growth of the IT industry and increased agricultural-production created an atmosphere of optimism, which led to the coining of phrases, such as Incredible India, India Shining, and India 2020 around the end of the millennium. The Indian growth story has been one of high Gross Domestic Product (GDP) growth but primarily driven by the growth in services sector.

Since the last decade of 20th century we saw huge economic fluctuations in the form of reforms. Not all sectors of the economy have grown at the same rate as is reflected in the relatively low agricultural growth rate, low-quality employment, poor education, inadequate healthcare services, rural-urban divide, social inequalities, and regional disparities. Therefore the focus of the government in recent years has shifted from promoting Incredible India to building Inclusive India. Inclusive growth basically means "broad-based growth and pro-poor growth". The broad-based growth is concerned with opportunities for the majority of labour force, poor and middle class alike. The pro-poor growth is interested in the welfare of the poor. Apart from reducing the poverty rate inclusive growth aims at allocation of productive resources with benefits incurred to every section of the society.

Inclusive growth needs to be achieved in order to reduce poverty and other social and economic disparities, and also to sustain economic growth. In recognition of this, the Planning Commission had made inclusive growth an explicit goal in the Eleventh Five Year Plan (2007-2012). The draft of the Twelfth Five Year Plan (2012-2017) lists twelve strategy challenges which continue the focus on inclusive growth. These include enhancing the capacity for growth, generation of employment, development of infrastructure, improved access to quality education, better healthcare, rural transformation, and sustained agricultural growth. Growth that is not inclusive affects the society, the economy, and the polity. A lack of inclusive growth can result in real or perceived inequities, which has its own social ramifications. Inclusive growth promotes economic growth partly by broadening the base for domestic demand and partly by increasing the number of people with a stake in reforms and in a stable government.

The objectives of an inclusive growth agenda is to reduce poverty, improve quality of life, and ensure to the extent possible, that all segments of society benefit from the economic growth of the country. A number of macro and micro level interventions have shown to be conducive to promoting inclusive growth. At the macro level, recommendations such as improving fiscal discipline, trade liberalisation, openness to Foreign Direct Investment, privatisation, regulation, tax reforms, labour market flexibility, providing social safety nets, reorientation of public expenditure, and legal and political reforms can be useful in guiding policy discussions for promoting rapid and inclusive growth in developing countries. At the micro level, reducing income and non-income related inequality, improving public infrastructure, healthcare, education, access to markets, accountability, women's empowerment, role played by civil society organisations, and good governance can help accelerate poverty reduction. Inclusive growth sets the direct relationship between micro and macro determinants of economy. These mainly include the structural transformation of the society along with growth in country's GNP and GDP. The Commission and Growth, 2008, notes that inclusiveness-a concept encompasses equity, equality of opportunity and protection in market and employment transitions is an essential ingredient of any successful growth strategy.

The inclusive growth strategy takes a longer term perspective as the focus is mainly on creation of productive employment for all without any kind of discrimination. However, for achieving inclusive growth, it is essential that the diffusion of opportunities been supported with good governance and accountability. In order to reduce disparity and promote inclusive growth, the Indian government has set state-specific targets for parameters, such as GDP growth rate, agricultural growth rate, new work opportunities, poverty ratio, dropout rate in elementary schools, literacy rate, and gender gap in literacy rate, infant mortality rate and maternal mortality ratio.

The pace of structural transformation and creation of productive opportunities highly depends on human capital and what is the role of state in creating human capital. It is rightly argued that the better transformation of economy poverty is to be reduced through increasing the productive efficiency of people. Better education is often an important means to better jobs, increased income, and a better quality of life. Over the past few decades, the global economy has shifted from being manufacturing-centric to a knowledge driven one. The services sector contribution of world production has grown from around 52per cent in 1970 to 68per cent in 2005. On the one hand, India's increasing integration with the global economy and the growth of sectors such as IT, BPO, and financial services have led to an increased demand for knowledge workers. On the other hand, the fact remains that its per capita income continues to be quite low. India has moved up the ranks, but is still the poorest among the G-20. The per capita income of India stood at $1,527 in 2011. The need of the hour is to provide opportunities for people living in poverty to transform their lives. Education is an important tool to achieve this task. The population of India, cutting across regions, languages, and socioeconomic status, has begun to appreciate the value of education in a global economy and demonstrated an increased willingness to pay for quality education.

This paper elaborates the need to build Inclusive India and emphasises why it is imperative to focus on inclusive growth now. It presents the opportunities available for building an inclusive India by identifying key levers education, especially higher education in the country. The present paper throws light on the potential effect on human capital accumulation and inclusive growth by keeping in view the composition of public expenditure in higher education sector in India. It has been proved that there is direct impact of education in creating human capital to reduce poverty and attain economic growth. Education enhances the efficiency and productive capacity of people. Many researchers have proved that investing in right kind of educational programmes has positive impact on short–term as well as long-term development process. People with elementary literacy level have failed to fight with the poverty. The total literacy rate of rural India is 58.7per centwhere as in urban India it is 79.9per cent. In rural areas, households with 'primary level and lower' education have the highest poverty ratio, where as the reverse is true for households with 'secondary and higher' education. The need of the hour is to increase the accessibility of people to higher education to attain inclusive growth in India.

Trends in India's Higher Education

There is good amount of transformation in Indian educational sector. The students' enrollment in higher education has increased from just 3.97lakh in 1950-51 to 169.76 lakhs in 2010-11. The following chart shows the growth higher education in India. There is noticeable progress in India's higher education.

Growth of Higher Education in India

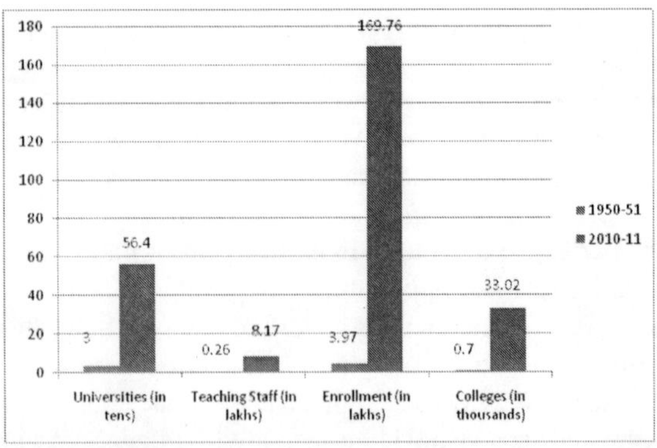

Source: Higher Education at Glance, UGC India, Feb 2012.

Since 1951, education has primarily been a responsibility of the states, but in the case of higher and technical education, a greater responsibility was placed with the Central government. The Constitution of the Republic of India made education a state subject. The responsibility of only certain categories of education/institutions and subjects continues to vest in the Central government (Central Universities, Sand T institutes of national importance, regulation of higher education were placed in List 1 of the Seventh Schedule of the Constitution dealing with subjects in the purview of the Central government). However, in 1976, the omnibus 42nd Amendment to the Constitution brought "Education, including, technical education, medical education and Universities" into List 3 of the Seventh schedule dealing with subjects in the joint purview of both central and state governments.

More recently, the Constitution 73rd and 74th Amendments have recognised the rural and urban local bodies in India as the third tier of government and "education, including primary and secondary schools", "technical training and vocational education" and "adult and non-formal education" have been placed in the purview of the local bodies in Article 243G of the Constitution. However, higher education is not in the purview of local bodies. While the State has been the dominant source of finance for higher education, non-governmental finance provided by religious endowments, charitable trusts and others has been an important source of funding. Many of these institutions are able to receive regular state grants to meet a large proportion of their recurrent expenditure after they meet eligibility criteria.

Public expenditure on higher education grew at a very rapid rate till the early 1970s but continued to exceed the rate of growth of national income till the mid-1980s. As a result, the share of public expenditure in higher education to GDP rose on this period. Thereafter, the trend is towards stagnancy or decline. The most noticeable feature is a decline in per student real expenditure on higher education in the period after 1992-93. Per student expenditures on higher education were low in India to begin with. With the modernisation of education, these should have grown at a high rate to provide infrastructural support of the necessary quality. This, however, did not happen.

Problems of Higher Education in India:

- Dr D.K. Bandyopadhyay, Vice Chancellor, Guru Gobind Singh Indraprastha University, said that on some areas we have performed well but there are areas where we are still lagging behind. He believes that one of the major crises faced by the country in terms of development in higher education is the crunch in faculty members.

- Deepak Pental, Professor, Department of Genetics, South Campus, Delhi University and Ex Vice-Chancellor at Delhi University, believes that there exists a major policy deficit in the country that is curbing the development in higher education. He adds that even though there are a number of committees and commissions set up, the implementation of the recommendations of these commissions happens at snail's pace. He also agrees that the major issue is the shortage of trained faculty.
- Our educational institutions are ready to collaborate with some of the best institutions in the world but we do not want to collaborate within ourselves. There is a lack of synergy between institutions within the country. Researchers performing outstandingly well abroad, lose their willingness to perform as soon as they land in India. The system's lack of reward and recognition initiatives for performing researchers in India could be a contributing factor behind the poor performance of higher education.
- There is great need of change in the pattern of education faculty wise. Practical oriented and technical education should be given more importance.

Suggestions

- The nature of research that is required for faculty hiring should be carefully looked into. There are very little incentives for researchers in India to publish their work in reputed journals.
- The existing number of Universities viz., around 400 and colleges viz., around 20,000 are definitely not able to cater to the increasing number of school pass-outs. Even if the number of Universities is increased to 1,500 and the number of colleges doubled, we will be able to cater to just 15 per cent of the population.
- There is a lot to be done in the field of higher education in India to meet the global demands in terms of quality, reach and access. The quality of teaching faculty is a key aspect that has been suffering in India due to dilutions of selection standards.

- The curriculum, content, teaching methods, assessment standards and methods have all to be revamped and upgraded. In order to make higher education competitive and global, the credit system is to be introduced.
- Research facilities have to be improved and students attracted to take up research work more meaningfully without any hurdles.
- Multiple regulatory authorities should go, replaced by a single, friendly regulatory authority, giving more autonomy to the Universities.
- The regulatory authority be least interfering, more supportive and follow well-defined assessment criteria for accreditation so that the Universities are globally accepted.
- There is a wide gap between the industry expectations and the university standards, on account of which millions of people are unemployed/unemployable, while thousands of jobs are lying vacant for want of the right personnel.
- The role of private operators in the field of higher education has increased and a meaningful private-public partnership is a must to cater to the increasing number of users.
- The churning of researchers and doctoral research candidates should be regulated.
- There is need of fast track sanction of funds for research in newer areas.
- Even though private Universities are doing well, they would require some government support.
- Good researchers working on good projects should be provided with public fund to support them as well as the national knowledge network should be made available to these researchers.
- Greater investment is needed in the physical and intellectual infrastructure to improve higher education in India. "India needs to widen its education base radically," said Prof Amartya Sen after receiving an honorary degree of Doctor of Literature from the National University of Educational Planning and Administration at New Delhi in July 2011.
- The value-based education is absolutely essential for the development of higher education in India.

From the above one can conclude that some concerted efforts is all that is required to improve the quality of higher education. Thus what is required is a systematic, accountable and transparent approach without piecemeal inputs. This would help to meet the challenges of universal access to quality education and our march towards INCLUSIVE GROWTH.

References

- Amartya Sen (2007): Development as Freedom, Oxford University Press, London.
- Annual Report 2006-07, Ministry of Rural Development, Government of India.
- Analysis of Budgeted Expenditure on Education, MHRD.
- Higher Education at Glance, UGC India, Feb 2012.
- Ramchandran Vimala, Rishi Mehrotra and Kamaeshwari Jandhyala (2007): Incentives in Elementary Education. Do they make a difference? Journal of Education Planning and Administration, Vol. XXI Number 2, April, 2007.

Global Perspectives in Higher Education

18

Internationaliasation of Higher Education: A Trajectory for Professional Development of Teachers

Bhanu Pratap Pritam

The most significant global change has been manifested in form of internationalisation, especially, of higher education in the post-war period and the most visible and important feature is trans-border student mobility. This further followed by the neo-liberal movement of late 70s in western world and of 90s in Indian scenario. Liberalisation, Privatisation and Globalization (LPG) have influenced higher education, more intensively the professional and technical education at large in post-90s period. The LPG movement supported by several governmental policies; private university bill, foreign education provider bill and also by allowing free entry of local private providers of IT and related areas. As a result, the mobility of students, being a potential manpower, to the international Universities and also the international students' mobility to the Indian Universities appeared at great extent in recent decades. The outward and inward student mobility has also mobilised the teaching manpower nationally as well as internationally. Students and teachers exchange programme with different international Universities, as a policy of bond of cultural relation between two or more nations, and vice-versa also registered at great extent in recent past. Therefore, the most obvious manifestation of internationalisation of higher education in India has become the increasing presence of international students in Indian university campus. But India, for a long time, has been slow in reacting to the wave of internationalization and Indian Universities have not been able to take advantages of the possibilities that internationalisation offers for improving the quality of education, for promoting Indian culture worldwide, deriving political and economic benefits.

Diversity increases quality in higher education, the most known and discussed issue, furthermore, leads to rethink about the diversity coming from international students to Indian Universities needs to be tackled through competent and professionally equipped teaching manpower. Here comes the issue of needs of professional development of teachers, who can carry forward international brains, considering them as international knowledge resource and produce such kind of manpower from Indian higher education institutions who can compete in global market of knowledge economy. The paper discusses such issues and concerns related to internationalisation of higher education and how this can lead to the professional development of teachers in higher education institutions? Here, internationalisation of higher education is considered as a tool for professional development of teachers.

Defining Internationalisation of Higher Education

(Knight and De Wit 1997 quoted in OECD,1999) "Globalisation is the flow of technology, economy, knowledge, people, values, ideas.... across borders and globalisation affects each country in different way due to a nation's individual history, tradition, culture and priorities". Basically, Internationalisation of higher education is one of the ways a country responds to the impact of globalization yet, at the same time respects the individuality of the nation. Thus, internationalisation and globalisation are seen as different but dynamically linked concepts. Globalisation can be thought of as the catalyst while internationalisation is the response, though a response in a proactive way. Internationalisation of higher education is the process of integration an international/intercultural dimension into the teaching, research and service functions of the institutions.

The National University of Educational Planning and Administration (NUEPA) deliberated upon issues pertaining to globalisation and response to internationalisation of higher education in a national conference and felt that; challenges of quality, modes of supply, access and equity in higher education, response to GATS and WTO, matters pertaining to identity, culture and curriculum and other concerns of the nations receiving foreign higher education need to be tackled. Whereas, University Grants Commission (UGC) in Tenth Plan (2002-2007) made internationalisation of higher education one of its thrust areas and projected a vision for promoting Indian higher education abroad as a response to the phenomenon of globalisation. The chairman UGC set up an expert committee to encourage the free flow of students from other countries to India and vice versa.

Internationalization quality issues can be addressed basically from three major approaches (OECD, 1999). The first sees the inclusion of the international dimension as a key component in the general academic quality review systems operational at an institutional or system level. This is based on the premise that an international dimension is part of the university/college mission and major functions and is thus included as one of many elements addressed in the quality review procedures. And, the second looks at the quality of specific internationalisation policies, procedures and programmes (i.e. International students, work study abroad, student/faculty exchanges, research, language instruction and technical assistance). Whereas, the third concerns the internationalisation of quality assurance procedures themselves. These procedures are generally policy based. It is increasingly acknowledged that quality assurance procedures benefit from an international input and approach.

Rationale for Internationalisation of Higher Education

As there are various ways of describing and defining internationalisation of higher education, there are also a number of different rationales for integration of international dimensions into higher education especially in developing countries like India. Basically, there are four categories of rationales for internationalisation of higher education (Knight and De Wit 1997 quoted in OECD,1999) and these categories are not exclusive with each other rather more interrelated in nature. The first category from a political point of view are perhaps more relevant to a national perspective than an institutional perspective. Globalisation, as contemporary world order, connotes borderless nation shrinking time, distance and free flow of knowledge economy. So in this scenario, internationalisation can be considered by some countries denationalisation and used as a way to strengthen and promote their national identity and therefore, it becomes an important political rationale. Second category from economic point of view refers that globalisation of world economy, growing interdependence among nations and the information revolution, countries are focusing on their economic, scientific and technical competitiveness in order to increase the productivity. The most effective way to improve and maintain a competitive edge is through developing a highly skilled and knowledgeable manpower by investing more and more in applied research. Therefore, it appears that there exists a close relation between internationalisation of higher education and the economic and technological development of the country. The third category from academic point of view, for internationalisation of higher education, is directly linked with quality improvement. Leading reason for internationalising higher education is the achievement of international academic standards for teaching and research by the presence of international students and faculties. It is further assumed that by enhancing the international dimensions of teaching, research and service there is value added to the quality of higher education system. Last category from socio-cultural point of view refers internationalisation of higher education to be outdated and the preservation and promotion of national culture are becoming a strong motivation for those countries which consider internationalisation as a way to respect cultural diversity and also to respond to the globalisation. The preparation of students who have strong knowledge and skill base in intercultural relations and communication, which facilitates the bilateral relations between two countries, may be considered as one of the strongest rationale for internationalisation of higher education.

Internationalisation as inbound Student Mobility

Universities and institutions of higher education in India have manifested a substantial growth in international students opting India as a knowledge hub in recent past. There are numerous ways of internalisation of higher education; formal agreements through MoU have been a common mechanism for international collaboration, the presence of international students in Universities and institutions of higher education impacts upon teaching, curriculum development, cultural interaction, etc., international research collaboration either through formal agreements or personal contacts, faculty exchange, borrowing for best practice in teaching and academic management and through curriculum change or adoption. Here, presence of international students in Indian Universities, as the most dominant approach for internationalisation of higher education in India, has been focused to show the trends of internalisation in recent past.

As Table-1 displays below, through the trends of international students' inflow, it appears that a typical growth has been taking place by increasing number of international students in Indian Universities and other institutions of higher education whereas a steep growth has also been registered from 2005-06 onwards by sudden increase of international students. As discussed above, there are several reasons for such increase in the number of international students but some of the major grounds are; India being one of the fastest growing economies in the world, Indian IT revolution, cheap labour cost, etc. attracted international students to

International Students in Indian Universities (Continent wise)

Continents	*2002-03*	*2003-04*	*2004-05*	*2005-06*	*2006-07*	*2007-08*
Asia	—	—	9849	10493	13400	15437
Africa	—	—	2005	2403	3616	3796
America	—	—	593	654	776	626
Europe	—	—	178	206	238	309
Australia	—	—	55	71	69	81
Miscell-aneous	—	—	587	629	592	957
TOTAL	10936	11934	13267	14456	18391	21206

Source: AIU and UGC (2007-08).

wards India in recent years. On the other hand, international students mobility towards India are also seen from the industrialised and developed countries; Australia, Europe and America. Although the number appears to be very low but an indication has been registered at global level that Indian Universities have the quality to teach, train and produce manpower for global competitive world. Majority of the international students have identified well reputed central, state and deemed Universities in India (shown in Table-2). These Universities have always shown better performance in terms of; teaching manpower, professional development of students as well as teachers, world class infrastructure, international students friendly environment, and quality education at every level as accredited by NAAC also. Most surprisingly, female have been contributing almost half of the total international students' mobility in Indian university/institutions of higher education. Among all the international students, most popular education they opt for are undergraduate and post-graduate especially in science/technology and other professional courses, but even at research level, as evidences reveal, a sufficient number of international students have opted for research studies and this number is increasing as well.

Table-2

Top 10 Indian Universities with International Students (2007-08)

	Name of the Universities	Male	Female	Total
1	University of Pune	2791	1016	3807
2	University of Mysore	859	453	1312
3	Manipal University	537	689	1226
4	University of Delhi	660	471	1131
5	Osmania University	559	123	682
6	Alagappa University	288	280	568
7	Jamia Hamdard, Delhi	337	172	509
8	Bharti Vidyapeeth, Pune	359	135	494
9	Aligarh Muslim University	300	65	365
10	Banaras Hindu University	221	77	298

Source: *AIU and UGC (2007-08)*

Professional Development of Teachers

Professional development of teachers refers to the generation of all those updated skills required to execute a task of teachers in academic teaching-learning situations. It means by which members of academic community at higher education level maintain, improve and broaden their knowledge and skills and, develop the personal qualities required in their professional lives. (Educational Resources Information Center, ERIC in Wikipedia 2009) database refers; Professional development may also come in the form of pre-service or in-service professional development programs. These programmes may be formal, or informal, group or individualised. Individuals may pursue professional development independently, or programmmes may be offered by human resource departments.

Professional development opportunities can range from a single workshop to a semester-long academic course, to services offered by a medley of different professional development providers and varying widely with respect to the philosophy, content, and format of the learning experiences. But, at the heart of professional development is the individual's interest in lifelong learning and increasing their own skills and knowl-

Higher education in India has scaled up gradually. The number of Universities has increased 18.8per cent, the teaching staff in colleges and Universities by 34.69per cent, the students enrollment ratio increased by 42.76per cent and the number of colleges increased by 47.57per cent from 1950-51 to 2010-11. Though the students' enrolment in higher education increased to the considerable extent but it is also important to know that in which faculty large number of students have enrolled. The employability of students from technical, commerce and science faculties is higher than the students from other fields.

Faculty-wise Students Enrolment in Higher Education 2010-11

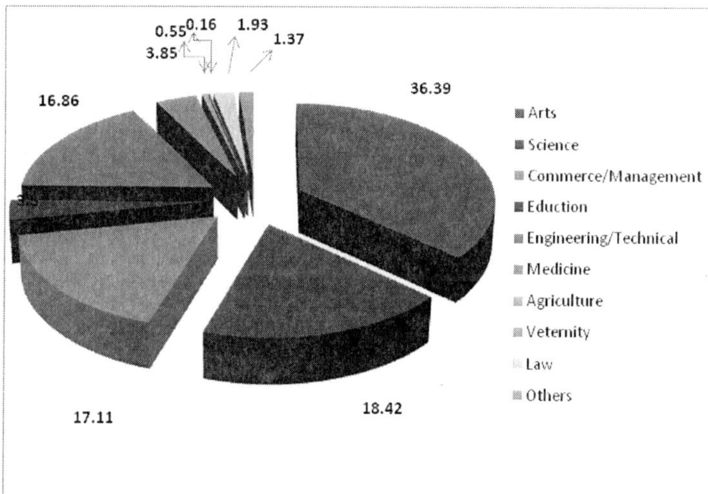

Source: Higher Education at Glance, UGC India, Feb 2012.

As per the above chart large number of students is found in Arts discipline whose technical efficiency is very poor. It is interesting to note that in India, where agriculture and allied constituents play a critical role in economic development, student enrolment in agricultural courses accounts for around only 0.5%. The students from science, technology and management have comparative advantage in understanding and adapting new or existing ideas in to the development process. The following chart reveals lots of loopholes in students' enrollment stage-wise also.

Students Enrolment by stages in Higher Education 2010-11

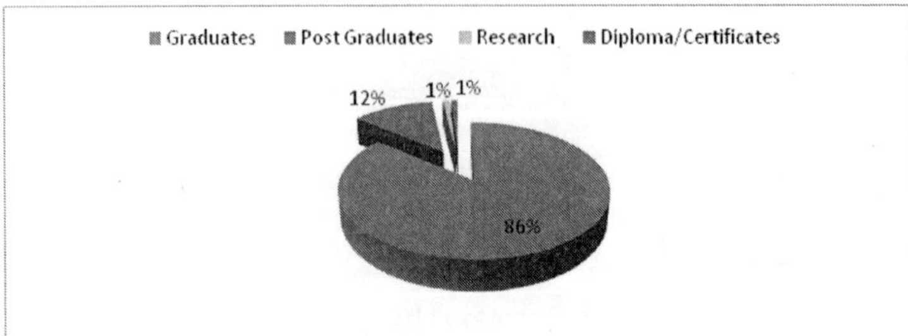

Source: Higher Education at Glance, UGC India, Feb 2012.

Hardly one per cent students are found in research field. This has reduced their practical approach towards many key issues of development. There is wide consensus that expansion in the skills, knowledge, and capacities of individuals increasing human capital is crucial for economic for reduction of poverty and growth. This is rare to find in Indian Higher Education system. Above this the most alarming is the Indian higher education system suffers from a large rural-urban divide in access.

Rural Urban disparities in students enrollement Ratio in India.

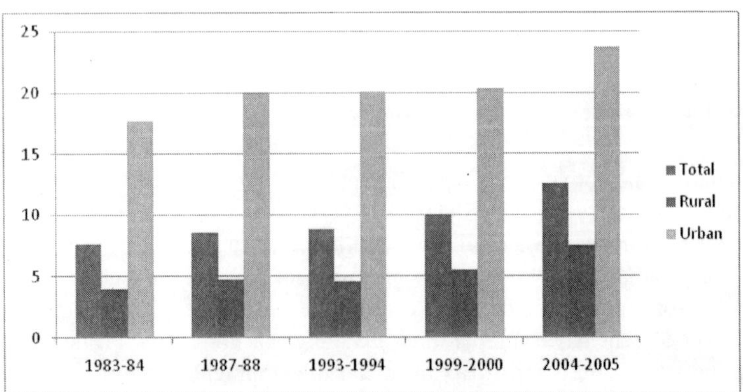

Though Gross Enrollment Ratio in rural India has increased, the gap between GERs in rural and urban areas has only widened. This is basically because of neglecting rural areas in allotment of good educational institutes by both private sector and government. There is need to have reforms which can strengthen higher education in our rural economy.

Public Expenditure on Higher Education in India

The emergence of a global economy due to increased trade, investment and mobility of people and, more recently, work across borders has forced nation states to adapt their systems of higher education to the changed global realities. Pragmatism rather than ideology is driving this change.

Many countries like USA, China, Russia, African Nations, United Kingdom etc, have diverted good portion of their expenditures on strengthening their higher education. The USA has major plans for investment in higher education. The United Kingdom has injected new dynamism in the higher education sector through competition and incentives. China has undertaken a package of comprehensive reforms in higher education for over the past two decades. The government in China has declared education, science and technology to be the strategic driving forces of sustainable economic growth.

From the early 20th century, there have been several high level commissions set up to provide policy orientation to the development of higher education in India. But results are not satisfactory. Yet, it is believed that a crisis is plaguing the Indian higher education system. While, the National Knowledge Commission (NKC) set up by the Prime Minister calls it a 'quiet crisis', the Human Resource Minister calls higher education 'a sick child'. Indian government is treating higher education as adopted child. The government's spending is often inefficient and inequitable with higher education outlays. At the same time given the budgetary constraints, many developing countries including India face important trade offs between higher education and other type of expenditure.

The fiscal austerity programmes frequently require countries to make difficult choices regarding which the components of public expenditures should be reduced or reallocated. Due to the government's tendency to formulate educational policies based on public pressure, often wrong policies are pursued. It is widely believed that technological advances and a shift in demographic provide India with a window of opportunity to productively engage its huge pool of human resources, and become a leader in both the rapidly expanding sectors of services and highly skilled manufacturing. This would, however, require revamping the higher education sector. Many efforts have been put under various reforms and even the National Knowledge Commission has made many recommendations but these efforts these efforts do not give a sense of an integrated reform agenda for Indian higher education. Government expenditure has also increased considerably but still there are many loopholes' in the policies. The following graph clearly shows the governments spending on higher education.

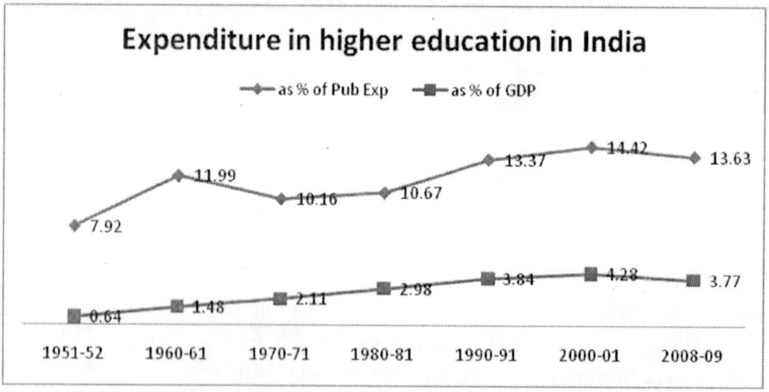

Source : Analysis of Budgeted Expenditure on Education, MHRD.

Education may not be the mother of growth, but it matters as much as any thing else, and probably a lot more. Hence promoting the right educational policy is key factor for inclusive growth. But in India public expenditure on whole education sector as per cent of total GDP is less than five per cent. This is revealed in the following chart.

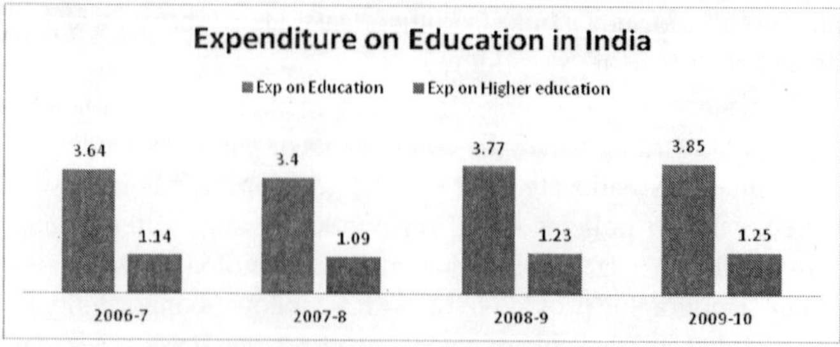

Source : Analysis of Budgeted Expenditure on Education, MHRD.

Since 1951, education has primarily been a responsibility of the states, but in the case of higher and technical education, a greater responsibility was placed with the Central government. The Constitution of the Republic of India made education a state subject. The responsibility of only certain categories of education/institutions and subjects continues to vest in the Central government (Central Universities, Sand T institutes of national importance, regulation of higher education were placed in List 1 of the Seventh Schedule of the Constitution dealing with subjects in the purview of the Central government). However, in 1976, the omnibus 42nd Amendment to the Constitution brought "Education, including, technical education, medical education and Universities" into List 3 of the Seventh schedule dealing with subjects in the joint purview of both central and state governments.

More recently, the Constitution 73rd and 74th Amendments have recognised the rural and urban local bodies in India as the third tier of government and "education, including primary and secondary schools", "technical training and vocational education" and "adult and non-formal education" have been placed in the purview of the local bodies in Article 243G of the Constitution. However, higher education is not in the purview of local bodies. While the State has been the dominant source of finance for higher education, non-governmental finance provided by religious endowments, charitable trusts and others has been an important source of funding. Many of these institutions are able to receive regular state grants to meet a large proportion of their recurrent expenditure after they meet eligibility criteria.

Public expenditure on higher education grew at a very rapid rate till the early 1970s but continued to exceed the rate of growth of national income till the mid-1980s. As a result, the share of public expenditure in higher education to GDP rose on this period. Thereafter, the trend is towards stagnancy or decline. The most noticeable feature is a decline in per student real expenditure on higher education in the period after 1992-93. Per student expenditures on higher education were low in India to begin with. With the modernisation of education, these should have grown at a high rate to provide infrastructural support of the necessary quality. This, however, did not happen.

Problems of Higher Education in India:

- Dr D.K. Bandyopadhyay, Vice Chancellor, Guru Gobind Singh Indraprastha University, said that on some areas we have performed well but there are areas where we are still lagging behind. He believes that one of the major crises faced by the country in terms of development in higher education is the crunch in faculty members.

- Deepak Pental, Professor, Department of Genetics, South Campus, Delhi University and Ex Vice-Chancellor at Delhi University, believes that there exists a major policy deficit in the country that is curbing the development in higher education. He adds that even though there are a number of committees and commissions set up, the implementation of the recommendations of these commissions happens at snail's pace. He also agrees that the major issue is the shortage of trained faculty.
- Our educational institutions are ready to collaborate with some of the best institutions in the world but we do not want to collaborate within ourselves. There is a lack of synergy between institutions within the country. Researchers performing outstandingly well abroad, lose their willingness to perform as soon as they land in India. The system's lack of reward and recognition initiatives for performing researchers in India could be a contributing factor behind the poor performance of higher education.
- There is great need of change in the pattern of education faculty wise. Practical oriented and technical education should be given more importance.

Suggestions

- The nature of research that is required for faculty hiring should be carefully looked into. There are very little incentives for researchers in India to publish their work in reputed journals.
- The existing number of Universities viz., around 400 and colleges viz., around 20,000 are definitely not able to cater to the increasing number of school pass-outs. Even if the number of Universities is increased to 1,500 and the number of colleges doubled, we will be able to cater to just 15 per cent of the population.
- There is a lot to be done in the field of higher education in India to meet the global demands in terms of quality, reach and access. The quality of teaching faculty is a key aspect that has been suffering in India due to dilutions of selection standards.

- The curriculum, content, teaching methods, assessment standards and methods have all to be revamped and upgraded. In order to make higher education competitive and global, the credit system is to be introduced.
- Research facilities have to be improved and students attracted to take up research work more meaningfully without any hurdles.
- Multiple regulatory authorities should go, replaced by a single, friendly regulatory authority, giving more autonomy to the Universities.
- The regulatory authority be least interfering, more supportive and follow well-defined assessment criteria for accreditation so that the Universities are globally accepted.
- There is a wide gap between the industry expectations and the university standards, on account of which millions of people are unemployed/unemployable, while thousands of jobs are lying vacant for want of the right personnel.
- The role of private operators in the field of higher education has increased and a meaningful private-public partnership is a must to cater to the increasing number of users.
- The churning of researchers and doctoral research candidates should be regulated.
- There is need of fast track sanction of funds for research in newer areas.
- Even though private Universities are doing well, they would require some government support.
- Good researchers working on good projects should be provided with public fund to support them as well as the national knowledge network should be made available to these researchers.
- Greater investment is needed in the physical and intellectual infrastructure to improve higher education in India. "India needs to widen its education base radically," said Prof Amartya Sen after receiving an honorary degree of Doctor of Literature from the National University of Educational Planning and Administration at New Delhi in July 2011.
- The value-based education is absolutely essential for the development of higher education in India.

From the above one can conclude that some concerted efforts is all that is required to improve the quality of higher education. Thus what is required is a systematic, accountable and transparent approach without piecemeal inputs. This would help to meet the challenges of universal access to quality education and our march towards INCLUSIVE GROWTH.

References

- Amartya Sen (2007): Development as Freedom, Oxford University Press, London.
- Annual Report 2006-07, Ministry of Rural Development, Government of India.
- Analysis of Budgeted Expenditure on Education, MHRD.
- Higher Education at Glance, UGC India, Feb 2012.
- Ramchandran Vimala, Rishi Mehrotra and Kamaeshwari Jandhyala (2007): Incentives in Elementary Education. Do they make a difference? Journal of Education Planning and Administration, Vol. XXI Number 2, April, 2007.

Global Perspectives in Higher Education

18

Internationaliasation of Higher Education: A Trajectory for Professional Development of Teachers

Bhanu Pratap Pritam

The most significant global change has been manifested in form of internationalisation, especially, of higher education in the post-war period and the most visible and important feature is trans-border student mobility. This further followed by the neo-liberal movement of late 70s in western world and of 90s in Indian scenario. Liberalisation, Privatisation and Globalization (LPG) have influenced higher education, more intensively the professional and technical education at large in post-90s period. The LPG movement supported by several governmental policies; private university bill, foreign education provider bill and also by allowing free entry of local private providers of IT and related areas. As a result, the mobility of students, being a potential manpower, to the international Universities and also the international students' mobility to the Indian Universities appeared at great extent in recent decades. The outward and inward student mobility has also mobilised the teaching manpower nationally as well as internationally. Students and teachers exchange programme with different international Universities, as a policy of bond of cultural relation between two or more nations, and vice-versa also registered at great extent in recent past. Therefore, the most obvious manifestation of internationalisation of higher education in India has become the increasing presence of international students in Indian university campus. But India, for a long time, has been slow in reacting to the wave of internationalization and Indian Universities have not been able to take advantages of the possibilities that internationalisation offers for improving the quality of education, for promoting Indian culture worldwide, deriving political and economic benefits.

Diversity increases quality in higher education, the most known and discussed issue, furthermore, leads to rethink about the diversity coming from international students to Indian Universities needs to be tackled through competent and professionally equipped teaching manpower. Here comes the issue of needs of professional development of teachers, who can carry forward international brains, considering them as international knowledge resource and produce such kind of manpower from Indian higher education institutions who can compete in global market of knowledge economy. The paper discusses such issues and concerns related to internationalisation of higher education and how this can lead to the professional development of teachers in higher education institutions? Here, internationalisation of higher education is considered as a tool for professional development of teachers.

Defining Internationalisation of Higher Education

(Knight and De Wit 1997 quoted in OECD,1999) "Globalisation is the flow of technology, economy, knowledge, people, values, ideas.... across borders and globalisation affects each country in different way due to a nation's individual history, tradition, culture and priorities". Basically, Internationalisation of higher education is one of the ways a country responds to the impact of globalization yet, at the same time respects the individuality of the nation. Thus, internationalisation and globalisation are seen as different but dynamically linked concepts. Globalisation can be thought of as the catalyst while internationalisation is the response, though a response in a proactive way. Internationalisation of higher education is the process of integration an international/intercultural dimension into the teaching, research and service functions of the institutions.

The National University of Educational Planning and Administration (NUEPA) deliberated upon issues pertaining to globalisation and response to internationalisation of higher education in a national conference and felt that; challenges of quality, modes of supply, access and equity in higher education, response to GATS and WTO, matters pertaining to identity, culture and curriculum and other concerns of the nations receiving foreign higher education need to be tackled. Whereas, University Grants Commission (UGC) in Tenth Plan (2002-2007) made internationalisation of higher education one of its thrust areas and projected a vision for promoting Indian higher education abroad as a response to the phenomenon of globalisation. The chairman UGC set up an expert committee to encourage the free flow of students from other countries to India and vice versa.

Internationalization quality issues can be addressed basically from three major approaches (OECD, 1999). The first sees the inclusion of the international dimension as a key component in the general academic quality review systems operational at an institutional or system level. This is based on the premise that an international dimension is part of the university/college mission and major functions and is thus included as one of many elements addressed in the quality review procedures. And, the second looks at the quality of specific internationalisation policies, procedures and programmes (i.e. International students, work study abroad, student/faculty exchanges, research, language instruction and technical assistance). Whereas, the third concerns the internationalisation of quality assurance procedures themselves. These procedures are generally policy based. It is increasingly acknowledged that quality assurance procedures benefit from an international input and approach.

Rationale for Internationalisation of Higher Education

As there are various ways of describing and defining internationalisation of higher education, there are also a number of different rationales for integration of international dimensions into higher education especially in developing countries like India. Basically, there are four categories of rationales for internationalisation of higher education (Knight and De Wit 1997 quoted in OECD,1999) and these categories are not exclusive with each other rather more interrelated in nature. The first category from a political point of view are perhaps more relevant to a national perspective than an institutional perspective. Globalisation, as contemporary world order, connotes borderless nation shrinking time, distance and free flow of knowledge economy. So in this scenario, internationalisation can be considered by some countries denationalisation and used as a way to strengthen and promote their national identity and therefore, it becomes an important political rationale. Second category from economic point of view refers that globalisation of world economy, growing interdependence among nations and the information revolution, countries are focusing on their economic, scientific and technical competitiveness in order to increase the productivity. The most effective way to improve and maintain a competitive edge is through developing a highly skilled and knowledgeable manpower by investing more and more in applied research. Therefore, it appears that there exists a close relation between internationalisation of higher education and the economic and technological development of the country. The third category from academic point of view, for internationalisation of higher education, is directly linked with quality improvement. Leading reason for internationalising higher education is the achievement of international academic standards for teaching and research by the presence of international students and faculties. It is further assumed that by enhancing the international dimensions of teaching, research and service there is value added to the quality of higher education system. Last category from socio-cultural point of view refers internationalisation of higher education to be outdated and the preservation and promotion of national culture are becoming a strong motivation for those countries which consider internationalisation as a way to respect cultural diversity and also to respond to the globalisation. The preparation of students who have strong knowledge and skill base in intercultural relations and communication, which facilitates the bilateral relations between two countries, may be considered as one of the strongest rationale for internationalisation of higher education.

Internationalisation as inbound Student Mobility

Universities and institutions of higher education in India have manifested a substantial growth in international students opting India as a knowledge hub in recent past. There are numerous ways of internalisation of higher education; formal agreements through MoU have been a common mechanism for international collaboration, the presence of international students in Universities and institutions of higher education impacts upon teaching, curriculum development, cultural interaction, etc., international research collaboration either through formal agreements or personal contacts, faculty exchange, borrowing for best practice in teaching and academic management and through curriculum change or adoption. Here, presence of international students in Indian Universities, as the most dominant approach for internationalisation of higher education in India, has been focused to show the trends of internalisation in recent past.

As Table-1 displays below, through the trends of international students' inflow, it appears that a typical growth has been taking place by increasing number of international students in Indian Universities and other institutions of higher education whereas a steep growth has also been registered from 2005-06 onwards by sudden increase of international students. As discussed above, there are several reasons for such increase in edge. Whereas, this paper has taken a very specific dimension of professional development; learning through diversity of international students.

Internationalisation and Professional Development

Any activity helps to improve the execution of job in better way and prepare teachers for improved performance in present and for the future leads to professional development. Higher education provide maximum opportunity and situation for professional development of teachers whereas, increasing number of international students in university campus offers a great and diversified opportunities for university teachers to academically renovate themselves before the international human resource. Each individual comes from different continents and countries of the world with graduate/post graduate degrees to study and learn in India must be considered as a rich source for international brains, knowledge and experience that can share and contribute to make international relations and extend their wisdom to the institutions and country they learn from. International students' mobility provides a diversified scenario to Indian Universities and their faculties. Since, international students coming from diverse countries, diverse background, diverse expectations and intensions so, it becomes very pertinent to prepare Universities and their faculties in such a way that they meet the expectations and demands of international students for which they have opted Indian Universities. Now meeting these demands of international students not merely lie with university teachers but it is also the responsibility of apex bodies of higher education which permitted inflow of international students and further, responsibility extends to the university itself to prepare such kind of academic manpower who can handle international students and tackle their academic concerns. In order to pursue the responsibility of international students' best achievement during studying in Indian university, university teachers require a different kind of teaching skills, classroom management and create international students' friendly climate in the institution to handle a diversified group of international students. Since, larger responsibility goes with university's academic administration to train their teachers in such a way so that they are equipped with all those knowledge and skill required for healthy acclimatisation of international students in university campus, here comes the role of Academic Staff College.

Academic Staff College was an establishment with the view of having a formal in-service training set up for university and college teachers require for the upgradation and updated knowledge according to changing time and need of the teaching-learning situations in higher education. Since Academic Staff College is the only formal institution in higher education system having the responsibility to train and teach in-service university and college teachers, the duty to orient teachers for dealing with international students entirely lie with it. Training university/ college teachers to understand the multiculturism and cope with international students having diversified academic background are the major responsibility of academic staff college as far as attracting and promoting internationalisation of higher education in India is concerned. Equipping with all those skills and knowledge require to adapt and sustain international students in university system with ability to convert these students as a global manpower are the most important dimension of professional development for university and college teachers. Therefore, this part of professional development, although accomplished by Academic Staff College only, has to be executed more rigorously to maintain accelerated growth of inbound mobility of international students in Indian university and institutions of higher education, not merely for quantitative growth of international students but also for the qualitative growth of bilateral relations with other countries as well as qualitative professional development of university teachers.

Although this dimension of professional development of teachers through internationalisation of higher education largely remained untouched in Indian University, but with a little more initiatives by Academic Staff Colleges to encourage a friendly environment for international students can contribute much to the development of higher education in India. Further, a by-product of developing this dimension of professional development among teachers can be seen in near future as developing a kind of sensitivity towards Indian diversity of students as well, in terms of social and economic base, by the university and college teachers. Because, it is very often seen in the context of higher education that if, it is international students, the kind of academic care and treatment appears in university campus for them is extraordinary, due to government policy and maintaining well reputation with other countries, whereas, students from within country with diverse socio-economic background are seen left without any special care and treatment of such kind. Here, the opportunity for professional development of teachers in the context of internationalisation of higher education extends its benefit to local Indian students with diversified socio-economic background. Most importantly, the ability to deal with such students itself can be the greatest quality indicators for university/institutions of higher education in a country whose policy specification is inclusive growth.

Concluding Remarks

Entire discussion in the paper has taken a stand from the point of view of professional development through inbound mobility of international students in Indian Universities and institutions of higher education. LPG movement since early 90s has manipulated entire sectors particularly the higher education and as a result, internationalisation has emerged as the most dynamic phenomenon of this era. Especially in 21st century, movement of international students not only from Asian and African continent but also from Australian, European and American continents were registered at great extent. This movement manifests the increasing bond of relations among different countries of the world which also results in infusing national boundaries in terms of knowledge and economy therefore, entire world has becoming a global village and higher education has been contributing upto maximum extent in this process. In this scenario, university system in India also needs to be a part of global development and expected to contribute in the national development through producing globally competent manpower. Since, higher education system has no such formal training institution, unlike B.Ed/Teacher Education an institution for school education, Academic Staff College remains the only institution that has to fulfill all the responsibilities and expectation to develop competent teachers who further can produce competent students. Therefore, Academic Staff College contains the overall accountability, indirectly, for attracting and sustaining international students by producing professionally developed and quality teaching manpower who can generate globally competent students.

References

- Anandkrishnan, M (2008) Promises and Perils of Globalized Higher Education. *Journal of Educational Planning and Administration.* Vol. XXII, No. 2, pp. 199-212.
- Sharma, K.A (2008). *Internationalization of Higher Education: An Aspect of India's Foreign Relations.* New Delhi: Gyan Publishing House.
- Powar, K.B (2004). *Internationalization of Higher Education: Focus on India.* New Delhi: Amity University Press
- University Grants Commission (2008). *University Development in India: Basic Facts and Figures, Enrolment of International Students in Indian Universities(2006-07, 2007-08).* New Delhi: UGC.

- Organization for Economic Co-Operation and Development (1999). *Quality and Internationalization in Higher Education: Programme on Institutional Management in Higher Education (IMHE)*. Peris: OECD.

  www.ugc.org

  www.wikipedia/internationalization.org

  www.aiuweb.org

19

World University Rankings: Status of Indian Universities

Prof P. F. Rahman,
and
Bhanu Pratap Pritam

Abstract

Quality is a process whereas excellence can be attributed as an indicator for outcomes. The thrust of knowledge and achievement has always been central force to receive attention of mankind since inception. Education has become the latest addition among all the sectors of governance in society with increasing importance of knowledge economy in recent past of modern history. This paper makes an attempt to show the global scenario in which world university ranking system emerged along with its methodological concerns consequently at global, continental as well as national level. Further it also describes the efforts of Asian and Indian institutions to come up with their pursuit of excellence in order to queue up in global rankings. Finally a critical outlook of some of the efforts of Indian agencies and government in the wake of world university ranking system have also been included for future plan of action in higher education sector. This paper is not meant for comparative study but largely a descriptive-informative paper.

Key Words: Global Rankings, Higher Education, Quality, Indian and International Institutions.

World University Rankings

Success through marketing has become the leading popular 'mantra' in the contemporary market oriented world irrespective of sectors. Higher education as a catchy sector for economic development also appeared in limelight in post-LPG era especially in last decade. In addition, the global movement of manpower, technologies, ideas, etc. has led to increase in competition among top notch institutions worldwide leading to rank institutions of higher learning at certain levels as a measure of excellence. The world Universities rankings help in stimulating competition, providing valuable information to teachers and policy-makers for taking appropriate steps for quality improvement, information to the prospective students about the quality of institutions across the countries and disciplines to opt for better university with a better placement reputation for the value of money. In past one decade university rankings have become increasingly important worldwide; the number of global rankings has grown and is predicted that it will keep growing (Marginson, 2011). This paper makes an attempt to show the global scenario in which world university ranking system emerged along with its methodological concerns consequently at global, continental as well as national level. The annual university ranking season begins prior to every academic session year at global level across the countries in order to provide stakeholders of the university to have greater options available (Altbach 2011).

World University Ranking agencies can be categorised based on their objective/ methodologies (Rauhvargers, 2011).

1. **Ranking with the purpose to prepare league tables of top Universities** –The Shanghai Academic Ranking of World Universities (ARWU) first to rank Universities in 2003, the Times Higher Education (THE) ranking initially in cooperation with Quacquarelli Symands (THE-QS) from 2004-2009, since 2010 THE in cooperation with Thomson Reuters (THE-TR); QS World University Ranking (QS) since 2010; the Russian Reitor ranking etc.
2. **University rankings concerning research performance only – with or without league tables** " The Leiden Ranking, The Netherlands; the Taiwan Higher Education Accreditation Evaluation Council university ranking (HEEACT); the EU Assessment of University-Based Research (AUBR); University Rankings by Academic Performance (URAP), Turkey.
3. **University rankings and classifications using a number of indicators with no intention of producing composite scores or league tables** –German Centre of Higher Education Development (CHE); the EU U-Multi ranking, Center for World University Ranking (Saudi Arabia), U21 (Australia).
4. **Bench mark Universities based on actual learning outcomes** - Assessment of Higher Education Learning Outcomes (AHELO), France.

5. **Rankings of Universities based on their visibility on web** – Webometrics, Spain.

The world university rankings of ARWU, QS-WUR and THE is most widely referred and popular among academics, analysts, students and policy-makers across the globe. Thus this paper considers world university rankings of only these three ranking agencies.

Parameters of world university rankings

Quality of institutions is observed/measured by both tangible and intangible indicators by all major global ranking agencies. Tangible indicators are lesser challenging in measurement compared to intangible indicators due to their abstract nature. Following are the common parameters of the ranking agencies with different proportions of factual and perception tools (Table 1).

- Teaching, learning and research leading to citation.
- Presence of students and faculty from abroad, in order to cater diversity as an indicator of institutional quality.
- Reputations of the university/institution, post education job prospectus/placements.
- Academia-industrial relation.

These ranking agencies keep revisiting the parameters as per the contemporary needs/demands of the stakeholders of Institution's changing nature.

Table 1- Parameters for ranking and their% of weightage by three world university ranking agencies

ARWU		QS WUR		THE	
1. Quality of Education(Alumni of an institution winning Nobel Prizes and Fields Medals)	10%	1. Academic Reputation	40%	1. Teaching	30%
2. Quality of Faculty (Staff of an institution winning Nobel Prizes and Fields Medals - 20%+ Highly cited researchers in 21 broad subject categories-20%)	40%	2. Employer reputation	10%	2. Research	30%
3. Research Output (Papers published in Nature and Science- 20% + Papers indexed in Science Citation Index-expanded and Social Science Citation Index- 20%)	40%	3. Faculty student ratio	20%	3. Citations	30%
4. Per Capita Performance	10%	4. Citations per faculty	20%	4. International outlook	7.5%
-	-	5. Proportion of international students	5%	5. Industry income	2.5%
-	-	6. Proportion of international faculty	5%	-	-

The ARWU focus is on research activities apart from, quality of education and per capita performance of the stakeholders of the university. ARWU parameters favour Universities that are very strong in sciences and English speaking countries which is language of research publications. QS world university ranking focuses much on academic reputation in addition to pupil teacher ratio and citation which is a part of research output. Apart from these, employer's reputation and international dimensions were also given weightages. Whereas, THE (Times group) focused much on research activities and output along with, teaching and international dimensions of the university. Both QSWUR and THE rankings remains focused on the world's top Universities from preselected lists.

Taking a glance at the methodological perspectives of world university ranking system, the observations direct towards the skewed research related activities (Altbach 2011) rather on the teaching and learning aspects. One of the limitations can be understood as complexity in measurement of such dimensions. Now keeping the imperial perspective of knowledge transaction and vision of Universities, the Universities in developing world i.e. countries below 20 per cent GER (approx.) are still suffering from inadequate GER in school education and low transition rate from school to higher education. Such scenario connotes much difficult position in leaning towards research but more on teaching and learning aspects which also causes in inadequacy of figuring among top institutions of world university ranking.

Top Ranking Universities of the worlds

World University rankings are now an annual popular exercise across the continents. The following Table 2 reflects the top ten world Universities ranked by the top three agencies from the initial years (2004) of their establishments, of recent past (2011) and also for the current years (2013).

Taking a glance at the Table 2, Harvard University always placed distinctly outstanding throughout the years and by all ranking agencies. Leading to this, University of Cambridge, Stanford University, Oxford University, Massachusetts Institute of Technology, University College of London, California Institute of Technology, Yale University, Princeton University were among the top league Universities. But, major variance found among the world university ranking list can be directly linked with the measurement criteria adopted by different agencies whereas the common appearance can be understood as few top 10-15 Universities somehow appears in all the rankings in three different years. So, on the basis of criteria made by different ranking agencies and their ranking list, these Universities can be generalized, anyway, as the best in the world. The list is largely dominated by Universities from USA and UK, where English is the language of teaching and research.

Table 2. List of Top Ranking Ten Universities of the World

World	ARWU			QS			THE		
	2004	2011	2013	2004	2011	2013	2004	2011	2013
1	Harvard University	Harvard University	Harvard University	Harvard University	University of Cambridge	Massachusetts Institute of Technology	Separate ranking was not started by THE	California Institute of Technology	California Institute of Technology
2	Stanford University	Stanford University	Stanford University	University of California, Berkeley	Harvard University	Harvard University		Harvard University	Harvard University
3	University of Cambridge	Massachusetts Institute of Technology	University of California, Berkeley	Massachusetts Institute of Technology	Massachusetts Institute of Technology	University of Cambridge		Stanford University	University of Oxford
4	University of California, Berkeley	University of California, Berkeley	Massachusetts Institute of Technology	California Institute of Technology	Yale University	(University College London)		University of Oxford	Stanford University
5	Massachusetts Institute of Technology	University of Cambridge	University of Cambridge	University of Oxford	University of Oxford	Imperial College London		Princeton University	Massachusetts Institute of Technology
6	California Institute of Technology	California Institute of Technology	[illegible] Institute of Technology	[illegible] Cambridge	[illegible] College London	University of Oxford		University of Cambridge	Princeton University
7	Princeton University	Princeton University	Princeton University	Stanford University	(University College London)	Stanford University		Massachusetts Institute of Technology	University of Cambridge
8	University of Oxford	Columbia University	Columbia University	Yale University	University of Chicago	Yale University		Imperial College London	University of California, Berkeley
9	Columbia University	University of Chicago	University of Chicago	Princeton University	University of Pennsylvania	University of Chicago		University of Chicago	University of Chicago
10	University of Chicago	University of Oxford	University of Oxford	ETH Zurich	Columbia University	California Institute of Technology		University of California, Berkeley	Imperial College London

Table 3. Continental Representation of Universities in 2013 Rankings (Top 200 and 400 Universities)

Agencies	ARWU 200	ARWU 400	QS 200	QS 400	THE 200	THE 400
North America	46%	37.3%	30.5%	25%	42%	32.0 %
South America	1.5%	1.7%	1.5%	3.5%	0.5%	0.75 %
Europe	37.5%	41.0%	47%	47.2%	42.5%	45.25 %
Asia	11.5%	15.0%	16%	16.8%	10.0%	15.25 %
Pacific	3.5%	4.5%	5.0%	6.2%	4.5%	6.00 %
Africa	0	0.5%	0.5%	1.0%	0.5%	0.75%

Continental representation data shows that Universities from Europe and North American continents are dominating in rankings followed by Asian, Pacific, South American and African regions (Table 3). ARWU and THE data is almost similar whereas QS data shows a bit different continental ratio figure.

Asian Universities in world university ranking

The Asian Universities representation from the world university rankings has been analysed (Table 4), to find the top Ten Asian Universities by the world university ranking agencies.

Table 4. List of Top Ten Asian Universities in World Ranking

	2004			2011			2013		
	ARWU	QS WUR-	THE	ARWU	QS WUR	THE	ARWU	QS WUR	THE
1	The Univ. of Tokyo(14)	The Univ. of Tokyo(12)	Separate ranking was not started by THE	The Univ. of Tokyo(21)	Univ. of Hongkong(22)	The Uni. of Tokyo(30)	The Univ. of Tokyo(21)	NationalUniv. of Singapore(24)	The Univ. of Tokyo(23)
2	Kyoto University(21)	Beijing University(17)		Kyoto University(27)	The Univ. of Tokyo(25)	The Univ. of Hong Kong(34)	Kyoto University(26)	Univ. of Hongkong(26)	National Univ. of Singapore(26)
3	Osaka University(54)	National Univ.of Singapore(18)		The Hebrew Univ. of Jerusalem(57)	NationalUniv. of Singapore(28)	National Univ.of Singapore(40)	The Hebrew Univ. of Jerusalem(59)	The Univ. of Tokyo(32)	The Univ. of Hong Kong(43)
4	Tohoku University(69)	Kyoto University(29)		Osaka University(82)	Kyoto University(32)	Peking University(49)	Technion-Israel Inst. of Tech.(77)	The Hongkong Univ. of Sci. and Tech. (34)	Seoul National University(44)
5	The Hebrew Univ. of Jerusalem(90)	Hong Kong University (34)		Nagoya University(94)	The Chinese Univ. of Hongkong(37)	Kyoto University(52)	Osaka University(85)	Kyoto University(35)	Peking University(45)
6	Nagoya University(97)	Indian Institute of Technology(41)		Tohoku University(97)	Hongkong Univ. of Sci. and Tech. (40)	Pohang Univ. of Sci. and Tech.(53)	Weizmann Inst. of Sci.(92)	Seoul National Univ. (35)	Tsinghua University(50)
7	Hokkaido University (101-152)	Hong Kong Univ. of Sci. and Tech.(42)		Hokkaido University (102-150)	Seoul National Univ. (42)	Hong Kong Univ. of Sci. and Tech.(62)	Hokkaido University (101-150)	The Chinese Univ. of Hongkong(39)	Kyoto University(52)
8	Kyushu University (101-152)	Nanyang Univ. Singapore(50)		National Taiwan University (102-150)	Osaka University(45)	Tsinghua University(71)	Nagoya University (101-150)	Nanyang Tech. University (41)	Korea Advanced Inst. of Sci. and Tech. (56)
9	National Univ. of Singapore (101-152)	Tokyo Inst. of Tech. (51)		National Univ. of Singapore (102-150)	Peking University(46)	Korea Advanced Inst. of Sci. and Tech.(94)	National Taiwan Univ. (101-150)	Peking University(46)	Hong Kong Univ. of Sci. and Tech.(57)
10	Tel Aviv University (101-152)	Osaka University(62)		Seoul National University (102-150)	Tsing Hua University(47)	Tokyo Inst. of Tech. (108)	National Univ. of Singapore(101-150)	Tsing Hua University(48)	Pohang Univ. of Sci. and Tech.(60)

Tokyo University, Japan is consistently dominated the list across the years as well as across the ranking agencies which directs in generalising University of Tokyo as the best in Asian Continent. Apart from this, majority of the top ranking Asian Universities are from Japan. Universities from Singapore, Hong Kong, Korea are also represented more frequently. Taiwan, Israel, China and Malaysian Universities are the other one represented in Top Ten Asian Universities.

It is pertinent to mention here that, the methodology adopted for ranking of Asian Universities is similar to world rankings. The QS ranking methodology is little different with lesser weightage for academic reputation (30 per cent) and research citation (15 per cent) for Asian Universities.

Table 5. Number of Asian Universities among Top 400 in 2013 World University rankings

Asian countries	*QS*	*ARWU*	*THE*
China	11	26	15
Taiwan	6		17
Hongkong	6	5	6
India	5	1	3
Iran	0	0	3
Israel	4	6	4
Japan	14	15	22
Lebanon	1	0	1
Malaysia	4	0	1
Republic of Korea	9	7	14
Saudi Arabia	3	3	3
Singapore	2	2	2
Thailand	2	-	3
Turkey	9	0	5
United Arab Emirates	0	-	1
Kazakhstan	2	-	-
Indonesia	1	-	-
Philippines	1	-	-

The Table 5 indicates the number of institutions/ Universities of Asian countries appeared in top 400 of world university rankings. Maximum contribution in the world university ranking from Asia comes from Chinese sub-continent followed by Japan, Israel, Republic of Korea, India, Singapore, Saudi Arabia, and Malaysia. Most of them are from developed economies.

Indian Perspective in World University Rankings

Post-independent era in India has witnessed a significant growth in institutional establishments in higher, technical, professional and other contemporary sectors. The accelerated institutional growth was witnessed post-1991 due to Liberalisation, Privatisation and Globalisation (LPG). India has entered in the global race of industrialisation, corporatisation, free economy with private sector involvement, which is extended to education sector as well. With provision of adequate resources, professional and technical education with its research and development priorities helped Indian Universities/Institutions to enter in the race of global university rankings.

The agencies like National Board of Accreditation (for technical courses), National Assessment and Accreditation Council (for non-professional courses), Medical Council of India (for medical courses), Accreditation board (for Agricultural Sciences) etc. are statutory bodies established by the union government for maintaining quality of higher education in respective disciplines in India. These organisations conduct periodical review of institutions /courses and grant accreditation which is a measure of quality. There is no system of ranking the institutions by these agencies. As far as ranking is concerned, firstly, India needs to think about the internal demand and supply of quality aspects/parameters leading to sustainable institutional quality culture within country then it can be extended to sub-continent and later at continental level.

Recently, Ministry of Human Resource Development, Government of India intervened at various occasions for improving the ranking of Indian Universities/ institution in World university rankings. These days Governments are becoming increasingly aware of the important contribution that high performance world Class University makes to global competitiveness and even economic growth of the country (Salmi, 2012). Apart from this, few national ranking agencies have also came into picture in recent years especially the India Today group for Universities and Colleges and Outlook, Mint, Data Quest etc for Engineering colleges in India. These agencies may have their own motives to market few institutions prior to the beginning of annual academic session where information dissemination to the students, guardian and society at large may just a by product of their agendas. Nonetheless, such efforts by these media organisations can be termed as new initiatives in the line of global university ranking agencies.

Indian Universities in World University rankings

The performance of Indian Universities in world university rankings of 2011 and 2013 are analysed (Table 6) for consistency in scoring ranks. The Indian Institute of Sciences, Bangalore is the only institution appeared in top 400 under ARWU ranking in both 2011 and 2013. Whereas, QS world university ranking shows all the early IITs in top 200-400 rankings. Some of the old Universities such as University of Delhi, Mumbai, Pune and Kolkata are ranked in the range above 400. THE world university ranking shows a surprising recent upsurge of University of Punjab at 239th rank leaving apart all the elite Institutions such as IITs, which are in the range of 300-400. The performance of University of Punjab is attributed to 'citation' parameter. The initiatives taken by the Panjab University in boosting the performance in world university rankings may have catalytic effect for other such quality institutions/universities in near future.

Table 6 : Indian Universities in World Ranking:

Ranking	ARW		QS		THE	
	2011	2013	2011	2013	2011	2013
100-200	-	-	-	-	-	-
200-300	-	-	IITD (218)	IITD (222)	-	Punjab University (239)
			IITB (225)	IITB (233)		-
			IITM (281)	IITK (295)		-
300-400	IISc	IISc	IITK (306)	IITM (313)	IITB	IITD
			IITKgp (341)	IITKgp (346)		IITK
			University of Delhi (398)			IITKgp
						IITR
400-500	-	-	IITR	IITR	-	-
				University of Delhi	-	-
500-600	-	-	IITG	-	-	-
			University of Mumbai			
600-700	-	-	University of Calcutta	IITG	-	-
				University of Mumbai		
700+	-	-	-	University of Kolkata	-	-
				University of Pune		

IITD-IIT Delhi, IITR-IIT Roorkee, IITK-IIT Knapur, IITKgp-IIT Kharagpur, IITM- IIT Madras, IITB-IIT Bombay, IITG-IIT Guwahati, IISc-Indian Institute of Sciences. Figures in brackets are exact ranks.

Data drawn from websites of ARWU, QS-WUR, THE

University Ranking by Indian Ranking Agencies

India Today partnered with The Nielsen Company to determine India's top Universities in the year 2010. The agency considered only Universities that offer postgraduate courses in arts, science and commerce were considered. The methodology is based on a 40 per cent perception score (from an in-depth interview conducted among academic experts) and 60 per cent an objective score (factual data furnished by Universities). The parameters considered for rankings are -University reputation, quality of academic input, student care, infrastructure, Job Prospects, faculty, research Publications, admission procedure, Global Exposure, Security arrangements, Innovation and Governance.

The University of Delhi, Jawaharlal Nehru University, Banaras Hindu University are consistent in their top ranks in all the years. Some of the old state Universities are also ranked among top 10 ranking in all the years such as; University of Calcutta, Osmania University, University of Madras and University of Mumbai (Table 7).

Table 7. Top 10 Universities of India ranked by India Today group

Ranks	2010	2011	2012	2013
1	Banaras Hindu University	University of Delhi	University of Delhi	University of Delhi
2	Jawaharlal Nehru University	Jawaharlal Nehru University	Banaras Hindu University	University of Calcutta
3	University of Delhi	Banaras Hindu University	University of Calcutta	Jawaharlal Nehru University
4	University of Calcutta	University of Calcutta	Jawaharlal Nehru University	Banaras Hindu University
5	University of Madras	University of Madras	Aligarh Muslim University	University of Mumbai
6	University of Mumbai	University of Hyderabad	Osmania University	University of Hyderabad
7	University of Hyderabad	Osmania University	University of Madras	Osmania University
8	Indian Institute of Sciences	Jamia Millia Islamia	University of Allahabad	Aligarh Muslim University
9	Jadhavpur University	Bangalore University	University of Hyderabad	Jamia Millia Islamia
10	Osmania University	MS University of Baroda	Jamia Millia Islamia	Pondicherry University

Conclusion

World university rankings have been emphasising more on the scientific temper of the Universities; teachers, researchers, students with scientific output by having large industrial relation leading to job markets, technological advancements, etc. Researches and its publications, citations, applied-technology are also a boosting proxy indicators in the current world university rankings which has been criticized at many occasions by the academia due to its negligence of other disciplines such as Arts, Humanities, Social Sciences etc. So, such rankings have become a science, medicine and technology oriented rankings rather a holistic ranking with all the courses and disciplines which a university basically stands for ultimately ignoring the specific mission of university establishment and narrowing the diversity (Tilak 2013). It is evident from above study that in both World ranking and Asian Ranking high income group countries, mostly from English speaking countries are able to produce high ranking Universities/institutions, which confirms the observations made by Millot, 2013.

In Indian context, some of the recent active initiatives taken by Indian authorities and agencies can be visualised as futuristic approach towards promotion of quality to achieve excellence in Higher Education (X, XI and XII Plans of UGC, MHRD). Measures such as attractive salaries for teachers in higher education, performance-based promotions, encouraging Universities and teachers with special financial assistance (such as Universities with Potential for excellence), liberal grants for research projects and travel, initiatives to establish world class/Innovative Universities taken by authorities towards promotion of research culture in general may achieve desired goal of getting better rankings. MHRD Govt. of India and some of the IITs have initiated an active discussion on the status of ranking of Indian Universities/Institutions at global level and also steps to be initiated either to mark in world university ranking or a separate ranking for Indian Institutions in Indian context (Director, IIT Delhi 2013).

The ideological complexity in understanding the benchmarking and world university ranking system from Indian perspective appears to be at infancy stage for now. There is also an arbitrary state of mind of some of the educational thinkers regarding educational development sector that all the other sectors of the country should run ahead along with the movement of globalisation including technology, medicine services, global managerial positions and also the notion of Millennium Development Goal, human rights need, and developmental issues etc. but the historical culture of the establishment of university higher education should remain tagged with conventional vision-philosophy of '*why university was established*?'. Such unclear state of mind not only shows an ambiguous vision and policy of the country but also widening the increasing gap between conventional and modern discipline of education in global world order. So, the cultural context of developing world and specifically of Indian sub-continent connote the classical struggle of educational development between a quasi-social democratic India and quasi-capitalistic India in the backdrop of Liberalisation, Privatisation and Globalisation.

India in its contemporary state of educational affairs is struggling from mass demographic structure to provide access at one hand and at the same time providing quality education in order to compete in the global race at other hand. Education in developing societies conventionally appear in hierarchy of developments such as; to begin with quantity-equity leading to expansion-quality and finally towards excellence. Here, policy need to be in cohesion with tackling pressure from both sides; priorities to extend mass higher education as internal demand as well as world class higher education for qualitative global movement. The proper synchroniration of socio-cultural needs of India along with meeting international challenges are the strategic need of the hour.

References

- Altbach, P.G. (2011). Ranking Season is Here. *International Higher Education*. No. 62.
- Altbach, P.G. (2011). The State of Rankings.www.insidehighered.com
- Indiatoday- http://www.indiatoday.intoday.in/story/india-today-universities-ranking
- Marginson, S. (2007). Rankings: Marketing Mana or Menace? The Big Picture.16th Annual New Zealand International Education Conference, 8-10 August 2007, Christchurch, New Zealand. Retrieved 11 Jan 2011 from: http://www. cshe.unimelb.edu.au/ people/ staff_pages/Marginson/KeyMar8-10Aug07.pdf
- Millot, B. (2013). University Ranking and Tertiary Education System Banchmarking- Divergant Methodologies, Convergent Results? *Journal of Educational Planning and Administration*. Vol. XXVII (2)
- QS world university rankings http://www.topuniversities.com/ university-rankings

- Rauhvargers, A. (2011). Global University rankings and their impact: EUA Report on rankings 2011. Brussels: European University Association
- Salmi, J. (2012). The Challenge of Establishing World-Class Universities. The World Bank
- Shanghai Ranking Consultancy- http://www.shanghairanking.com/
- Tilak, J.B.G. (2013). Review of Edited Book *University Rankings: Theoretical Basis, Methodology and Impacts on Global Higher Education*, Springer: London. (2011) in *Journal of Educational Planning and Administration*. Vol. XXVII (2)
- Times Higher Education-http://www.timeshighereducation.co. uk/world-university-rankings/

Note: This paper is already Published in University News (University News, Vol (Nov. 2013) **ISSN-0566-2257)**

Indian Higher Education

20

Indian Higher Education: A Way Forward

Prof (Dr) Khwaja M Shahid
and
Bhanu Pratap Pritam

Introduction

India has traversed through a long ways in the last six decades of independence. Post-independent era has witnessed several ups-downs in all the developmental sectors in the country including education in general and higher education in particular. Chronologically looking at the last six decades in Indian higher education sector, three different phases can be identified. The first phase of two decades of independence has witnessed the industrial development of Nehruvian period leading to formal establishment of Indian higher education sector. It can also be identified by formal structure of different statutory bodies of higher education along with several commissions and committees of education in order to provide philosophical basis to this sector at large. Whereas, the subsequent two decades can be considered as decades of transition, complexity and especially as the stage preparation for the modern world. Here it is important to note that little political instability has caused several threats to all the developmental sectors including education during these periods. The contemporary two decades (1990-91 to 2010-11) can be considered as the most volatile, progressive and exploited phase of education sector due to its basis on liberalisation, privatisation and globalisation leading to modern Indian higher education.

The huge success and transition from school education sector, increasing enrolment in higher education sector, achieving professional education sectors in majority of the states across to the level of saturation and the contemporary demographic dividend and its management have located Indian higher education sector at the most critical juncture. Now, the management and administration of such transformation is the immediate need of the hour with the new political shift in the country.

Liberalisation, Privatisation and Globalisation in Higher Education

Change is inevitable in any society that comes routinely with timely interval. Such change may be pushed/influenced by many factors and one of the important factors in post-war period is due to politico-economic upsurge. 1991 can be considered as one such paradigm shift in Indian politico economy of that time. Indian higher education has experienced optimal growth and development especially in professional education sector in last two decades. Post 1991 has manifested several initiatives such as revival of AICTE, establishment of NCTE as a statutory body for teacher education, establishment of NAAC for quality assurance in higher education sectors and private institutions participation at large scale in this sector.

Nonetheless, last two decades have seen many ups and downs in higher education sector largely including quantitative growth and development along with quality deterioration in higher education. Mushrooming of higher education institutions led to accelerated growth in enrolment and has also shown a rosy picture of development in this sector along with other developing and developed countries of the world. Besides, low performing private institutions largely meant for profit purposes merely started by local initiatives without any vision further led to extreme deterioration of quality in such institutions. Such institutions are quite large in number which started posing threat to entire higher education sector in the country. Now tackling such institutions became a great challenge especially for the state government and their concerned bodies. Here it is important to note that the government might have dilemma about interfering such private sectors because, these private institutions have contributing towards increasing quantitative growth in enrolment and strengthening statistics in higher education.

Liberalisation as a policy and globalisation as a phenomenon in post modern world order manifested privatisation as the strongest policy for both; first for the maximum exploitation of available resources for economic development and second as to unify the scattered world as a global village. Unlike in any other sector in the country, education in general and higher education in particular has also been influenced optimally by privatisation and private initiatives.

RUSA and 12th FYP

Rashtriya Uchchatar Shiksha Abhiyaan (RUSA) was a much awaited planning to rejuvenate entire sector of higher education in the country. Largely it is led by continuously increasing budgetary allocation of 11th and 12th Five Year Plan respectively 2007-2012 and 2012-2017. The huge financial outlays for higher education sector along with increasing demand of higher education also initiated programmes like RUSA. RUSA targets mainly at achieving 30 per cent GER in higher education sector by the end of 2020 which largely appears to be an achievable targets because by 2014 India has already achieved 22 per cent GER in higher education. Looking at increasing GER, also due to large scale private sector participation, achieving 30 per cent GER is much deserved targets for India. On the other hand, RUSA also focuses on several aspects of private participation in higher education along with quality assurance through bodies such as NAAC and state specific NAAC .

Although growth in enrolment in Indian higher education sector has been steadily constant of an average one per cent per year especially since 11th five year plan, but the target of achieving 30 per cent by 2020 is still a difficult goal to reach. There are two different directions appear looking at indian higher education; first is about the saturation point of professional/technical education sector shown in recent past and the second; transition from success of Universal Elementary education leading to universal Secondary Education through Rashtriya Madhyamik Shiksha Abhiyaan may lead to successful achievement of the Target of RUSA by 2020. And the recent political shift in the country started focusing on vocationalisation of education supplementing manufacturing sector of production rather than merely towards higher education sector leading to educated unemployment in the country.

Recent Shift in Higher Education towards Vocationalisation

The world has taken major shift from financial economy to knowledge economy in last few decades. Earlier financial economy largely used to lead as well as impact on all the sectors of a nation whereas now, the knowledge has became wealth of nation. Knowledge economy has also potential of boosting financial economy is a well accepted concept in the contemporary world. When higher level of knowledge/education started impacting the world economy, it also created different layers of knowledge and its implications. Professional knowledge at higher level of achievements and vocational knowledge/skill based knowledge at direct industrial/productivity level is the need of the hour.

Several researches, reports and government documents revealed that 75 per cent of Indian professional education graduates are not sufficiently equipped with knowledge and skills required for employment in their concerned sectors. The recent initiatives of vocationalisation of education may lead to harness the potential of Indian demography leading to productive population contributing directly to national development. Higher education sector need an immediate shift from merely mushrooming IT & Engineering related education to job oriented skill-based vocational and education.

Contemporary Politico-Economy of Higher Education

Indian politics have manifested durability with stability in the last decade along with recent political shift in 2014 from UPA regime to NDA regime which received a clear majority in government formation shows the similar political stability as in previous government. Such political stability of one complete decade has been realised after a long time in last three decades which also resulted in several policies related strong decisions in education in general and higher education in particular. Some of the significant policy initiatives can be seen in school education sector in terms of Sarva Shiksha Abhiyaan (SSA), Rashtriya Madhyamik Shiksha Abhiyaan (2008-09), Right to Education (2009), Mid-Day Meal programme apart from huge financial allocation for school education sector continuously in 10th, 11th, and 12th Five Year Plans. Whereas in higher education sector, the initiatives of private Deemed Universities, National Knowledge Commission (2005-06), Rashtriya Uchchatar Shiksha Abhiyaan (2012-13) apart from huge financial allocation for higher education in 11th and 12th Five Year Plans can be termed as boosting initiatives in last one decade by government of India. India has so far achieved nearly 100 per cent GER in elementary education sector as well as 22 per cent GER in higher education sector through recent policies for growth and development by the government in last decade.

As we are aware that every political shift in the country comes with different socio-economic orientation in order to bring desirable changes. The current government also seems to be oriented towards economic development as a prime motto leading to development of other sectors in general. The recent initiative of vocationalisation of education along with focus on manufacturing sector in India certainly leads the country towards higher development through productive manufacturing sector.

Privatisation of Education Sector

Privatisation in higher education can largely be traced in professional/technical education sector rather in general higher education sector in India. Here it is important to mention two sectors; engineering education as well as teacher education sector, both of which have reached upto the level of saturation point. This can further be traced through several institutions of engineering and teacher education in the country laying vacant without admission as a resultant, several institutions has applied for closure in last few years or the authorities have banned establishment of the new institutions.

Unlike technical/ engineering education sector along with the growth of professional education sector, teacher education in particular has been lately adopted to be studied as a discipline largely during last decades of twentieth century. Emergence of several professional areas of studies as a discipline including teacher education/teacher training or education as such was also manifested with market driven sectors leading to multidisciplinary and interdisciplinary education. In this context, even teacher education is not a unified area/single course of study because this subject/discipline itself has to be studied at different levels of understanding such as; early childhood care education (ECCE) which is also called pre-schooling teacher education, elementary teacher education, secondary teacher education and courses for teacher educators (M.Ed) again for different levels. Such a complex and vast area of studies is still not figured as a complete discipline due to its lack of full fledge curriculum, lack of contribution of different discipline in teacher education and vice-versa, adequate research support from other discipline, duration itself which denotes for its professionalism and many others.

Apart from the above mentioned concerns in teacher education and lack of its identity in the arena of school education or higher education have also contributed much in shaky establishment of teacher education as a discipline unlike other professional education sectors. Although, private sectors have identified teacher education and especially secondary teacher education as a noticeable area of investment in last one decade. Privatisation in teacher education is not as spontaneous as privatisation in other professional education sector. Secondary teacher education got late attention due to its non-linkage with job sector in the market until Sarva Shiksha Abhiyaan (SSA, 2001). SSA has given rise to increasing enrolment in elementary schools for which teachers were also required in order to fulfill the norms of SSA throughout the states. So, SSA as the largest mission to achieve universal elementary education created the demand for teacher education in the country. Fulfilling such demand by government sector was not financially viable because of its project mode nature and also due to speculation of achieving a saturation point after few years. Further government opened up this sector for private players by easing the norms and standards to establish teacher education institutions. Therefore, decreasing norms and standards of teacher education institutions, increasing demand of trained teachers, direct linkage of teacher education with school teaching jobs, identification of teacher education as low investment and high profit by private sector and larger phenomenon of liberalisation, privatisation and globalisation have established teacher education as an area of great concern of this decade.

Privatisation in teacher education has its linkage with supply and demand in school education as well as teacher education institutions (NCTE, 2009-10). Until recently, teacher education was not even identified as a sector rather included somewhere in elementary education-school education sector of MHRD. Since there was not a specific sector of teacher education so there is no specific financial data available for this sector. The understanding of teacher education can only be traced by its quantitative growth in last one and half decade and its resultant also reflected by several reports such as; Sudeep Banarjee Committee Report (2007-08) and Justice Verma Commission Report (2012) regarding degrading quality of teacher education due to extreme mushrooming privatisation leading to commercialisation in this sector.

Privatisation in secondary teacher education can also be traced by its accelerated quantitative growth in last one decade which results in 600 per cent increasing in number of teacher education institutions from 2002-03 to 2010-11. The number of institutions of teacher education has grown from 1050 in 2000-01 to 8000 (appox) in 2010-11 with increasing share of private institutions upto 92 per cent or even more during 2011-12. The share of private teacher education institutions were somewhere around 40-45 per cent during 2000-01 which has reached more than 90 per cent in just less than 10 years of time. Whereas on the other hand, the overall higher education institutions has grown from nearly 5000 during 2000-01 to nearly 21000 during 2010-11. Such a huge growth also shows a 400 per cent increase in higher education sector with around 80 per cent share from private sector alone in India. Now looking at such a comparative figure, privatisation in teacher education appears more intense as well as critical compared to privatisation in other sector of higher/professional education in India.

Quality of education is another critical concern of entire education in general and teacher education in particular. Privatisation has increased commercialisation and negatively impacted on majority of self-financing teacher education institutions (Pritam, 2009). There are several empirical instances in higher education which reveals that privatisation leading to commercialisation further leads to degradation of quality in education sector. Self-financing model of institutional management has become the most popular mode of privatisation in education sector. Here investment by the private providers needs an extensive examination in order to probe its profit or non-profit nature. Although all private institutions are established under Society Act 1860 which means a non-profit charitable nature of the organisation/institution, but it is important to note here that majority of these institutions are a for-profit institution at practice level. What makes privatisation in teacher education more lucrative investment for private providers compared with other higher education sector is the short duration of the course and direct linkage of the degree with teaching jobs at school level. Here it is significant to note that some of the stand alone self-financing teacher education institutions are performing much better in terms of providing quality education in the country.

Quality Concerns in Higher Education

Quality as an exclusive phenomenon appears to be the contribution of post-modern society. Few decades ago, quality used to be the integral part of any phenomenon/activity and without which there was a sense of incompleteness. In this globalised world, value degradation from all living and non-living things have became the most routine and visible occurrences. Today we discuss about issues like quality separately, for example, quality education, quality parenting itself, and so on. When we think of education or parenting, it has to be good education and careful parenting; there cannot be an issue of the word "good" or "quality" in it. These days such attributes are used in order to compete in the market driven world and simultaneously, education and higher education also has became a valuable good for the market in this contemporary world especially after LPG of 1991.

There are more than twenty statutory bodies to regulate professional education sector apart from large bodies such as UGC and NAAC to ensure quality education across the institutions and states. Even though, quality of education in seventy percent of the Universities in India and almost ninety per cent colleges in India is at poor state of affairs as opined by NAAC in its report of assessment and accreditation of Indian institution of higher learning. Prime Minister of India (2007) in his remark expressed the concerns that not only quality of education is degrading in Indian Universities and colleges but also it is infected by with widespread corruption in appointments of Vice Chancellors in state Universities which caters more than 90 per cent enrolment in this sector.

President of India in his Vice-Chancellors' conference on 4-5th February 2015 also expressed his concerns for quality issues in higher education along with consistence laying vacancies in institutions of higher learning as a matter of great concerns. While only a handful of Universities in India are maintaining standard of education, others kept routine education without worrying about development of students in particular and entire education in general.

Conclusion: A Way Forward

Higher education in India has been facing multifaceted challenges especially for last two decades in post-1991 era. At one hand, increasing demographic profile and challenges to manage such demography by transforming them into human capital in order to make them contribute in national development, whereas on the other hand universalisation of school education leading to increase in higher education enrolment are some of the major concerns in this area. The gradual increase in educational achievement through DPEP(1994) for universal primary education, SSA (2001) & RTE (2009) for universal elementary education, RMSA(2008-09) for increase in enrolment of secondary education led to establish policies such as Rashtriya Uchchatar Shiksha Abhiyan (RUSA) 2013 are among critical area of concerns of educational management.

India is witnessing demographic dividend with having more than 60 per cent of its population of young age below 35 years. Such a huge young age population itself is a national asset who have optimal potential to contribute in national development further making India into the league of developed nations. Country needs to channelize such potential population into human capital by intervening through education in general and vocational/professional education in particular. Nonetheless in the last two decades, India has successfully achieved universal primary and elementary education by launching programmes like DPEP, SSA and RTE. It further opened the scope of secondary education for which RMSA programme was launched in order to increase enrolment in secondary education. Finally in the year 2013 RUSA was launched to achieve GER of 30 per cent by the year 2020. Keeping these developments in mind, the issues of quantitative achievements are largely met by the government of India but problem remains in the area of quality which is alarming these days by both national demand as well as international pressures.

Apart from this, privatization leading to commercialization in higher education sector is posing threat to entire education system in the country. India can no more enjoy the celebration of merely quantitative growth with the help of private sector alone ignoring the larger issues of degrading quality and also the increasing educated unemployment in the country. RUSA also proposed for the larger role of private sector in higher education in order to achieve the goal of 30 per cent GER in this sector. Government has to revisit the entire policies of approving/affiliating private institutions to offers programmes/courses with provision of terminal inspection/supervision to check the delivery of education with quality. The false infrastructure and manpower in private institutions are to be strictly checked by the governmental agencies. Nonetheless, merely government alone cannot check such problems unless all the concerned stakeholders are involved in reforming entire education system in the country. Therefore, ensuring quality in such educational institutions can largely be a shared responsibility rather on government alone. Let us represent the ethos of Indian democracy through shared responsibility in order to restore the quality of higher education.

References

- Agarwal, P (2009). Indian Higher Education: Envisioning the Future. New Delhi: Sage.
- Agarwal, P (2012). A Half Century of Indian Higher Education: Essays by Philip G Altbach. New Delhi: Sage
- Chattopadhyay, S (2013). Education and Economics: Disciplinary Evolution and Policy Discourse. New Delhi: Oxford.
- Ministry of Human Resource Development (2013). All India Survey of Higher Education. Government of India.
- Ministry of Human Resource Development (2013). Rashtriya Uchchatar Shiksha Abhiyan. Government of India.

- National Council for Teacher Education (2013). Institutions and Enrolment. Government of India.
- Pritam, B.P. (2014). Rashtriya Uchchatar Shiksha Abhiyan: A Trajectory of Indian Higher Education Policy and Implementation Challenges. College Post, (April-June 2014).
- Pritam, B.P. (2014). Teacher Education at Crossroads: Critical Reflections from Justice Verma Commission Report. University News. Vol.52, No.45.
- Pritam, B.P. (2009). A Study of Challenges posed by Privatisation to Teacher Education in India. An unpublished M.Phil. Dissertation. New Delhi: NUEPA.
- Tilak, J.B.G. (2014). Private Higher Education in India. *Economic and Political Weekly*. Vol. (XLIX) No. (40)
- University Grants Commission (2013). Education at Glance. Government of India.